BEING FIRST

An Informal History of the Early Peace Corps

Robert Klein

Published by Wheatmark®
610 East Delano Street, Suite 104, Tucson, Arizona 85705 U.S.A.
www.wheatmark.com

ISBN: 978-1-60494-457-0
LCCN: 2010925686

It is not for you to complete the task,
But neither are you free to desist from it.
—*Pirke Avot*

Travel and See
(Slogan on a market lorry in Ghana 1961)

TABLE OF CONTENTS

FOREWORD...ix

INTRODUCTION xi

The Circle xi

Being First...xii

Why I Joined the Peace Corps...xii

CHAPTER 1: CREATING THE PEACE CORPS........................1

Defining the Towering Task...1

The Mentors of Ghana I: George Carter and David Apter 4

Shriver Meets Nkrumah (and Ghana I is Born)......................7

CHAPTER 2: FINDING THE VOLUNTEERS 9

Sorting the Mail 9

Me and Sarge Start the Peace Corps....................................11

Why Did YOU Join the Peace Corps? 12

CHAPTER 3: TRAINING...19

Ground Work: Washington, Ghana, Berkeley 19

Answering the Call 21

Getting to Berkeley...22

Outside Warren Hall...23

Scraping Off the Callow..26

Problems in Ghana..30

Selecting, Rejecting, Dejecting..32

CHAPTER 4: HERE TODAY, GHANA TOMORROW...................................41

Meeting President Kennedy 41

Above the Trees and on the Ground, Ghana at Last 44

Dancing the High Life 46

They're Taking Tom Away...................................46

CHAPTER 5: LEARNING TO TEACH...................................53

But They Didn't Tell Us About That in Training...................................53

Trying to Be a PCV 56

Not Quite Tom Brown's School Days 60

Becoming Teachers...................................65

CHAPTER 6: THE FIRST YEAR AT SWSS...................................71

Exit Mr. Amissah-Arthur; Enter the Banana Man 71

Pop's Death...................................74

The Juaboso Connection...................................75

The Invisible Man Meets The Prisoner of Zenda...................................78

Adult Ed—Outside the Walls with the Extra-Mural Department...................79

The Farm Disaster—Blame It on George...................................83

CHAPTER 7: WE HAVE COME TO TEACH 91

The Ur–Ghana I...................................91

From Accra to Navrongo (with a Stop in Kumasi) 93

An African Student Asks His Science Mistress...................................96

Teaching at a Catholic School...................................98

Three's a Crowd—Five's a Party...................................99

CHAPTER 8: THE VIEW FROM ACCRA...107

    The Lumumba Thing..107

    Desist...109

    Paris or Bust; We Vote with Our Feet...112

CHAPTER 9: THE SECOND YEAR...115

    Changes...115

    SWSS: The Second Year..116

    All Politics Is Local (So Maybe George Carter Won't Hear About It)............121

    Not Quite Ready to Leave...123

    All Days Are Not Equal...126

CHAPTER 10: IMAGE VS. REALITY: GHANA I SPEAKS UP...............133

    How Many Ghanaian Friends Do You Have?.................................133

    The Termination Conference...137

    A More Personal Assessment, Thanks to Brewster and Rafe.......137

    SWSS and the Banana Man Say Goodbye.......................................139

    Finally Getting to Meet the Wizard...140

    Were We Successful?..141

CHAPTER 11: THEN WHAT?..143

    After 1963...143

    Back to Ghana and SWSS...146

    Through the Years..151

APPENDIX: 1961 Roster of Ghana I Peace Corps Volunteers.................159

ACKNOWLEDGMENTS...163

Peace Corps Ghana training program, Berkeley, July 1961

FOREWORD

This book is dedicated to the Ghanaians who had the grace and charm to put up with us—they have been our students, our teachers, our friends.

The Ghana I Peace Corps group is unique only by accident of history. We weren't first because we were special but we became special because we were first. In telling this story, I want to celebrate what we did but also want to encourage people today to seek a similar challenge. The Peace Corps now offers the same opportunity for service and adventure that it did in 1961.

The Peace Corps has continued to operate with projects now in more than 70 countries. After five decades the Peace Corps is an established program of the United States—that this would happen was certainly not apparent in the bold, innovative days of the early '6os. This book is about the beginning of the Peace Corps from the point of view of those who were its true creators—the volunteers in the field, not the Washington staff. If their risk was political, ours was highly personal. Many books have documented the Peace Corps/Washington history; other pioneering Peace Corps volunteers are preserving their experiences, such as the Colombia I and Tanganyika I projects. In *Being First*, within the context of the origin of the Peace Corps project in Ghana in 1961, I tell my own story and those of others in Ghana I.

This book interweaves three narratives. First, to place it in historical perspective, it tells how the Peace Corps project in Ghana came into existence, with a touch of awe over the fact that a full-blown federal agency achieved full functioning in only six months (President Kennedy signed the executive order creating the Peace Corps on March 1, 1961; Ghana I stepped off a plane in Accra, Ghana on August 30, 1961). Second, it is a personal account of my service as a Peace Corps Volunteer in Ghana I. Third, it provides a partial description of the service of several others in the Ghana I group (limits of time, resources and ambition have prevented me from interviewing and collecting material from every member of Ghana I, some of whom chose not to be interviewed; others were not accessible).

In preparing this informal history, I have used interviews

1. From the John F. Kennedy Library Oral History Interviews.

2. Collected by M. Brewster Smith and Rafe Ezekiel in 1962 and 1963 as part of a research project about Ghana I.

3. Collected by me for this book (and for the Returned Peace Corps Volunteer [RPCV] Collection at the John F. Kennedy Library).

In *Through the Looking-Glass*, Humpty Dumpty says, "When I use a word, it means just what I choose it to mean—neither more nor less." And so it is with our memories. Past experiences become real as we choose to remember them and thereby reconstruct the past. This is memoir. (Humpty Dumpty would have been deselected by the Peace Corps because of a tendency to fall apart under stress.)

I have indicated in brackets the year of the interviews that are quoted from, out of fairness to those interviewed. Remembering events after less than a year is different than doing so thirty-five or more years later when the Humpty Dumpty Effect becomes operative.

INTRODUCTION

The Circle

It is noon on a sunny June day in 1996 in Gloucester, Massachusetts, with a cloud-fringed sky of deep, distant blue. The clouds stand out so starkly that the sky beyond seems without end. The air smells fresh with a hint of salt water and seaweed. The spray from the ocean glistens on the rocks by the edge of the sea. In the background can be heard the soft rushing sound of waves washing across the boulder-strewn beach. Standing in a rough circle on these rocks is a group of people who have gathered in reunion. An African man steps into the circle to pour libation according to Ghanaian tradition. As he slowly pours the ceremonial drink onto the ground, he calls forth the spirits of the ancestors and the memories of friends and relatives who have died:

"*Nyame nsa; Asase nsa; Abayifo nsa . . .*" [God, come and drink; Earth, come and drink; Spirits, come and drink.]

It is a quiet moment that serves to create an inner moment of reflection. People and events drift into memory and the emotions of past times echo again. Between tears and laughter, one by one, individuals step forward into the circle to speak, remembering a lost friend, retelling an old familiar incident, giving voice to their feelings. The circle confirms a bond that has evolved out of a special experience thirty-five years ago. This is Ghana I, the first Peace Corps Volunteers to go overseas in 1961 and I am one of that group. We've held reunions every five years (though recently it's more like every two years). Week to week and month to month, many of us are in touch, but the reunion, increasingly through the years, has become a special occasion. Although few formal activities are planned, we end the gathering at mid-day on Sunday in this circle. It is a magical moment that touches the heart.

Ghana I is special because we feel ourselves to be so and because what we did in 1961 was special. In many ways we are ordinary people who, by our own individual choice, became involved in extraordinary events. In that short, frenzied period of time from March first to August thirtieth of 1961, the Peace Corps moved from an idealistic notion to a reality. On March first nothing existed but the idea; six months later the fifty of us, Ghana I, were in Accra, Ghana, to begin service as Peace Corps Volunteers. Our behavior and performance over the next two years helped to establish the viability of the Peace Corps. Those directly involved as volunteers, training faculty, and administrators were all aware of the significance of being first. That challenge created a sense of uniqueness which has lasted through the years. Through time, at least in the minds of some of the group, Ghana I has gradually been transformed into "Legendary Ghana I."

Being First

Standing within that circle at Bass Rocks in Gloucester, Massachusetts, in June of 1996, I felt the emotional bond with the others. Remembering DeeDee Vellenga and the sweetness of her being brought tears to my eyes. Hearing Alice O'Grady again tell her "Filling up the mammy lorry" story made me laugh. Seeing George and Newell and Marion and Meryl made me want to hug each one of them. I thought of how we share present lives and past memories. In the weeks following that reunion, I developed the conviction that the story of our experience should be recorded—part history, part recollection and reflection about the experience, part celebration of "being first." By God, we did it! It is worth celebrating.

In retirement since 1994, restless and seeking new challenges, I became the secretary-convenor of the Ghana I group. This means that I try to keep the address list accurate and current and circulate letters with information about upcoming reunions. Inspired by the 1996 reunion, I also began to organize an archival project, with the encouragement of the archivists at the John F. Kennedy Library in Boston. Because our group is still identifiable and in active mutual contact, it seemed possible to create a Ghana I archive within the Returned Peace Corps Volunteer Collection at the Kennedy Library. To promote this idea I sent letters to the group requesting materials for the Library.

An early response from David Apter motivated me to begin thinking more seriously about writing the Ghana I story. He wrote:

"In retrospect, it [training Ghana I] was one of the best things I was ever associated with. . . . If someone from Ghana I has the time perhaps we could sit down with a tape recorder. The original [program] had a verve and commitment that one can only call historic."

Reading that, I thought to myself, "Hey, why not? 'Historic' may be a bit thick but the tape recorder sounds like a good idea. I certainly have the time. Might even write a book."

So, in May 1997, I began collecting archival materials and taping interviews with the Ghana I group, the training faculty from Berkeley 1961, and various Peace Corps administrators who had direct involvement with us.

Why I Joined the Peace Corps

In meeting people through the years, whenever I mention that I had joined the Peace Corps in 1961, I usually get two responses. The first is the comment, "I wanted to join the Peace Corps after college/before I got married/when I first heard about it/when my children were grown but. . . ." And I think to myself, "I'm sorry you missed such a wonderful opportunity." The other is the question, "Why did you join the Peace Corps?" Since this memoir is a result of my having done so, I think it proper to start by answering that question.

It all had to do with the 1930s movie, *Beau Geste*, in which brave young men, faced with incredibly complicated personal lives, joined the French Foreign Legion. Shunning close friends and civilized comforts, they next appear in remotest North Africa, there to become involved in legendary exploits. This image sustained me in moments of personal stress, as I settled into being a junior high school teacher in New York City in the late 1950s. When I had to deal with an impossible class, or when I wanted to untangle myself from a romantic involvement, I would think to myself, "They can't do this to me—I'll go and join the French Foreign Legion!" By 1961, I had carried the fantasy out only so far as to grow a beard. If you looked at me, in dim light at a distance of thirty to forty feet, I did look a bit mysterious.

I was in my fifth year of teaching at Harriet Beecher Stowe, officially known as Junior High School 136 Manhattan, under the New York City Board of Education. I taught Social Studies to grades seven to nine in what was a doubly segregated school—all Black (by circumstance—it was located in Harlem) and all female (Board policy then). Although there were problems related to teaching, the late 1950s, even in New York City, was a gentler time. The school motto was "Every Inch A Lady" and we chose a Lady of the Week. The students, their families, and the faculty took these things seriously.

That it was a different era is also illustrated by what happened when I first grew a goatee over the summer vacation in 1960. It was the first day of class and my students, amidst a lot of giggling, good-naturedly commented about the change in my appearance:

"Hey, Mr. Klein, are you a beatnik?"

"I think that's cool, tell Mr. Nussbaum [the principal] to grow one too."

"Are they going to let you keep that thing?"

I was pleased with their responses because I personally liked the beard and intended to keep it. Arlene, my current girl friend, thought it made me look distinguished. As the United Federation of Teachers (UFT) representative in my school, before reporting to school that September, I had checked Board regulations which stated that teachers must be neatly attired (men wore jackets and ties, women skirts or dresses) and well groomed, but said nothing about beards.

As I was congratulating myself on how well my students had accepted the change in my appearance, I heard a rapid knocking at the classroom door. Looking through the door window, I saw a frantically gesturing Mr. Nussbaum, waving me out of the classroom. I stepped out into the hall.

"You can't teach wearing a beard!" he said.

Mr. Nussbaum was the quintessence of New York Jewish intellectualism. He wore horn-rimmed glasses, had a scholarly and distant look, and was, at all times—except this one—calm and cerebral. His receding hairline, which emphasized his shiny forehead and his quizzical eyes, made him look like a cross between Adlai

Stevenson and Woody Allen. In ordinary conversations, he seemed to be reading from prepared remarks, based on some scholarly work, rather than simply talking with you. But now he was apoplectic. I tried to respond quietly.

"Sir, I feel that I'm properly dressed and my students seem to like the change."

"But it isn't right; it will upset the class. How can you teach like that?"

"Certainly if my appearance causes a noisy classroom, I would immediately shave off the beard. But that doesn't seem to be the case, does it? May I return to my class?"

Mr. Nussbaum turned and slowly walked down the hall, no doubt to return to his office where in Talmudic isolation he could try to gain some perspective on the changes occurring around him. So began my fifth year of teaching in New York City. Along with it were pressures toward responsible domesticity from my parents. Mom and Pop kept saying, "You're old enough to get married now; you're thirty-two. Come home next weekend and meet Maxine. Her folks think you are wonderful and she's such a nice girl" (surely the most unromantic phrase in the English language). In my head I was already hearing the martial strains of the drums of the Legion.

My first attempt to answer those drums did not turn out well. In seeking a new teaching challenge I applied for a Fulbright Teaching Fellowship at a secondary school in Northern Rhodesia. With an M.A. in History from University of Chicago and five years' teaching experience, on paper I was a highly qualified candidate. Within weeks of applying, I was called for an interview at Columbia University with a U.S. foreign aid specialist and a professor of African Studies. They were both serious-looking men, conservatively dressed, with the stern, unsmiling demeanor of a fifth grade teacher who is grimly modeling self-discipline. I had done nothing to prepare for the interview.

The first question was:

"Why do you want to teach in Rhodesia?'"

Although it was mid-February, I immediately began to feel cold sweat uncomfortably tickling my armpits, and in a panic realized that these interviewers might not be impressed with my Beau Geste story.

"Well, I really enjoy teaching . . . um . . . um."

"Do you have any special interest in or knowledge of Rhodesia?"

I could find it on a map but I felt that this was not the kind of answer that they were looking for.

"No, I am interested in a new challenge and would like to teach overseas."

"Are you at all familiar with Northern Rhodesia's current status?"

"Uh . . . no . . . uh."

"Can you name the major colonial powers in Africa and discuss their influence?"

"Uh . . . England! No, the British; uh . . . Great Britain."

"Yes?"

Silence and then, trying to be helpful, the African Studies professor:

"Of course, you've heard of Timbuktu."

Of course, I had. Mom always used to tell me that if I didn't do my share of the household chores, she'd run away to Timbuktu. I didn't think that was the reference the Professor had in mind. The interview ended shortly thereafter and the Fulbright Fellows lost a good, though ill-informed, prospect to the Peace Corps.

It was about this time in early 1961 that John F. Kennedy was inaugurated as President and, in his inaugural speech, offered the challenge, "Ask not what your country can do for you, but rather what you can do for your country." I heard the speech on television and was moved by it. It added a moral dimension to my restless, romanticized adventurism.

Much of my motivation to join the Peace Corps came from my experiences while serving in the U.S. Army in Korea from 1952 to 1954. Having completed my M.A. in History, I was drafted in August 1952 when my deferment expired. Within six months I was assigned as Company Clerk in a Forward Ordnance Depot about ten miles behind the front lines in Korea. I worked with First Sergeant Burl Grant, an African-American who had worked his way up through the ranks during this period when the armed forces were being integrated, a process that was far from complete in 1953. Sergeant Grant dealt with the world through his eyes—they were brown, deep set, and full of life. They could be cold and unblinking, flecked with fire, as he dealt with diehard racists in our company. He would never raise his voice but his eyes signaled the anger and contempt he felt; that, and his rank, forced men to accept and follow his orders. We shared a tent and in the evenings, listening to jazz and be-bop (Errol Garner, Shorty Rogers, Dizzy Gillespie), I'd look at Grant and his eyes were soft and mellow.

As Company Clerk I worked together with Grant in the company Orderly Room. We became personal friends. We shared a dislike of those racists who turned their bigotry against the Koreans who worked for us in the depot as clerks, houseboys, and kitchen attendants. Our houseboy was Yoo Yung Shik, whom we called Pak. He was 15, with black hair and black eyes, broad-faced with a very expressive mouth. In anger or in joy, his lips always parted into a smile, giving him a pleasant appearance. When he was upset, the smile would freeze into a grimace, but when he was happy it would be accompanied by a slight giggle. Pak came from a small farming community in central Korea that had seen combat several times in the course of the war. As with many other young people, he had attached himself to a U.S. Army unit as a means of survival. When we paid him, he would take off to his village to share with his family, buying whatever he could with the MPC (military payment certificates) that we all, Koreans and Americans, used as currency.

Grant and I treated Pak decently and he became a friend, taking us to his village to meet some of his family. This kind of relationship was discouraged officially and scorned by many of the Americans in the company who would only deal with the Koreans by thinking of them as "gooks" and treating them as inferiors.

About six months after I had arrived in Korea, Pak came to me one day in the orderly room tent where I worked. For the first time since I had known him, his face was dark and somber. I even noticed tears in his eyes. He told me what had been happening in the company mess hall.

Our mess hall was typically American with a superabundance of whatever ill-prepared food we were being served. There were no shortages and much food was wasted. Sergeant Grant had started the practice of allowing the local-hire Koreans either to eat or take home the surplus of prepared food from each meal. What I found out from Pak was that Mess Sergeant Rousselot—Southern, white, and racist—had been verbally and physically abusive to the Koreans as he reluctantly gave them the table surplus. Rousselot had even gone so far as to throw the food into the trash cans before allowing the Koreans to take any. I immediately told Grant, who stormed out of the orderly room to find Rousselot. I was not witness to their encounter, but Pak happily reported to me within a few days that all was *Dai Jobi* [okay] in the mess hall.

After some time, Pak asked me to help him. He said that he and some of the other houseboys wanted to learn to speak and read English; knowing that I was approachable, they wanted me to be their teacher. As Company Clerk I did have a lot of free time I could devote to teaching rather than just drinking at the enlisted men's club. With no training or preparation other than the fact that I had used the language for 25 years of my life, I became a teacher of English. It felt good and right to be working with these young men, to be a bridge between cultures, to be expressing my feelings and attitudes about commonality among people. I also found that I enjoyed being a teacher. When I finished my military service in 1954 and could find no want ads in The New York Times for "Historians," I changed careers and became a teacher of Social Studies.

Korea and Pak and even Rousselot were on my mind as I went to the Post Office on Broadway and 68th Street in Manhattan to pick up a Peace Corps Questionnaire in April 1961. I remember filling it out. It included a lengthy list of personal and professional skills to be checked on a scale from "highly skilled" to "unskilled." With five years' experience, I hoped to become a Peace Corps teacher but wasn't sure what Peace Corps was looking for (they weren't either). I pondered how best to mark:

"Milk a cow"

"Drive a tractor"

"Service an automobile transmission"

"Use a welding torch to repair equipment."

Where, I thought to myself, did the application list the skills I was totally confident about? Items such as:

"Interpret a New York City Subway map"

"Control a class of 8th grade students on Friday afternoon"

"Read the Sunday edition of The New York Times"

were nowhere in evidence on the application.

Even if I wasn't ready to announce to the world that I was "joining the Legion," I went ahead with it and mailed the form to Washington within a few days. I had no trouble in responding to the item in the questionnaire that asked, "Why do you want to serve with the Peace Corps?" I wrote the following:

"My experience as a teacher in New York City and in the Army in Korea both convince me that it is important to reach out to people. We Americans are a privileged people and too many of us go overseas and become 'Ugly Americans,' arrogant and insensitive. I would like to teach in another country because I am an experienced teacher and I would like to live in another country so I can learn more about it."

On June 24th I was invited to the University of California in Berkeley to train to become a Peace Corps Volunteer teacher in Ghana. Training was to start July 2 and we were expected in Ghana by the end of August. I barely had time to meet with Arlene and tell her, "I'm joining the French Foreign Legion and going to Africa."

1

CREATING THE PEACE CORPS

Defining the Towering Task

Legendary in its own way, the story of the people who originated the Peace Corps is, for Ghana I, like tracing a family tree. If we were the first generation of Peace Corps Volunteers, they were the progenitors who brought us into that life. Their boldness and our adventurousness combined to help create the Peace Corps.

Peace Corps began to be organized immediately after John F. Kennedy's inauguration in January 1961. He assigned R. Sargent Shriver to head a task force to develop proposals for the new agency. Shriver met with academics, heads of voluntary agencies and old mentors such as Father Hesburgh of Notre Dame; but it wasn't until he encountered Warren Wiggins that the roller coaster began its ride. Wiggins came from ICA (the International Cooperation Agency, so titled in 1961 but soon to be re-titled AID—Agency for International Development) and brought with him like-minded colleagues who wanted to get new development programs into the field quickly under what they perceived were the innovative approaches implied in the name, Peace Corps. Shriver responded positively to their ideas, which he presented to the President. The next day, on March 1, President Kennedy signed an Executive Order creating the Peace Corps and appointed R. Sargent Shriver to head the new agency.

Within weeks, like determined squatters, the Peace Corps staff had taken over more and more space in the Maiatico Building at 806 Connecticut Avenue, only two blocks from the White House. Appropriately enough the offices were formerly occupied by ICA. Shriver took more than desks and offices from ICA. Led by Warren Wiggins, a group of ICA officers had joined Peace Corps staff. It was Wiggins' conceptual paper, "The Towering Task," that had jump-started the Peace Corps study group in February. The paper had recommended massive (1000+) programs such as teachers' aides for the Philippines, suggesting that the new agency directly operate overseas programs. Co-author William Josephson had the idea to begin work immediately under presidential executive order and not wait for specific enabling legislation.

Some of the early participants gave descriptions of the chaotic character of the Peace Corps' beginnings and Shriver's quickly defined role. Harris Wofford talked about the early suggestion that Peace Corps not do any projects directly but that they be contracted out to universities and other agencies. Wofford commented in an oral history interview:

"There's not much chance of that with Shriver running an agency. . . . Sargent Shriver clearly tended toward a fast moving, hard hitting, core central organization. He put enormous weight on speed and the more he saw of the complaints about the State Department and AID particularly—how long it takes in their pipeline to get anything done; how, in many projects, the time for them has passed by the time the experts and the money arrive—he was determined that in four months we'd be able to produce volunteers to fill jobs that took fourteen months in the old agencies. He just felt that with Kennedy's backing he could build a corps that would do it."

Four months was about right. It was April 24 when Ghana requested Peace Corps teachers and it was August 30 when we arrived in Accra.

Ed Bayley, who was the first Director of Information, told what happened right after the Presidential Executive Order:

"Then all hell broke loose, of course. And we really didn't know what the Peace Corps was at that point. . . . There was a sort of division there between the bureaucrats and the people coming in from outside. And Wiggins and Josephson and Charlie Nelson, a couple more of that bunch, they came over from AID. And they really thought they knew all about this, and we were a bunch of amateurs."

Some ICA professionals were skeptical about the Peace Corps, an attitude that was often reflected in the field as Peace Corps Volunteers began work in various developing countries. The telephone log of a senior ICA official, Dennis A. Fitzgerald, has notes from February 1961 of a conversation with David Bell, about to be appointed Director of Bureau of the Budget:

"When I talk [with Sargent Shriver] I will ask what is the PC, have you thought about getting any ideas on political problems involved and where you will put people and for what—understand it [PC] is full of fire. . . . He is collecting a lot of eager beavers—Wiggins, etc., etc., from our shop—they are already occupying the whole sixth floor of this building and every day [we] get a request for another bunch of people. Have talked to Shriver and he is groping—Bell said he is an intelligent guy—he feels he has a real operation that will change the future of the world—is not inclined to be over-impressed with the problems. . . .

"The real squeeze is the time—everyone thinking you have to pick up all the bright boys graduating this year in June—by March or April they generally have jobs lined up—this is what makes them frantic—I could care less but would rather hit next year's graduates than this one but Shriver feels the President has put a lot of emphasis on this and idea of waiting one year would not appeal to the President."

One of the ICA "eager beavers" was twenty-three year old Richard Thornell, a graduate of Fisk and the Woodrow Wilson School at Princeton. Richard is low key in manner, soft-spoken, cerebral. You almost have to strain to hear his comments and responses but it's well worth the effort. His eyes sparkle with humor and good will as he talks about his early involvement with the Peace Corps, but flash with anger when talking about racial injustice. I sought him out in 1998, knowing that he had played a significant role in the birth of the Ghana project, although his involvement was cut short by illness at the time.

After serving as a summer intern during graduate school in international affairs, Thornell went to work for ICA. He had developed an interest in Africa, Ghana particularly, and by 1961 was preparing for his assignment to Accra as an assistant program officer in the USAID mission there. In our interview he explained how he became involved with the Peace Corps:

"Once John Alexander was asked by Wiggins to come over—he was the person at ICA I was dealing with—I followed him with one condition. If there's a prospect of a request for Peace Corps from Ghana that I would go out there because I'm giving up the job that I really want in ICA. He said, 'Of course, yes' because—and I have to emphasize this—because nobody who was working on Africa, ICA or Peace Corps, thought that Ghana would be the very first country to receive volunteers."

Thornell characterized the group around Wiggins: "Those coming out of ICA were progressive people who understood and believed in economic development for the sake of raising standards of living. They were not into this 'buying people off.' Most were economists, not political hacks. Half of them had a background in the Marshall Plan which, for them, was a monumental achievement of assistance." [1999]

To staff the new agency, Sargent Shriver had attracted and recruited two dissimilar groups. One was the pragmatic, hard-headed ICA types; the other idealistic, visionary politicos, attracted to the Kennedy presidency. From the point of view of those of us who became volunteers, the differences in approach were played out in the nature of Peace Corps programs, the role to be played by the volunteers, and the training needed to prepare them for overseas. It was Shriver's genius to attract dynamic staff and challenge them to confront each other and then come to him with the best ideas about policies and programs from which he would choose.

Writing in 1966, George Carter, an early Peace Corps staffer, commented: "In choosing his advisers, he selected men of widely differing temperaments and abilities and then encouraged competition among them in handling various issues. Finally, on a lesser level, he titled memoranda on PC policy 'Interim Policy Directives' as a further admonition to any who believed that current policy was the last word. PC programs and programming are products of this environment of institutionalized uncertainty."

Bradley Patterson, then Executive Secretary of the Peace Corps, described Shriver:

"... Sarge is not a very systematic person; he's a charismatic administrator, a guy who leaps into the breach and gets things done, crossing channels or speeding things up or taking short cuts or cutting corners and so forth, in any manner that he feels necessary.... The Shriver idea of the Peace Corps was the Peace Corps because he ran it out of the palm of his hand."

Shriver was building a staff and soon would do a flying tour of the developing world to promote this new agency. Bayley described the early strategy:

"The Peace Corps was a precarious idea and we felt that it would be much less precarious if it were a living body instead of just an idea, if it was embodied and we were under way. The risky thing was that Congress might resent this [beginning operations quickly], however. The second risk would be that something bad would happen in the first months that would let Congress say, 'It doesn't work.' But against that was the gain of momentum and the feeling that in the first hundred days we did have the power to do things like that which made us very strong when we started. Shriver was itching to go."

The Mentors of Ghana I: George Carter and David Apter

During that early developmental period George Carter and David Apter became involved with the Peace Corps. They were eventually to play influential roles in the life of Ghana I. Their stories are intertwined.

In 1960 George Carter, an African-American in his mid-thirties from Pennsylvania, was working for the Kennedy campaign. Harris Wofford was Kennedy's adviser on civil rights matters and in the midst of the campaign he convinced Kennedy to make a phone call to Mrs. Coretta Scott King after the Reverend Martin Luther King had been imprisoned in Reidsville State Prison in Alabama. Afterwards, George Carter and other activists suggested they fully publicize Kennedy's call and bring it to the attention of African-American voters. Flyers were printed and on the Sunday before the election were distributed outside predominantly black churches throughout the country. Some analysts and certainly some of the Kennedy people felt that the African-American vote for Kennedy was crucial in that very close election.

How did George Carter get from Pennsylvania and the Kennedy campaign to Peace Corps/Ghana? It was that phone call and what followed as Sargent Shriver set up the Talent Search project for the incoming administration. Since 1958 Carter had been information director of AMSAC (American Society for African Culture), a group that promoted improved American understanding of African politics and culture, both of which were undergoing dramatic change. He was married to a Parisian woman, Michelle, was fluent in French, and he traveled extensively throughout Africa for AMSAC, organizing conferences, meeting with leaders, establishing avenues of communication. After the Kennedy election it was his ambition to get an ambassadorial appointment to a small, French-speaking, newly independent country, such as Guinea, Mali, Niger, or Upper Volta. Given his background, his experience, and his skills, it was not an unrealistic goal. His main Washington contact was Harris Wofford, who was part of the new administration's transition team. Wofford, as well as Sargent Shriver and others, was part of the talent search team whose job was to identify and vet potential government appointees for all departments and at all levels.

When it was first proposed in January 1961 Carter did not think much of the Peace Corps idea. In our 1997 interview, I asked him:

"What did you think was their [Shriver et al.] vision for the Peace Corps?"

"Crossroads Africa became in my mind the model they were somehow gravitating toward. I think it's one thing for Crossroads to take groups of 8, 10, 15 kids to maybe a dozen villages across West Africa, with the idea—live with the people, work with the people . . . of course work means, do small construction projects which were capital non-intensive, labor high-intensive. That's kind of the vision. The other thing that bothered me . . . was the idea of these [Peace Corps] youngsters, who I assumed incidentally would be middle-class, mostly white, college kids, going over there with a kind of naive dumbness: 'how can we help?' And I thought that it was going to be counterproductive and create problems for the kids, for their hosts and for host governments. I just did not see what kind of positive value that was going to bring to the mess of U.S. relations with Africa. I'd seen a lot—Ghana and so forth—what the hell are a group of kids going to do?"

After Kennedy's inauguration, Carter arranged through Harris Wofford to spend time in Washington to lay the groundwork for a possible appointment to a position in foreign affairs, hopefully even an ambassadorship. What happened next?

"Then how did you get involved with the Peace Corps?"

"Wofford was my connection; he was the one who got me into this. I was waiting to go over to see Chester Bowles [Undersecretary of State] but the meeting was delayed, so Wofford took me over to see Sargent Shriver at the Mayflower Hotel [the temporary headquarters for the Peace Corps Task Force]. This was about March tenth or so. First thing, Shriver comes out and says, 'My God, George Carter! You're the guy who won the election and you're the guy who knows all about French Africa. Why don't you wait around. Bill Attwood [editor of Look Magazine] is coming over here and we could all go to dinner together.'

"I looked at Wofford and then said that I was supposed to be meeting with Chester Bowles. We did later get together for dinner: Sargent Shriver, Wofford, Attwood and me. That dinner went on until they chased us out of the Mayflower Restaurant. I spent that two or three hours [fighting] tooth and nail, going head to head with the three of them about the Peace Corps. A piece of nonsense, I in fact told them. I said, if you guys know anything about what it's like in Africa or Southern India with a group of unsophisticated, well-meaning but naive Americans running around there trying to do good, you wouldn't even be talking about this.

"I was playing the role—I'm the professional, I've seen it, and you don't know what the hell you're talking about. We walked out of the hotel, Wofford and I walking just a little ahead. At one point, Shriver called Wofford back to where he was. Then I overheard Shriver say to Wofford, 'We have got to get this guy Carter working for us....' " [1997]

By the end of March, Shriver had talked George Carter into serving as a consultant to Peace Corps on a short-term basis, with the specialized assignment of helping to develop programs in French-speaking Africa. It was part of Shriver's genius as an organizer that he could convince early opponents of the Peace Corps to come on board. Shriver would say to them that he fully understood their reasons for opposing Peace Corps and thus didn't it make great sense for them to be part of creating it to avoid the pitfalls so eloquently described. It worked. Carter soon found himself on a trip to Africa. He accompanied Vice President Lyndon Johnson to Senegal for its independence celebration and served as Johnson's interpreter and guide for the two-day visit. Carter then continued on to Bamako, Mali to do Peace Corps work.

David Apter, Ph.D. from Princeton University, was Professor of Political Science at the University of Chicago and author of *Gold Coast in Transition*. He was about to transfer to the University of California at Berkeley in mid-1961. He became the Director of Studies for the Ghana I training program that summer and that is when I first met him. Apter was in his early thirties, a well-dressed man of medium height, with neatly trimmed hair, never quite combed flat. He had impaired vision in one eye which gave him a quizzical look that was somehow appropriate—his speech and manner were questioning, his outlook slightly jaundiced. He was by no means the absent-minded professor. Apter was experienced and knowledgeable about African affairs and had lived in Ghana (then Gold Coast) in the years leading up to its independence, 1956–1957. He spoke about events and personalities from personal experience. He was an academic to the extent that his writing was a bit murky to one not versed in such styles, but in talking about things Ghanaian he was clear and impassioned.

Like Carter, Apter had at first been opposed to the idea of the Peace Corps. They knew each other and had on occasion discussed it. I asked Apter in an interview in 1997:

"Did you feel that Ghana and other African countries could use some kind of help, like Peace Corps?"

He answered, "I couldn't imagine anything worse than about 2000 callow young Americans running around Africa at this very sensitive moment. It seems that Americans have a certain random quality about the way they act. The English-style school system in Ghana as it was imposed by missionaries and colonialists is quite rigid and organized. Peace Corps could be catastrophic in such a setting.

"I had just come away from writing a book on Ghana, being totally involved and getting to know the Ghanaians involved in the political drift to the left around Nkrumah [President of Ghana in 1961]. This was a Cold War period in which the Ghanaians were moving to the left towards a more authoritarian system where the radicals, I thought, would be just delighted to seize on situations where they could nail an American making a fool of himself. Politically I thought Peace Corps is not a wise thing to do because it would strengthen the extreme militants. I was afraid that Peace Corps would be foils of a dynamic they had very little to do with."

In April 1961 Apter was in Bamako, Mali, as a guest of the government, consulting on development of local political institutions. In the same interview he described the following phone call:

"I was sitting in my hotel in Bamako and I get this phone call. 'George? George Carter? Where in the world are you?' I thought he was calling from the United States. He said, 'I'm downstairs at the hotel.' He said, 'I've been to the Senegalese celebration.' I'll never forget this, he said, 'Lyndon Johnson wanted a Black face for the celebration and here I am.' So I said, 'That's pretty poor—a whistle from a vice president and you join the Peace Corps.' [Kennedy had appointed Johnson to head the Peace Corps Advisory Council.] George said, 'It's not like that. I want to talk to you.' After we talked I agreed to speak to Shriver when I returned to the U.S."

The outcome of Apter's conversation with Shriver was that Apter agreed to become Director of Studies for the Peace Corps training program for Ghana. Apter described it:

"Sargent Shriver said that all the reasons I'd given about the dangers of Peace Corps are valid and then added—shouldn't you be the one then to put together a program for Ghana? The conversation was about Ghana, strictly Ghana—I knew it was to be the first program, a model perhaps for other programs. I was aware that it would be important—being first it would automatically serve as a model." [1997]

Shriver Meets Nkrumah (and Ghana I is Born)

As reported in Shriver's memo to the President, there were four potential Peace Corps programs as of late March 1961: Chile; Colombia (in cooperation with CARE); Tanganyika (a modest request from visiting President Nyerere for some road-builders); the Philippines (Warren Wiggins' favorite as originally proposed in "The Towering Task"). However, by mid-April no country agreements had been signed and Shriver, not one to sit still very long, wanted to get things rolling. He decided to make a quick tour of Africa and Asia. Ed Bayley, Director of Public Information for the Peace Corps in 1961, describes this tour in his 1968 oral history interview:

"It was a very important trip. The whole Peace Corps was launched with such speed and without, really, sufficient backgrounding if you were going to do the thing under ideal conditions. I think it was the right way to do it: you had to strike while the enthusiasm was there. But if it had been a typical AID project, or something, they would have spent two years of diplomatic negotiations on this thing, and it probably never would have gained the same momentum. But we didn't really know anything about the other countries [developing nations].

"But [for] most of these countries, I think it was probably an adjustment of thinking. They were used to foreign aid, and they liked the idea of experts coming in, they liked to have money coming in, but to have a bunch of enthusiastic young people—even though almost every one of them recognized the need for teachers—it was a strange idea, and they were negative at first usually. But Sargent Shriver, again, being a good salesman, sold them on these things.... But we didn't know what the Peace Corps was going to be until we made that trip."

By April 18, the U.S. Embassy in Accra was cabling that it ". . . welcomes the opportunity discuss PC with Shriver and introduce him to key GOGhana officials. Have requested appointment Nkrumah morning April 24. Reaction GOGhana unpredictable."

Unpredictable, indeed. On April 22, the Ghanaian Times had an editorial headlined, "Peace Corps: Agency of Neo-Colonialism," which was described in Embassy cable traffic:

"As world told on paper, and as Mr. Sargent Shriver will want us to believe, PC meant offer voluntary aid to so-called needy countries. Under it, USG will send scores young yankee graduates to Africa and Latin America as teachers, social, and industrial technological workers and the like.... We reject all twaddles about its humanitarianism and declare this nothing short of agency of neo-colonialism ... instrument for subversion less developed countries into puppet American economic imperialism."

That same day Nkrumah urgently requested a meeting with our Ambassador, Francis H. Russell. The report of that meeting states:

"Nkrumah said he deeply regretted editorial attacking PC ... agreed would be desirable receive Sargent Shriver and hear his explanations PC. Nkrumah commented press often got out ahead of the government and made unauthorized statements. He would be happy to receive Sargent Shriver. Added obviously nobody had to accept Peace Corps if he did not like it and whole question should be judged on its merits."

That ambivalence about utilizing Peace Corps assistance continued throughout the two years of our service in Ghana.

And then R. Sargent Shriver and Kwame Nkrumah met. Ed Bayley's notes on the meeting provide an interesting introductory snapshot of what was to become the Ghana I project:

"Nkrumah   splendid idea
Teaching schools
Electric & water engrs & sanitary
Shd be subject to Ghana govt direction
Need 270 secondary s teachers
Don't want executives, want workers"

In a later interview, Bayley commented:

"We found a reluctance to accept ordinary university and college graduates as teachers. I remember the Minister of Education in Ghana told Sarge, 'We'll take some of your people if they have Ph.D.s from your better universities.' And Sarge said, 'Well, they won't have Ph.D.s. Some will but most won't. And what do you mean by the better universities?' He says, 'Yale, Harvard, and Princeton.'"

The follow-up cable reported the Ghanaians "stressing desperate need secondary schoolteachers in science and mathematics. Need 270 secondary teachers by next September. Stressed importance August arrivals for orientation prior September school opening." By May 1, Ghana formally requested discussions about Peace Corps "recruitment of science teachers, engineers of all grades, and university teachers" and set two conditions:

"1. Peace Corps was in Ghana at the invitation of the government and will be responsible to government of Ghana and take their instructions from the ministers.

"2. Ghana expects Peace Corps members to accept and carry out operational and executive duties in the field, and not regard themselves in the role of advisers."

Neither Shriver nor Wiggins could have given a better description of how Peace Corps was going to be different from previous U.S. foreign aid programs.

2

FINDING THE VOLUNTEERS

Sorting the Mail

How prepared was Peace Corps to answer Ghana's request by the end of August? Not very. While R. Sargent Shriver was out selling the goods to the developing world, the newly assembled staff in Washington was frantically building the factory to produce them. But conventional foreign aid wisdom was that these things could not be rushed. Professor Thomas Blaidsell of University of California at Berkeley visited Peace Corps in early April 1961 to explore program possibilities for the university. In a report to the Chancellor, he wrote:

"Just as the Point IV Program was an old idea in a new form, the Peace Corps idea is an old idea in a new form. To make it something more than the collection of spot activities which have been undertaken by many individual private agencies will require months of hard work and thought.... It is difficult to refrain from praising the enthusiasm and idealism which were evident, particularly in talking with some of the younger people associated with the staff."

There was enthusiasm and idealism both in Peace Corps/Washington and throughout the United States, as was attested by the thousands of letters of interest received from January to April. However it wasn't until the very end of April that the formal application questionnaires were available in post offices, on college campuses, and elsewhere. Within a month 8500 completed forms had been received; more than 5000 of those indicated availability for training and service by the summer. So, at least there was an apparently adequate supply of raw material, although no one had yet devised the exact design of the final product. That was a task that would be done by the early groups of volunteers, such as Ghana I.

Tom Quimby, who was the first head of recruitment, describes the challenge as of late March in an interview in 1968:

"One of the very first jobs, of course, was that just after the thing was announced, we immediately got something like twenty thousand letters of interest and application, and sorting these out and getting them answered and setting up a structure for formalizing applications and receiving them and considering them, these were the jobs that occupied us the first few months. I can remember one night not getting home until 3 o'clock in the morning and being back at the office at 7 the next morning."

The letters were transformed into formal applications through individuals completing the Peace Corps questionnaire; along with the completed questionnaire, the applicant was expected to arrange for six letters of recommendation as well as formal transcripts of college work. Another taste of what the Peace Corps office was like in those days comes from a college paper, prepared by a graduate student in Public Administration who worked as an intern in mid-1961:

"There was an immense amount of pressure, even on the people in lower positions. Consequently, several secretaries actually had nervous breakdowns. Almost everyone put in a lot of overtime work, including the top men, but the backlog of work kept piling up. . . . The most pressing need of the Peace Corps last summer was to get a project organized, through training, and in the field proving itself. Because of this, Selection was probably the key division in the whole process, and it caught hell from all sides."

These comments almost lend credence to one of our oft-repeated jokes about Ghana I during training. Although we were constantly told how select a group of trainees we were, the haste with which we had been gathered led us to believe that, in fact, we were probably the first 58 people who had applied to the Peace Corps.

An April 21, 1961 review of the first 4000 questionnaires received showed that 2907 potential volunteers were available as of June 15 but analysis of college transcripts indicated only 36 with college credit of 60–90 hours in education; there's no indication of science or math majors. By May 23 there were 4800 potentials and the pool had enlarged to include 1203 with one or more years of graduate school and 137 with 40 to 90 hours in education. But questionnaires did not one-for-one equal Peace Corps volunteers. The questionnaire was one of several steps in the selection process. There were six letters of recommendation to be checked, as well as college transcripts, and then applicants had to take the Peace Corps Qualification Examination which, as of May 2, had not been made up (the exam was first given on May 27).

Ghana's Ministry of Education was on a different schedule. As early as May 2, following their own traditional expatriate teacher screening procedures, it was requesting that Peace Corps immediately provide "biographic data including transcripts of 75–100 applicants, primarily science, math, French for review," expecting to fill a minimum of 30 positions. Of course, we knew none of this. Individually we may have been thinking about what it might be like to join the Peace Corps but at the end of April, 1961 the 58 of us looked as follows:

    15 were completing a Bachelor's degree;

    10 were in graduate school;

    24 were teaching (mostly junior and senior high);

     9 were otherwise working or traveling.

How did we stack up against Ghana's request of May 2? Off the top, the Yale,

Harvard, Princeton total was 7. There were 24 experienced teachers but only 7 in math or science and only 4 had an M.A. degree. There were no Ph.D.s but there were 21 who admitted to some fluency in French.

Me and Sarge Start the Peace Corps

Little did I know that Shriver's timing in Ghana was perfect for me. As he was setting the wheels in motion for the teaching project there, I was in the midst of my restless fifth year of teaching. During the 1960–61 school year, I was busy as the union organizer in my school district for the United Federation of Teachers, following the first-ever teachers' strike in New York City in November. It had been a one-day strike to get the Board of Education to accept a system-wide collective bargaining election to be held within a year and succeeded in winning that goal. I was on the Executive Board of the UFT and was considering applying for full- time work as a union organizer. I'd also thought about starting the long, bothersome administrative route to becoming a supervisor or principal in the New York City school system. I had a strong desire to be doing something more challenging or, at least, different. I was ready for a change.

By the end of April 1961, I was aware that the Peace Corps existed (in case the French Foreign Legion didn't pan out), and that it offered another possible avenue of escape (with what seemed like a lower level of risk). I hastened to complete the application as soon as it was available at my local post office. It was fun to fill out; after two years as company clerk in the Army and almost five years in a New York City classroom, I was expert at filling in the blanks in whatever form or report I was presented with. I remember requesting a project in teaching and giving a preference for Africa (I was still trying to undo the Fulbright Fiasco). I was also in the midst of the process of soliciting letters of reference from my principal at JHS 136, a YMCA secretary on Long Island, fellow teachers, and a lifelong friend, Pete Strand; also sending for transcripts from Northeastern University and the University of Chicago. All this entitled me to an admission card to the first Peace Corps written examination on May 27.

Once I had requested the letters of recommendation in late April, I began telling my friends and family that I might be joining the Peace Corps. It was a vague enough notion to them and I was equally vague with the details of when/where/how—no one questioned me closely. I went ahead with teaching, union organizing, enjoying the company of women, and making plans for summer employment on Long Island with the YMCA summer day camp program.

At the same time, Thornell was in Accra, trying to nail down the details of the project and Shriver was approaching David Apter about running the training program.

By mid-May I had a notice and admission card to report on Saturday, May 27 to take the Peace Corps Examination. It was held at the New York Daily News Building on 42nd Street in a large, plain, institutional room containing 75–80 table desks in spaced rows, and little else. The room was filled with test takers, proctors, and newspeople, mostly cameramen. There was a certain amount of confusion in sorting us all out, checking identifications, assigning desks—a process made more difficult by the intrusive news camera wielders. I felt strongly, though naively, that my interest in the Peace Corps was a personal one. I resented, and always have, people who shove cameras in my face. Rather than just stew about it, I called for one of the proctors and said,

"Not all of us want to be photographed; I came here to take an exam."

"What can we do? Plenty of people don't mind having their pictures taken."

"Well, I do mind. Can't you do something?"

After some consultation, "OK. I'll announce that if someone does not wish to be photographed, they can place a blue 3 x 5 index card on the upper corner of the desk."

And he proceeded to set it up.

One of the other test-takers, Jim Kelly, remembered being a bit apprehensive about the Peace Corps and the testing. Settling at his desk, he looked around the room and saw me—horn-rimmed glasses, goatee, with jacket and tie, but wearing Hush Puppies—then, as he told me years later after we had become friends, thought to himself, "Well, if Peace Corps is going to let just anyone join, I'm not so sure."

The exam was long. The only part I remember was a foreign language aptitude section, based on Urdu. But there was lots more—history, current affairs, math, logic, language. It took over six hours. After six years of college and five years of teaching, if nothing else I had learned the skill of test-taking. I felt I had done well.

Why Did YOU Join the Peace Corps?

The motivations to join the Peace Corps in 1961 were as varied as the individuals who did so. In taking what from the outside might have looked like a foolhardy, even misguided step, those who became Ghana I had a mix of personal reasons for joining. Often it was a sense of adventure, fueled more by curiosity than derring-do, and a desire to 'help others'—a feeling that was enhanced by the charismatic words of President John F. Kennedy.

In 1997, on a trip through California, I visited Tom Livingston. At the time, Tom was the proprietor of an antique shop in the downtown San Francisco Antiques Row on Jackson Street (I almost wrote "owned and operated" but that doesn't do justice to Tom's relation to his store; it's much more personal). Tom is unassuming in dress and modest in manner, with a neatly trimmed mustache and an open smile. It is when he begins to talk of individual antique pieces of furniture that Tom reveals his elegance, charm and wit. In my own life I've been completely indifferent to antiques and have none in my home. However, when I visit Tom's shop and he begins to describe a piece there, I'm as enchanted as I was as a kid listening to Hansel and Gretel for the first time.

I see a chair—looks a bit old, pleasant fabric, definitely not your 'relax and kick back' style of seating. Tom says, "Notice the delicate carving of the legs and the detail in the ball and claw finials. The damask fabric beautifully contrasts with the rubbed patina of the cherry wood and is upholstered with hand-wrought brass pins. The overall lines, especially the curve of the arms, are suggestive of the later Queen Anne style. Look, especially, at the carver's mark incised on the under side of the seat. It tells us that this piece was probably made in the 1750s."

When Tom is done I feel remiss in not being able immediately to plunk down $5000 for this gem of a chair (but then, I already own a chair.) We had agreed to meet at the store for the taped interview at 10:00 a.m. when no customers were expected, Tom had said. "People shop for antiques later in the day, after they've read the early Dow Jones reports." We sat on a lovely sofa to talk. I sat gingerly on the edge of the cushion—being large in size and weight, I have a neurotic fear of my relaxing bulk suddenly making a pile of interesting scrap wood out of a $12,000 piece of furniture (just my luck it would be Queen Anne).

I asked Tom where he was and what he'd been doing in early 1961 before he'd even heard of the Peace Corps. He said that in his second year of teaching after getting a B.A. in English Literature from University of Illinois at Champaign, he had been teaching in Itasca, Illinois, seventh and eighth grade English and French. Tom had spent his college junior year abroad in Paris. It was a great eye-opener for somebody born and raised in the Midwest who'd never even been to New York City. It was a great experience getting away from Illinois—he also learned to speak French fairly well.

Tom then talked about his developing interest in teaching overseas and how he decided to join the Peace Corps:

"I'd thought about it a little because I'd always been interested in the American Friends Service Committee. I have a very active Quaker aunt and she was interested in encouraging 'Friendly' activities on the part of her nephews. So, I had thought some time of maybe going to Quaker work camps and I think that's what prepared me for Peace Corps. When it was announced, it wouldn't be just for a summer but for a longer duration and it appealed to me that way."

"Then how did you first become aware of the Peace Corps?"

"I think it was early March because it was played up in the newspaper—in the Chicago Sun-Times. I remember reading about it and immediately became interested. I made some phone calls and they said pick up the forms at the post office."

"What was the reaction of family and friends?"

"My aunt, the Quaker lady, was rather interested and thought it was about time the government did something like this rather than just eternally building up arms. Colleagues of mine at school thought it was a bit bizarre."

On the same California trip, I went to see Peter Dybwad in Berkeley. When I think of Pete—my 1961 memory of him—the first thing that pops into my mind is the obscure New England prep school phrase, "That's real shoe." (According to *The Official Preppy Handbook*, it means top-drawer, very acceptable.) In neither New York City nor the U.S. Army had I heard anyone use that expression. I admired Pete because, with complete unselfconsciousness he'd describe someone as "shoe." He was the only person I have ever met who could do so. However, for all his preppy facade, he was timid. Pete was twenty-one years old when he started Peace Corps training but he looked to be fifteen or sixteen, a little gawky, with a prominent Adam's apple.

When I visited Peter in 1997 I had to readjust my image of him. He did still look young to me—during my visit when he left his house to go to work, in proper suit and tie, he looked like someone who had dressed up for a make-believe occasion. But Peter is President of the Wright Institute in Berkeley, a well-known doctoral training institution in psychology; he's married and the father of teenagers. We talked about January 1961 when Peter was in college at Wesleyan University:

"I was a senior in college. The previous fall someone had come to campus to talk about teaching in West Africa and that had got me interested. I applied but was turned down because you had to have a Master's degree to be the equivalent of the English university degree they were accepting in former British colonies."

"Was this just a lark with some college buddies?"

"No, I had idealistic missionary grandparents. It was a good and noble thing to do. It was in that tradition of Protestant missionaries going off to do good and save the world. I remember being skeptical of the Peace Corps but deciding to go along and look into it. I'd been accepted at law school, Yale and Harvard."

With some people there was an early curiosity about Africa. Laura Damon, a graduate of Smith College, remembered that in grade school she performed in a play that was based on Alan Paton's Cry, *The Beloved Country* and was just fascinated with the idea of Africa. While at Smith, she went on a summer study tour of East Africa, led by Gwendolyn Carter, a noted teacher of African Studies.

Steve McWilliams, who had completed a degree in Conservation at University of Colorado at Boulder, admitted that he had had a lifelong (though irrational) ambition to go to Africa. As he said:

"There wasn't any doubt in my mind that somewhere along the line soon I'd be there—I have no explanation for it but it goes back to—I remember this clearly—in the fourth grade in Iowa, a friend of mine and I—we were what, nine years old?—and we were both talking about getting to Africa. I don't think he was serious; I was serious." [1997]

Ruth Whitney, struggling with a troubled family environment, turned aside their resistance to her joining. She spoke of it in 1997: "I decided that this is who I was and that not to go would be a violation of who I am, my idealism, my wanting to help people."

With Alice O'Grady it was her family, her mother actually, who encouraged her:

"I was teaching in San Francisco and my mother in Chicago sent me a clipping from the newspaper about Peace Corps. She thought I might be interested. Why did she send the article? I think she was an adventurous woman at heart who'd never had the opportunity, and she saw an opportunity for me and maybe for her, vicariously." [1997]

George Coyne was a veteran of four years' service in the Navy, which enabled him, through the GI Bill, to complete a degree in Forestry at Rutgers University. After graduation George became a middle school science teacher. In our interview he described himself as a real immigrant success story. "When I came to the U.S. [from Ireland] I didn't have a dime in my pocket and couldn't speak a word of the language. Of course, I was only ten months old." Like many of us in the group, in the early '60s, George was restless and had explored overseas teaching opportunities but was discouraged at each attempt. With the American Friends Service Committee, he had applied and was interviewed but was put off by the interviewer who asked whether he smoked or drank. As a Catholic, he thought that Papal Volunteers for Latin America might work but was dissuaded by the requirement that he would have to recruit donors from his local parish to pay for his transport to Latin America.

George continued: "Kennedy's inaugural really appealed to me. My family was skeptical of any new government project as just another boondoggle, saying that even if it does get off the ground, Peace Corps won't amount to anything. But I looked to a different possibility. As a teenager I had met some people who'd been with the New Deal's Civilian Conservation Corps and I was impressed with the kinds of experiences they described. I thought this was what might be possible with the Peace Corps."

George applied and took the exam. He spoke of what happened when the acceptance arrived: "I got no encouragement from my family, whose feeling was that in his late twenties it was time for George to settle down, get a job, marry. My father was waiting to get me into a secure lifetime position with the electric company where he worked. However, there was Sister Mary, my sixth grade parochial school teacher who had always spoken with great emotion about missionaries in Africa. When I went back to the school to tell her about the Peace Corps, she was very excited for me and said she would pray for me and I should write her. I did." [1999]

Ophelia DeLaine was a junior high school science teacher in New York City. In July 1999, she spoke at the Chautauqua Institution as part of a panel discussion on the Peace Corps:

"I personally was a child of the segregated South; segregation in the schools had actually not been ended in many places and I had come from South Carolina and was living in New York City. But my brother had been in the Army in Korea, my cousin had been in Germany. And members of the family had served in the armed forces in various countries. I was not prepared to take a chance on my life and join the service but I wanted to do something. Most of the people here can remember very well that when the Star Spangled Banner came on, you took off your hat and you covered your heart and you did all of these things and you recited the Pledge of Allegiance and you really felt something down inside. That was no different for me just because I came from the segregated South; I was still an American and I felt like this was my country. However, President Kennedy's call didn't strike a chord in me. I was already looking for somewhere to go. When people asked me why did you join the Peace Corps, my answer was always, my feet were itchy. I wanted to know how the rest of the world lived. I wanted to go somewhere—I really didn't care where it was and I had looked into a variety of different places. Where I went to school, the maps in the geography book had no map of Africa. I knew almost nothing about Africa though I had some African friends. When I joined the Peace Corps, I was not looking necessarily to go to Africa. My motivation was to go someplace and to see something about how other people addressed the problems of the world. And I found that out."

Newell Flather, Harvard, New England, has more of the attendant virtues than vices associated with each. If there are pillars that uphold Western Civilization, surely one of them has the name, Flather, engraved on it. Newell grew up in Lowell, Massachusetts; his father owned a textile mill there; he was Second Marshal of his senior class at Harvard and participated in Crew, Wrestling, and Dramatics. To a parochial New Yorker like myself, that put Newell in a remote place, populated by ethnocentric aristocrats with names like Cabot and Lowell and Saltonstall. He wasn't an elitist, but he couldn't help himself from being correct and well informed—upright is in his genes. His greatest strength, rectitude, is also his greatest weakness. Newell tends to believe that others are as sincere and well intentioned as he is. When he finds out that they are not, his disappointment fuels his own renewed efforts at doing the right thing. When I interviewed Newell in 1999, he readily recalled 1961 and his decision to join the Peace Corps:

"I do remember deciding I would take the Peace Corps test because I was very curious. I recall feeling it was something very new and I wanted to know about it. I thought the test would be an interesting way to find out. I wondered how they were going to recruit and get people to give up everything to go into this thing. So I took the test and I remember thinking, 'I don't really want to do this so why am I taking the test?' It was in May. I know it rained that day in Boston."

Newell had just graduated Harvard and been admitted to the University of Virginia Law School. "I majored in being in college. I ended up doing everything at college and was fully occupied doing it and I enjoyed sampling everything." In listening to him talk about it now, I get the feeling he was ready for a "real" challenge in his life after his wide-ranging but insulated success at college. He believed then, as now, in the importance and the challenge of doing right in the world. Newell is worldly enough now to be a bit embarrassed talking about this but he's honest enough to be forthcoming.

He talked about getting invited to training in June while he was visiting a friend on Cape Cod. As soon as he arrived, the following conversation occurred:

"Your father called."

"Oh, he did?"

"Yes, he said you got a telegram; something about going to work in Ghana for a few years and he said, call soon. He assumes you'll want him to call and inform them you're not coming."

"My father was very quick about this—he knew I was going to law school. I called him and said I'd come home that night and we'd talk about it. When I got home, it was one of those lovely, classic experiences—a father-son talk. He never really dug in with me but on this one he was pretty much dug in. He used all of the wonderful parental persuasions—go to law school and, if you still want to do the Peace Corps you'll have the credential. That makes more sense. We probably stayed up to two or three in the morning talking about it. The next morning we both got up thinking it was a good idea. I felt that it was an extraordinary idea. To my father, I said, 'I'm a privileged person, have a great education. I'm at that moment in life when I can go; if I don't go, then who does?' It now sounds so righteous but I felt that way."

Marion Morrison is from San Francisco. In meeting with Marion in 1997, my initial impression was that, as is true with many of us, there's a lot more Marion today than there was in 1961. She is tall, with a pretty face and friendly smile; she seems very approachable. However, her winning appearance belies her flinty intellect. In either personal or political discussions, Marion walks the fuzzy line between assertive and aggressive. She is self-confident to the point of stubbornness. That an opinion might be conventionally labeled as biased does not deter Marion from expressing it, smoothing the way with an engaging smile and a sideways glance. This is enhanced by the trace of a Southern accent in her speech which is punctuated with expressions like, "Well, my goodness," "Oh, heavens, no," "Now you just listen to this."

But her inner strength and ability to disagree allowed her in 1961 to swim against the tide in joining the Peace Corps. When she first suggested it to her father, his immediate response was, "No way!" Marion was fresh out of college at Rice University:

"I dawdled for several months, enjoyed my mother's company and we held off Daddy's concerns that I start working, a career. When President Kennedy made his speech, later in the winter, broaching the idea of the Peace Corps, I do remember I was absolutely enthralled by it. I just fell in love with the idea—in the sense that it sounded like something I wanted to do. I wanted the adventure, I wanted the excitement. My view was [laughing] this kind of romantic going off to save the noble savage kind of thing. This was very much part of it. The other part—it was opposite to what all my friends were doing. I simply didn't want to settle down and pursue graduate school or pursue a job. I just didn't want to settle down—it's just that simple. I could have gotten married right out of college but I just didn't want to lead a normal life. I just didn't see myself going into any kind of regular routine." [2000]

Dick Maze was the first person in the Ghana I group that I interviewed. It was a beautiful, sunny day in Phoenix, Arizona. We settled into lawn chairs in his backyard, with a couple of 'brewskis' at hand and began to talk. As I replay the tape, I hear the sound of garden birds, wind chimes, and the friendly hiss of beer cans being opened. Except for the fact that he's from Iowa, Dick Maze is "as corny as Kansas in August." He is open and enthusiastic and, even as an adult, talks to you with the eagerness of a young child. His speech is still punctuated with "Gee" and "Golly" (without the least affectation). Dick is of medium height and stocky. An accident years ago rearranged his nose, giving him a bit of the appearance of a not-too-successful boxer. Rather than making him look menacing, the crooked nose and a constant half-smile give him a comfortable and approachable look, like a friendly policeman or bartender.

"In January 1961 I was getting ready to graduate Iowa State Teachers College and I was trying to land a teaching job. Quite frankly I looked fairly young for my age. I was having a difficult time in interviews. I started out looking primarily in the state of Iowa but then I began to develop this idea in my head—I took some philosophy courses—I began to expand my mental horizons.

"So what I did then—saw a notice at school, ICA teaching in East Africa; so I signed up for an interview in Chicago. About in March. Some chap from the U.K. was doing the interview. When he saw this young, immature-looking neophyte from Iowa—well, it didn't go well. He asked questions like, 'Compare British and Portuguese colonial policies in Africa.' I knew nothing and fumbled my way through. He thanked me and that was that. But I was still going to look overseas, strictly for the adventure of it.

"One day on the bulletin board was this notice about people taking an exam for the Peace Corps. I didn't know anything about it; had no clue what it was. Essentially it was on a beer bet with this guy I lived with at the boarding house. He chided me into that but I was still very much interested in going overseas to Africa; primarily at that time it was the romanticism but I didn't say that out loud. We took the exam at Waterloo. After we left the exam we went over and talked to an army recruiter. I don't know who he was but to this day I thank my lucky stars. He said, 'You guys are teachers and there's a shortage of teachers. The country needs you more as teachers than they do as soldiers.'

"Anyway, took the test and didn't hear anything more about it. When I was finishing my last semester I proctored an undergrad class in science. It was near the end of the course and the prof couldn't complete his grades on time. He made an offer to us, the assistants; he said, 'You stay and get the grade work done and I'll take you out to dinner.' We did that, went to a restaurant and were all sitting around. There were four of us, getting ready to graduate. Everybody had a teaching job except me.

"The prof opened the conversation—we were waiting to be served—and said, around the table, 'What do you plan to do?' One fellow, well, he and his girl friend were going to get married that summer and were going to California. He had a job at some nice high school there—for an Iowan that was really terrific—so, success number one. Another was going to teach business somewhere; success number two. Then the third was going to Iowa State graduate school with a scholarship.

"Then it came around to me. 'What are you going to do?' 'I'm going to look around and see if I can't get something overseas. Hell, I've grown up in Iowa and this is all I really know.' It was embarrassing. But then the prof, his mouth dropped open and he said, 'Goddamn it, Maze, if I had my life to live over again, I'd do exactly the same thing.'

"Another professor when I was an undergrad—he spent time in Colombia. He did all kinds of stuff and he talked about the wasted life—if you don't go out and do something outside your own dimension." [1997]

Probably all of us who reported to Berkeley in July for Peace Corps training were a bit like Dick Maze—we weren't going to waste our lives and we were certainly about to go outside our own dimension.

3

TRAINING

Ground Work—Ghana, Washington, Berkeley

During May and June while Thornell was in Accra working out the details of the program, the Washington staff was creating a screening, selection, and training process for the potential volunteers. The first Peace Corps qualifying examination wasn't given until May 27; invitations to participate in the Berkeley training program didn't go out until June 24 (to begin July 2). In early May Sargent Shriver had met with David Apter to invite him to head up the training faculty for the Ghana program. Apter was just transferring from University of Chicago to the University of California at Berkeley. He recalled the meeting:

"I knew it was to be the first program and a model perhaps for other Peace Corps programs. I told Shriver I would do it but I set down five conditions. One, no CIA; two, I select the faculty; three, we design the curriculum; four, there be no interference from Washington; and five, faculty have an opportunity to screen candidates; although that last point proved not to be practical. We put together an interdisciplinary team: L. Gray Cowan, a comparativist in West Africa; Robert Lystad, an anthropologist; St. Clair Drake, a sociologist; myself, a political scientist. Drake knew Nkrumah personally, as did I, and he had worked on Blacks in the U.S., in his book, *Black Metropolis,* and in Africa. He was just an engaging human being with a commitment both to Ghana and to students."

Apter characterized what he felt was the faculty's approach to training:

"We wanted to guard the volunteers against American mawkish nonsense and hype that go so often with good things that take away from the real quality of the program. We really were concerned to sustain as much as possible a certain kind of moral tension—commitment not to the Peace Corps in general but to the idea that they were really doing something for Ghana at this moment, in a school system which needed them and keep it at that level—which meant their relationship to both the teaching program and the job they would be doing would be a personal one. We didn't want outsiders making big speeches about higher purposes—these guys had enough sense of higher purpose to join the Peace Corps in the first place." [1997]

As an active Kennedy supporter, Padraic Kennedy (no relation) had been recruited by his friend, Lemuel Billings, to become part of the initial Peace Corps staff. Like others at that time, he was available for a variety of administrative assignments, whatever tasks were needed to get the agency up and running. Among his other duties in the ad hoc organizational structure in Washington, Kennedy inherited the job of training officer for Ghana I. He convened the group that was to become the faculty:

"They all had a great deal of interest in Africa. They were scared to death that Americans would go in and mess it up—somehow they would blunder in there. At the same time they were also excited in being asked to help in the creation of something new. In those days there were few Africanists and they all knew each other and looked forward to the opportunity of working together on this." [1997]

In Washington, as the agency began to develop, Shriver provided the leadership but his executive style encouraged the tension between "hard-heads" and "soft-heads" (so titled by George Carter) on his staff. He had brought together practical, positive-thinking former foreign aid administrators like Warren Wiggins and John Alexander and balanced them against more idealistic global thinkers such as Harris Wofford and Bill Moyers. Their differing points of view were expressed as Peace Corps/Washington tried to define the role of the Peace Corps Volunteer and the nature of overseas programming. One side felt that the Peace Corps should serve as a catalyst for change in the developing world according to the model described in the book, *The Ugly American*. The volunteer was to be an exemplar of American entrepreneurial values, live and work in the villages, not the capital, sleeves rolled up, cheek-by-jowl with host country counterparts, egalitarian to the core. The other view was less dramatic but more practical. It looked to modest successes in programs which would draw on foreign aid experience but with the enthusiasm and idealism generated by the Peace Corps dynamic, a chance to do things slightly differently. In the short run at the beginning of Peace Corps' existence, both groups were ultimately hostage to the reality that it was people like me, less ideological and more activist, who would actually decide what a Peace Corps Volunteer was by being one.

In Ghana Thornell was getting a mixed reception in his negotiations with Ghanaians about the Peace Corps. It was one thing for President Nkrumah to respond favorably to this dramatic new American initiative but quite another for the bureaucrats and civil servants to try to implement the program. The Director of Secondary Education at the Ministry of Education and his deputy, who was British, were proceeding cautiously and following the established procedures for screening and recruiting individual expatriate teachers even though the Peace Corps was being offered as a package—X number of Peace Corps teachers, screened, trained, and delivered by Peace Corps as a group. This disparity led to misunderstandings that were not resolved until late in August, literally days before our planned departure for Accra. Our college credentials trickled into the Ministry, with transcripts from U.S. schools such as Kansas Wesleyan University,

Montclair State College, Johnson C. Smith University, North Texas State College, Spring Hill College, showing degrees with majors in education, forestry, political science, government, astronomy, conservation, philosophy, mechanical engineering. The Ministry did not know what to make of it, having almost no familiarity with the American post-secondary academic system. By mid-July the Ministry decided that their standard for acceptance was to be an Ivy League bachelor's degree or a Master's degree; no one else was acceptable. This standard would have reduced the group to approximately 20 of the 58 then in training.

In relation to the Peace Corps, the Ministry of Education was not the only interested party in Ghana. In 1960 Kwame Nkrumah wanted to extend secondary schooling to make it available to far more young people. He created the Ghana Educational Trust, with a mandate to build new secondary schools throughout the country and to coordinate with the Ministry of Education on matters of staffing and academic program. The G.E.T. received generous funding from revenues produced through the Ghana Cocoa Marketing Board, which controlled the international marketing of Ghana's leading cash crop, cocoa. Nkrumah did this partly out of frustration with the traditional and slow-moving civil service establishment which would not act boldly on such an initiative. The G.E.T. was political, free-wheeling and ready to contract for new construction on short notice, rewarding political loyalists in the process. Most secondary schools were boarding schools, and needed classrooms, dining hall, faculty and administrative space, dormitories, and houses for teaching staff. Many of these schools were located away from major urban areas in the more rural districts, previously unserved by secondary education institutions. Local politicians, loyal to Nkrumah and the Convention Peoples Party, were influential in choosing both school sites and building contractors. Within two years, the G.E.T. had added at least 20 new secondary schools and soon thereafter they (and the Ministry of Education) had a serious problem in staffing these schools.

Answering the Call

We first gathered at the University of California in Berkeley on July 2, 1961. There were 58 of us reporting to the training program. We had been summoned by telegrams sent out June 24 to 26 and, in little more than a week's time, we were there. The telegrams read:

CONGRATULATIONS. YOU HAVE SUCCESSFULLY COMPLETED THE INITIAL REQUIREMENTS FOR THE PEACE CORPS. YOU ARE NOW INVITED TO APPEAR ON JULY 2 AT THE UNIVERSITY OF CALIFORNIA AT BERKELEY FOR PHYSICAL EXAMINATION, SELECTION PROCESSING AND TRAINING FOR POSSIBLE ASSIGNMENT TO A SECONDARY SCHOOL TEACHING POSITION IN CHANA [sic] (CONTINGENT UPON FORMAL AGREEMENTS NOW UNDER DISCUSSION), OR TO ANOTHER WEST AFRICAN COUNTRY. DURATION OF TRAINING AT BERKELEY, CALIFORNIA WILL BE EIGHT WEEKS. TRANSPORTATION WILL BE FURNISHED BY THE PEACE CORPS. PLEASE REPLY BY RETURN WIRE

COLLECT TO: PEACE CORPS (PCV-2) WASHINGTON, D.C., INDICATING
WHETHER OR NOT YOU ARE AVAILABLE LETTER AND DETAILED
INSTRUCTIONS FOLLOW. BEST WISHES
ROBERT SARGENT SHRIVER JR
DIRECTOR PEACE CORPS

Of course, the typographic error, 'Chana,' led to some wild speculation. The geography books at my school, JHS 136 Manhattan, like most of the maps and atlases in the United States at the time, only showed a British colony, Gold Coast, which we soon figured out was the independent country of Ghana. Frank Guido said that it didn't matter to him whether it was China, Chana, or Ghana; he was just ready to do something and go somewhere. Carol Waymire's family was initially concerned that she was being assigned to godless and wicked communist China and were relieved when they found out that it was really Africa. Carol said, "I think it was a plus that it was Ghana—we knew nothing about it. Whereas with China we had a lot of preconceptions."

The training program might have ended up a bewildering three-ring circus with acts in each ring meeting the expectations of disparate interests—Peace Corps/Washington, congressional critics, political opponents of the idea. However, thanks to David Apter and his colleagues, the program had a central and unifying theme—a challenge to us to identify individually what we were about in becoming Peace Corps Volunteers in Ghana. The enthusiasm with which Apter, Lystad, Cowan and Drake spoke of Ghana was contagious. It enabled us to put up with the other circus acts spinning around us—lessons in world communism, a short course of American Studies (including review of the U.S. Constitution), an extended exposure to tropical health data and epidemiology, lectures on international affairs, with an emphasis on the United Nations and the Congo Crisis.

Getting to Berkeley

I was late reporting to Berkeley because the telegram had left little time for arranging personal matters. The instructions indicated that we might be going directly from training to Ghana so I had to see about sub-letting an apartment, storing household goods (a bed, an easy chair, and an electric frying pan) and selling a car. We were told that Berkeley was for training and 'final selection' but it never occurred to me that I wouldn't qualify—after all, I had a Master's degree and five years' teaching experience; all that was lacking was any knowledge of Africa. That had been amply proven at my ill-fated Fulbright teaching interview a few months earlier, but I figured that Peace Corps training would erase that deficiency.

My first-ever jet flight (New York to San Francisco), above the cloud cover, was exhilarating. The startling clarity of the sky and the endless carpet of clouds created a fresh canvas in my mind's eye on which I could paint adventuresome fantasies. Snuggled into a window seat, I spent a lot of time staring out the window. I thought too of my family, knowing that I went with their blessings. Mom was convinced that there was as good a chance of my meeting someone to marry with Peace Corps in Ghana as there was at Junior High 136 in Manhattan. After my thirty-second birthday she began to lose her enthusiasm for matchmaking—I can still hear her saying, "Just call Pauline up, take her to dinner; you don't have to marry her!" My father had dedicated his life to the family business and, with a touch of envy, warmly supported my joining Peace Corps. We had talked seriously about it when I first applied, since he was recovering from a second heart attack and I was now planning to go off to some remote corner of the world. Without hesitation, he had said, "Bob, do what your heart tells you to. You've been teaching in Harlem for five years; you love teaching; you'll be good for the Peace Corps. We know you'll never make a good roofing and air conditioning man so go and help the Africans." Both Mom and Dad felt I was a bit of a missionary anyway, since I had been teaching at what was considered a difficult junior high school in Manhattan.

Outside Warren Hall

I revisited the Berkeley campus in 1999 and walked from International House, downhill along the curving walks of the main campus, through the eucalyptus grove—the smell of the fallen leaves that I crushed in my hand reminded me of the pause I used to take in the long walk to class, stopping there to catch my breath (and light a cigarette!), and finally to Warren Hall. In training, the three-quarter-mile walk twice a day was my phys ed program—no soccer, calisthenics, or running laps for me. It wasn't required and I had never needed it to face the rigors of New York City teaching, so why now?

We had most of our lectures at Warren Hall. It was an ordinary large-scale college lecture hall, no windows, with a steeply raked interior, tiers of seats with fold-down desk arms; in front, a wide lectern, sliding whiteboards, retractable movie screen, high, even, unpleasant fluorescent lighting, made even crueler by the warmth of green vegetation and sunlight just outside its doors. Stepping back out of Warren Hall in 1999 I felt this visceral tug to reach into my shirt pocket, find a cigarette, and light up. Nearby was a slight, grassy knoll, bordered by low concrete walls—this was where we gathered on lecture breaks, to smoke, chat, and relax. It was also the site of our first group photograph. (*See* Frontispiece)

Studying the faces in the photo forty-plus years later reminds me that, although we were the Ghana I training group, we were also individuals, cliques, clusters, sets and subsets, young adventurous adults, exploring new experiences and relationships. For no particular reason, I was close to Sue Hastings and Peter Dybwad outside of class but, once seated in Warren Hall for a lecture, I'd seek out Bob Krisko and Sue Bartholomew (the peanut gallery). The photo was taken while we were on break from our training, probably a lecture by either David Apter or Gray Cowan (sitting, suited, front right in the photo; both with arms resting on knees). To their right, in center front, in the light suit and dark tie, is Ted Brown, who worked for the AFL-CIO, and had been introduced to us as the person who would be in charge of the program in Ghana, as the field representative. Within a few days, he left Berkeley and we heard nothing further about him, other than that there had been an administrative decision to replace him, with no further explanation. In mid-August we were introduced to George Carter who did become the field rep in Ghana.

The occasion of the photo is most likely another visit from another Peace Corps/ Washington type, no doubt accompanied by a photographer (probably Rowland Scherman). We look like a happy crew and we were. At this midpoint in the training we were slowly developing a sense of definition in relation to becoming Peace Corps Volunteers; we were awash in lectures, discussions, and informal talks led by enthusiastic, highly informed Africanists who, if they were skeptical about the "larger" mission of the Peace Corps, were most comfortable with this not-so-raw bunch of recruits. Like us they were caught up in the quiet excitement of being pioneers in the development of the Peace Corps. Though our behavior and motivation may have been less than ideal, we knew that we were, at that moment, the very model of what a Peace Corps Volunteer was (and would be) since we were then just about the only Peace Corps volunteers in existence. It was a burden lightly borne, thanks to the guidance of the faculty and our own exuberance at what we were doing and the delightful setting in which it was unfolding. The only dark cloud was the question of selection since we knew that ultimately someone else would make the judgment as to whether we were fit or not to serve as teachers in Ghana, although we were also encouraged to "self-select" (Ask yourself: Do you really want to be doing this? Commit to two years?).

As I look at the photo, years later, some in the photo are close friends, some strangers (then and now), some have died, some have disappeared (at least from my view). Of course, I look first for myself (back row, fourth from the left). There I am, dark-haired and with a goatee, horn-rimmed glasses, and a smile. I am thirty-two years old, veteran of the Korean War, veteran of five years' teaching in a New York City junior high school, with an M.A. in History from the University of Chicago. I am thoroughly enjoying being in Berkeley, learning about Africa and Ghana, being part of the Peace Corps—the prospect of two years' teaching in Ghana is a pleasing one. I'm pretty sure this photo was taken during a visit to the training program by Charlie Peters, just beginning to emerge as Inspector General/Chief Evaluator for Peace Corps/Washington. He was a West Virginia journalist and Kennedy political activist. Charlie was soft-spoken, a Southern gentleman. He was short and stocky with a chubby-cheeked face, unevenly punctuated with an off-center grin that underlined crinkly, mischievous eyes. You half expected him to take you aside to tell an off-color story.

The day before this photo, Charlie, who was wearing a blue seersucker suit and a conspiratorial air, had taken me aside at International House.

"Bob, we'd like you to shave off the beard. It's not good for the image of the Peace Corps at this time."

(To myself: "Shades of Al Nussbaum! What the hell does the beard have to do with my being a PCV? mutter-mutter-mutter.") To Charlie, "I don't think the beard interferes with my ability to teach. I had it when I taught Junior High in New York and it wasn't a problem." Then, worrying about Charlie's possible influence on the selection process, "I really feel qualified to be a Peace Corps teacher and I want to go to Ghana."

End of conversation but the next day, Charlie again approached me, and said, almost as an aside, "Bob, when group photos are being taken, would you mind standing in the back?" I assured him that it wouldn't be a problem. This Berkeley photo then was my first excursion as a "back-of-the-crowd" subject. Later photos (the Pan Am departure, arrival in Ghana) tend to show just the top half of my face (dark glasses, dark hair)—Charlie must have been proud of me.

Back to the photo. Standing prominently in the center back is Newell Flather. His place in the history of this training program was assured by a single, outstanding feat of strength. One evening, coming home from the Rathskeller, a mellow group of us witnessed Newell doing a horizontal handstand on the stanchion of a parking meter. It was done off-handedly but, to me, was so unlikely and startling that I can still picture it. In recent years, as I visit with Newell, I have not asked him to repeat the maneuver. Next to Newell in the photo is Maureen Pyne, twenty-two at the time, daughter of a Chicago policeman, graduate of Spring Hill College in Mobile, Alabama, employed by Illinois Bell Telephone in customer relations. And to Maureen's left, like a guardian bookend (or football left end), Bob Krisko, eighth grade science teacher as well as high school basketball and track coach, graduate of Kansas University, Kansas born and bred. He was quiet and soft-spoken, with an irreverent sense of humor. Sue Bartholomew, Bob, and I sat close together during lectures, high up in Warren Hall, sharing oversized black-and-white cookies from the local bakery and sophomoric jokes. Bob is the creator of "The Evil Files of Dr. Stiles," "A page of Fage is better than a chapter of Apter," "The Cyprus Citrus Surplus" and probably our team motto, "Here Today, Ghana Tomorrow." Krisko spent long hours of training worrying about his fiancée, Pam (who was not in the training program) and whether it made sense to go to Ghana and defer a wedding for two years. Bob went and spent the next two years worrying; it tended to tinge his humor with a slight but gray and gloomy cloud. Today Bob still worries and the cloud is still there. He never did marry Pam.

All the way to the right in the photo, kneeling, is Dick Maze, looking very much as he does today. To his right is Loretto Lescher of River Forest, Illinois, an experienced teacher and world traveler who saw the Peace Corps as an opportunity to continue to do both. Next to her is Ruth Whitney of Quincy, Illinois who became tennis partner to Newell Flather during training in spite of their initial conversation:

"I'm Ruth Whitney from Quincy, Illinois."

"We have a city of that name in Massachusetts but we pronounce it Quin-zee."

"Yeh, you snobs from the East have a different way of saying everything."

Ruth's feistiness was startling and refreshing to encounter but her directness later caused her problems in the selection process.

To Ruth's right is Carol Waymire of Santa Rosa, California, looking a bit school-marmish. She was very serious-minded and a bit intimidated by the high-powered training program. And next to her is Marion Morrison.

We look overwhelmingly collegiate, bright-faced, eager. We didn't worry about credentials and previous teaching experience. The training, in spite of the nagging tension about selection, was, in and of itself, a challenging, informative, and enlightening adventure. Some of us suspected that Peace Corps in June 1961 needed to fill in the Ghana project pronto and did not have sufficient candidates with teaching experience. Applicants like Marion seemed attractive—good academic credentials, excellent recommendations and good results on the Peace Corps exam. Marion had even traveled outside the United States and had taught during several college vacations at the Berlitz Language School as a part-time English tutor for adult Japanese businessmen. Such a profile applied to several in the group. Although devoid of formal classroom teaching experience, they did have degrees from good colleges and "other" assets. Peter Dybwad, degree from Wesleyan, accepted at Yale Law School; Laura Damon, degree Smith, traveled to Africa on student trip with noted scholar, Gwendolyn Carter; Susan Hastings, Stanford; Sue Bartholomew, Boston University, summer with Crossroads Africa in Guinea; Sam Selkow, Columbia; Valerie Deuel, Berkeley (at age 17, no less).

A word on the demographics of the group, although we were far too small a sampling to draw any broad statistical conclusions. We did not reflect anything of the larger whole, just the individual and clustered chunks of demographic bits from the pool of early Peace Corps candidates. In no particular order and with no attempt at completeness, of the 58 trainees, three were from Kansas, eight were Jewish, six were Harvard graduates, two were African-American, twenty-four were experienced teachers (of whom only seven were Science or Math teachers, Ghana's original request) and only one was from a state south of the Mason-Dixon line (Virginia). Among us was a poet, a journalist, a union organizer, a football player, a pianist, a Phi Beta Kappa, an Eagle Scout, and five veterans of military service. The age range was from 18 to 35, with the preponderance in their early twenties; there was one married couple, Ann and Richard Port. Except for Ann, we were all college graduates, eight with a Master's degree (Ghana had requested that all teachers have the Master's degree); about half had traveled outside of the U.S. and one had never traveled outside of Illinois.

Scraping off the Callow

Much had happened between the Executive Order of March 1 and July 2 when we reported to Berkeley, but many of the specific details were still up in the air. How do you prepare someone to be a Peace Corps Volunteer? What are the criteria by which to judge an individual's qualifications—faculty evaluation? psychiatric screening? credential vetting by the Ghana Ministry of Education? These questions were being decided by three institutions amongst whom there was less than perfect communication. One was the evolving Peace Corps staff in Washington, just beginning to decide how to organize this new agency internally; a second was the Ghana Ministry of Education, which would be assigning and supervising these teachers; third was the specially convened training faculty at Berkeley. But there was a fourth 900-pound gorilla in the game—the 58 individuals who reported to Berkeley to train to become Peace Corps Volunteers. When David Apter first met us, he described what he understood to be the goal of the next eight weeks. He said that the faculty, all experienced Africa scholars, saw us as "callow youth" and that their role was to scrape off the callow and to send us to Ghana, a bit humble but well-informed. But we would have a say in that process, too.

Training was wonderful because we trainees were so focused (about to go to Ghana in a few weeks) and motivated (for whatever reasons, we did join the Peace Corps). It was all new to me. I knew nothing of Africa other than the conventional, "Natives, jungles, lions and tigers." I quickly learned that the jungle is "the rain forest" and covers less than 5 percent of Africa; that there is almost no wild life in West Africa and the tiger's habitat is Asia; that 'natives' is considered pejorative. That was just the beginning. It was easy to unlearn these things because we were anxious to know how to avoid being Ugly Americans.

During a 1997 interview of a member of Ghana I, I switched from interviewer to interviewee and answered my own question, "What was the impact of training on the group?"

In that taped interview I say, "Through the seven weeks, we built up confidence in our ability to be Peace Corps Volunteers and an overwhelming sense of challenge at being volunteers at this moment. That came from the faculty. I don't know that we were any more naive than Shriver about the role of Peace Corps and its potential impact on foreign policy and world change. The difference was that we had this faculty that helped us, enabled us, to realize that we could become part of the process that was going on in Africa. Ghana was developing and we were lucky to be allowed to participate and there was a role for us as teachers. Washington on the other hand took it a step further and implied that we were agents of change and could play a significant role in shaping the process going on in Africa. I don't think any of us saw ourselves that way."

When I visited him in Overland Park, Kansas, 38 years after training, Bill Austin still had a complete set of lecture notes and handouts from the training (even though he did not get to go to Ghana as a PCV). Riffling through them provides some snapshots of what we were taught during the seven weeks of training. We started with the geography of Africa on July 5th: "The continent is like an inverted saucer"; zipped through colonial history: "British vs. French administration." And by July 14th were learning about cocoa production: "Money grows on trees." Professor Lystad was the point man for anthropology: "Ghana cultures, traditional roles, linguistic groups, family life in a traditional village," spiced up by several lectures by Meyer Fortas on Northern Ghana. Drake specialized in Pan-Africanism and the sociology of Ghanaian secondary schools: "It's rote learning completely. There is a right answer for everything." Every one of his lectures was accompanied by at least an hour of informal commentary for those willing to hang around and listen (and keep supplying Drake with cigarettes). Apter on politics with three lectures alone on Nkrumah's Convention Peoples Party of Ghana: "Government really lies in the party organization (CPP) and not in Parliament."

St. Clair Drake is a strong part of everyone's memory of training. He was a Professor of Anthropology at Roosevelt University in Chicago; he was the co-author of *Black Metropolis*, a study of Negroes on Chicago's south side. In June, 1961, Drake had just completed a three-year stint as chairman of the Department of Sociology at the University College of Ghana at Legon. He was a bulky man, his clothes slightly rumpled as though he had just gotten off the overnight Greyhound from Chicago, with a tracing of cigarette ash drifting down his suit vest. He had an imposing mantle of hair in what was later called the Afro style. Drake was an African-American and had devoted much of his life to Black and African causes and studies. His father had been a follower of Marcus Garvey. In his years at the London School of Economics Drake had befriended Kwame Nkrumah, Jomo Kenyatta, George Padmore and other early African independence leaders. He happily spent hours after his lectures spinning anecdotes about the people and places we were soon to encounter. He would only stop talking if we ran out of cigarettes. A lit cigarette was, unfortunately, his constant companion. He provided us with endless stores of informal and personal facts about Ghana and Africa, putting flesh on the bare academic bones of the lectures.

Some in Congress had expressed concern that we, unsophisticated and naive youth, would be easy prey for communist supporters overseas who would make us look like fools in discussions of world affairs. This deficiency was to be overcome through a series of lectures by knowledgeable 'experts' that would alert us to these dangers and suggest strategies for dealing with them. The training segment was called ASWAC (American Studies, World Affairs, Communism). We were taught about communist theory and practice, Russians in Africa, and the Congo crisis. Julian Towster called us "Peace Warriors" and warned us, "The Russians think Peace Corps will be Ugly Americans no matter what their personality."

The health program under Dr. Warren Stiles was a crash course in tropical medicine which taught most of us far more than we really wanted to know about mosquitoes, other disease vectors, and fecal-borne parasites. The high point of this segment of training was a guest talk by a missionary couple who had served in Sierra Leone. The husband told us what to do if we were attacked by a boa constrictor: "Quickly lie down on the ground and wait until the snake has swallowed your leg up to the knee. Then, take out your knife and attack the snake." After 39 years, no one has reported to me having to use that advice so it stands as one of the untested Berkeley gems of wisdom (or wit). The language training was a last minute mandate from Washington and three Ghanaian graduate students were hastily recruited to be instructors. Bill's notes include a list of sentences we were taught to speak in Twi:

I wish I could speak Twi well.
Please call the doctor for me.
Where is the party?
Does anyone here speak English?
I want to be alone for a while.

In a letter home I wrote, "The heart of our training is 3 professors who work with us each day. They are all young, alert, and take their learning lightly (not pedantically). It's a pleasure to sit through their lectures." By the fifth week of the program, I commented, "If they train us to any finer a pitch than we now are, many of us may just start swimming to Ghana." "We are developing a strong esprit de corps, thanks mainly to our professors. We have our private jokes and special characters, we talk very little about the why of the Peace Corps but think and talk more about how to best serve when we get to Ghana."

I felt relaxed about the program once my possible medical disqualification was settled. What the doctors suspected might be gout, an enlarged big toe, turned out to be a manageable form of arthritis. The next barrier was the psychiatric interviews. I reported back to my family, "My first interview: Why did you join the Peace Corps? What will you do for dates in Ghana? After New York City, aren't you afraid of being isolated, living under hazardous conditions, away from the familiar?" Although I had my doubts and fears, my answer was guarded but straightforward, "I won't be isolated. There'll be teachers and students at the school." The second interview was similar but with the added question, "Why did you grow the beard?" I said something about thinking that it looked nice since I wasn't willing to share my Beau Geste look-alike fantasy with a psychiatrist who was deciding whether I should go to Ghana as a Peace Corps Volunteer.

Berkeley was an enjoyable place to be—cool and fresh, close to San Francisco. The demands of training weren't so great that there wasn't leisure time. I went into San Francisco twice, once just to wander around and stare at the tall buildings, next to go to a performance of the New York City Ballet. During the week we often went to the Rathskeller. I wrote home, "We were paid Monday—$14.00. Since beer costs only 45 cents for an 18-ounce schooner, no one in the group is panicky yet. As far as the beer hall is concerned, the group is divided—those who go, those who don't, and those who wouldn't." The Rathskeller, in the cold light of an April day in 1999, is a ratty, dank downstairs bar, dimly lit and with the throat-catching sour smell of stale beer. But the magic of memory brings it back as a cozy college hang-out where we could share pitchers of 3.2 beer and endlessly sing, Michael, Row the Boat Ashore. Not quite Rick's Cafe but a reasonable way-station on my road to Africa.

Ed Mycue recalled the Rathskeller: "I remember someone confronted us one time downstairs at the Rathskeller. There were words and they were going to bar our way going up the stairs. Bob Eisenman, who seemed to me to be like Norman Mailer, was ready to fight. I said, Bob, we really can't get into a fight; we have to avoid it because it wouldn't really look good for the so-called Peace Corps people having to fight their way out of the Rathskeller. We somehow managed to exit. They were just local kids who didn't like the idea of the Peace Corps and they'd had too much to drink. They were rowdy; they probably heard us talking maybe loudly. I wondered what novel Eisenman was going to write." [1999]

What Barney Chessin remembered best about Eisenman was that, at age 26, he did not have a driver's license. What Eisenman did have was four years' experience wandering through Europe, being a free spirit, writing poetry, living more "bohemian" than "beat." He was more like Hemingway than Kerouac. When I interviewed Bob in 1999, he was able to find a copy of a poem he had written about the challenge to the U.S. represented by the election of John F. Kennedy. Bob was not selected to become a Peace Corps Volunteer, to his and others' disappointment. As he left Berkeley, Bob had given copies of this poem to some of us. A selection follows:

America I Call Upon You
by Robert Eisenman

And if thy time has ever come, it has come now, it is on thee now—
And if thou art to live or die, the time is now, the choice is thine.
What has passed is past no more to come, but a new era,
No longer Europe or America,
no longer every man his own backyard, but all the world.
And if you are to live or die, that time is now, the choice is thine.
If you are to raise yourself, pull yourself once mighty from out that
    slumber, the time is now.
For the whole of man awaits you....
(Paris, San Francisco, 1960–61)

Problems in Ghana

On July 11 Thornell cabled to Peace Corps/Washington:

"Aug. 30 arrival acceptable ... must receive PCV credentials in next pouch for presentation MinEd. Otherwise cannot assure approvals, school assignments, housing ... Suggest you reiterate each PCV that his coming here contingent upon Ministry prior approval of credentials. Unless PCV has BA from high ranking university or MA his chances of being approved are not certain."

By that standard Ghana I would have been reduced to approximately 20 volunteers. This led to a direct contact between some members of the training faculty and Kwame Nkrumah himself. Apter described it:

"We got word that Nkrumah wasn't going to accept the group. So Drake and I decided we'd call up Nkrumah. So we went up to International House [Peace Corps office at Berkeley] and I remember thinking—Do you think we can just make a call to the President? Why not? We know him. In fact, we just called up and got him on the phone. I knew Joyce Giddens, his personal secretary, very well and I said, 'Joyce, we just have to talk to him.' And she said, 'Sure just hold.'

"We both talked; we didn't have an extension so we took turns. I spoke first saying, Kwame, look, we're in a situation here where we've heard this [program cancellation] and I don't know if it's really true. He said, 'What the hell—this guy [Shriver] comes through saying he's the brother-in-law of the President so, of course, I have to meet with him but I don't want—who needs these people? I don't want them running around here; it's not the right moment.' I don't remember all he said. Then I said, 'This is really an exceptional group; I give you my word and you know me well enough that I wouldn't do this sort of thing if it wasn't OK.'

"I wouldn't have convinced him by myself. It was Drake who knew him much longer than I did and was a lot older than Nkrumah. So Drake said to him, 'Well, Kwame, you're going to have to do this.' Finally, Nkrumah said, 'All right.'"
[1997]

At about the same time in mid-August, G.E.T. and Ministry of Education officials and headmasters began to realize how many unfilled teaching positions existed, with schools due to open within a few weeks. It was difficult to recruit Ghanaian university graduates, already in short supply, or expatriate teachers, who were willing to accept any teaching assignment not within or near the urban triangle of Ghana—Accra, Kumasi, Sekondi-Takoradi. Some schools had been turning to untrained secondary school graduates to fill vacant slots but it was not considered a desirable alternative.

Matters were soon resolved. The Ministry of Education agreed they would accept the teachers that Peace Corps provided on the assurance they were qualified to teach and that, as reported from Berkeley, they were an outstanding group. Thornell returned to Ghana August 16 to finalize the agreements and to work out school assignments for the group. St. Clair Drake also went to Ghana at this time at Shriver's request. Shriver wrote to Ambassador Russell:

"We were particularly pleased that you were able to resolve the problem of placing the Peace Corps volunteers in the secondary system. I have asked Professor St. Clair Drake to come out to Accra for a period of about two weeks [he stayed more than a month]. It was felt both here in Washington and in Berkeley that there would be merit in having some one intimately involved in the training program at Berkeley serve as a bridge between the two training sessions (Berkeley and Accra). Professor Drake will of course serve in Ghana under your direction."

Drake was uniquely qualified by experience and temperament to smooth the way. He had lived and worked in Ghana from 1957–1960, as head of the Sociology Department at the University of Ghana at Legon. He had known Nkrumah and others in the top government circles from the time, before Ghana's independence in 1957, when they were all in England. Drake was thoroughly familiar with Ghana's schools. He knew us from having been faculty and informal counselor and cross-cultural informant in the training program. He was able to interpret our college transcripts and attempt to assign us appropriately within the Ghanaian secondary system. Given the history of the development of the Ghana project, it's no surprise that most of us were assigned to G.E.T. schools. Because many were new and in remote areas, it was these schools that faced serious staffing problems, just a few weeks before the scheduled opening date for the academic year. To the education establishment in Ghana our credentials were likely no more obscure than the locations and prospects for many G.E.T. schools, so the match was appropriate. By August 26 (only 4 days before our arrival) Thornell was able to inform Peace Corps: "All 50 PCV's placed. Drake and I believe placements very good."

Ambassador Russell wrote to Shriver:

"The Peace Corps program in Ghana is one of the first, if not the first, of the programs to be instituted. It therefore involved the breaking of new ground and the handling of questions for which there was no precedent. In addition, this work had to be undertaken against ambivalent attitudes on the part of Ghanaians: in part, there was the suspicion, voiced in the Government-controlled press, that the Peace Corps operation was an imperialist device; in part, there was a recognition of the desperate need of the schools for teachers, especially in science and mathematics."

Selecting, Rejecting, Dejecting

In researching this book I tried to find the eight of the 58 trainees who were not selected to go to Ghana in August, 1961. I was able to find all but two. One went to Ghana as a Peace Corps Volunteer within a month of our arrival. That was Arnold Zeitlin, who had been a newspaper reporter with a degree in Journalism, a major that did not match any of the Ministry of Education's subject specialty requests. Arnold has told his own story in the book, *To Peace Corps With Love.* Of the other five, Bill Austin was immediately invited to join the Philippines II Peace Corps program for teacher aides to middle schools. He served as a volunteer there until mid-1963. Bob Eisenman, Charlie Dirks, Bruce Bloomfield, and Frank Michalski all went on to graduate school and careers in teaching. For those deselected (Peace Corps language in lieu of 'rejected'), the process still rankles and many, both volunteers and staff, have unpleasant memories of the process.

In the 1961 report on the training project, Apter said:

"The ingredients of the problem included notification of non-acceptance on the penultimate day of training (this was handled in interviews by Dr. Hobbs) and the extraordinarily high level of group solidarity that quickly marshaled support behind rejected volunteers once it became known they were not to go to Ghana. The rejected volunteers seem to have found their last-hour rejection 'brutal'; in at least some instances they appear to have selectively misunderstood the rationale given them for being rejected in ways likely to have unfavorable repercussions."

Professor M. Brewster Smith in 1961 was a research psychologist teaching at Berkeley. We first met him during training and through the years none of us ever spoke of him as "Professor" or "Professor Smith" or "Smith." He was Brewster and may well be the true progenitor of Ghana I through both negative and positive influence. It was easy to see why he chose research rather than clinical psychology—he had a slightly awkward affect, shy in manner, with a wide-eyed bespectacled gaze and short but unruly hair; his speech was hesitant and came out in short, explosive clusters. On first meeting him, I pictured him as the kind of person who, in childhood, might be the last one picked when teams chose up sides. Initially it was not easy to warm up to Brewster, especially because of his perceived role. Nicholas Hobbs, a well-known clinical psychologist from Vanderbilt University, was the Director of Selection in Peace Corps/Washington. He had known Brewster through the years as a professional colleague.

In 1997 Brewster remembered, "Nick wanted someone he knew and had personal confidence in to be the point person for him at Berkeley. He also mentioned to me the possibility of my conducting a follow-up study of this group of Peace Corps Volunteers."

Brewster was first introduced to us as a psychologist who was going to administer a series of tests as part of both the training and a long-term study. This led to his negative contribution to the creation of a group spirit in Ghana I—most of us, the secure and the insecure, reacted negatively to this psychological probing and what seemed to be its implications for selection. We coalesced against Brewster; it was as much, if not more, against the process of which he was the most visible representative than against Brewster himself. Although outright rebellion did not occur, we rose to embarrassing heights of rudeness during several of the testing sessions. Esprit is not always built on the high ground of virtue and valor. Brewster's positive contribution to Ghana I came later when he began his follow-up study during and after our Peace Corps service.

The series of tests at Berkeley included:

1. Two separate psychiatric interviews (the Langley-Porter gang);
2. Taylor Manifest Anxiety Scale, based on the Minnesota Multiphasic Personality Inventory;
3. Barron Ego-Strength Scale;
4. Stein Self-Description Test;
5. Levinson F Scale;
6. Social Science Research Council Schedule:
   a. Form P 860
   b. Form I 860;
7. Mock Autobiography.

It was the psychiatric interviews, conducted by the Langley-Porter shrinks, that were used for selection purposes. The data that Brewster and Rafe Ezekiel, his graduate assistant, collected were used for the study only. Brewster was given a grant by Peace Corps to do a two-year follow-up study of Ghana I, later visiting us on site in Ghana for extended interviews.

In 1997 Brewster commented:

"The Peace Corps itself, particularly the Sargent Shriver wing of it, was awfully impressed with the image of the All-American boy or girl who was extroverted, out there drinking beer with the natives, participating in ceremonies. The introverted person with some personal quirks would be excluded as not right. Whereas it turned out that frequently in many of the Peace Corps situations the more introverted sort of person was the one who was really doing the job."

Through the years, Brewster has kept in touch with the group—both the introverts and the extroverts—because he developed a personal friendship with many of us and because he was trying to write a book about the group, based on his two years of research. It was during the years after our Peace Corps service that Brewster made his positive contribution to sustaining Ghana I—periodically he would circulate the current address list he had of the group, asking for corrections and updates. It was a small step from that to someone—Newell Flather, I think—saying, 'Why don't we have a reunion' and out of that evolved our tradition of gatherings every five years. We commemorate not our successful completion of service but rather the year of our birth—1961.

Peace Corps had chosen psychiatrists from the Langley-Porter Neuro-Pyschiatric Institute of the San Francisco Medical Campus of the University of California to be involved in selection; none had ever been to Africa. The institutional name alone guaranteed that it would be a weighty and serious process and one that intimidated most of us. The memories are still fresh.

Sue Hastings Bryson: "I remember only because, as I entered the room, I had to select a chair to sit in from a group of chairs around a table. I felt certain my choice was of great significance and I fretted about it afterwards."

Steve McWilliams: "I still remember the first time, the whole thought of seeing a psychiatrist—I knew I was filled with hangups and my concern was to hide them from him. I was very uptight. I must have had some guy that was straight out of some real strict upbringing just staring at me and he says, in a low voice, 'Is there anything that you want to tell me?' And I thought to myself, No! Then there was just this silence and the silence went on and on. It seemed like for years—I wasn't going to tell him about my intimate life any more than I'd tell the mailman."

Alice O'Grady: "I remember two psychiatrists and one of them said, 'Tell us about yourself.' Since I love to talk about myself, I launched into this story about how my mother died when I was born and I had a stepmother and my mother was Jewish. I think it's a very interesting story and I went on and on and, finally, stopped for a breath and one of them said, 'You've been talking for ten minutes and you haven't once mentioned your father.' And I thought, Oh my God! So I said, 'I-really-love-him-very-much.'" [1999]

From a perspective a bit more removed in time, M. Brewster Smith wrote in 1964 in the final report of his research on Ghana I:

"In general, the psychological tests and psychiatric appraisals employed with Ghana I were not very useful as a basis for predicting the effectiveness of the volunteers' subsequent performance. Several of the volunteers who were sent to Ghana on administrative decision in spite of psychiatric reservations did very well. A very few who were held back from Ghana on similar grounds seem likely, in retrospect, to have functioned quite adequately, had they been given the chance."

All of this offers little solace to someone like Bill Austin whose outlook on life seems as even and uninflected as his speech. I had little memory of him from the training program but immediately recognized him from the Outside Warren Hall photograph. He's short and wiry with close-cropped hair, pleasant features—a very straightforward person with an offbeat sense of humor. Later, in studying the tape of our conversation in 1999, I noticed that he was the easiest interviewee to transcribe because he spoke in short, measured phrases, with a flat unadorned mid-West accent. Bill was twenty-six in 1961, a U.S. Army veteran, with two years' high school teaching experience in WaKeeney, Kansas, and a degree in History from Kansas Wesleyan.

Bill's story is like many of the others in the group but he has an easy, folksy manner in telling it:

"I saw no reason why I should not take the test, apply, and let the chips fall where they may. I really think I was looking at it more from a selfish standpoint than I was taking Kennedy's 'Ask not ...' challenge. I was not superpatriotic but I had read some stuff, you know, like Lederer and Burdick, *The Nation of Sheep* and *The Ugly American*. I felt like the United States could use a little better public relations worldwide than they were getting. I was looking for adventure too. I have to say that the train would come through WaKeeney and there were a lot of nights I would have liked to get on it.

"In April I resigned from teaching and so, I really only had one iron in the fire, the Peace Corps. Bob Scheuerman and I took the test, probably in Salina. I was very discouraged by noon on that test because it was some kind of Civil Service exam and the thing was all day long and you're so doggone tired by the time you got to the math and the chemistry and the physics and all that stuff, and I wasn't going to do any good in that anyway. I finally gave up about mid-afternoon. I just turned my paper in and walked out.

"I went back to my room and was packing up to return home to Bennington. I was going to probably work in the harvest field that summer and then go try to get into a grad school in Kansas someplace in the fall. I had given up on the Peace Corps after that test. I was sure that they didn't want me and I would never hear from them again. Back in Bennington I was working with one of the farmers there who had a lot of acres of wheat. We were getting ready to cut wheat which comes along about the end of June. Then this telegram came and the drunken depot agent, Shelby Cleland, came to my front door with it. I was dumbfounded really. It bowled me completely over and I thought, well, I'm going to go. I went to the farmer and told him you're going to have to find somebody to fill my spot on your harvest crew 'cause I got to get my gear together and report to Berkeley on the second of July. He said, "Well this is an opportunity for you, so go ahead.' What else could he say?"

I asked Bill about the reaction of family and friends:

"My father was always one not to give advice, not to make decisions for you. He was always one that wanted you to make up your own mind and suffer, if you had to, and maybe you'd learn something. Maybe you'd make a better decision the next time. You see, I'd already been in the army and I think most people in Bennington thought I was crazy because I wasn't really drafted. At that time you could go to the draft board and move your name up, right to the top of the list. That's what I had done. My mother was a little bit concerned about my going to Africa because she was a graduate nurse and probably worried that I'd pick up some tropical disease. Peace Corps being a Democratic idea and of course everyone in my family was Republican and thought that a Democratic president was just something you had to endure. I had a lot of Christian friends who thought I was going to be a missionary. I had the blessings of the whole town behind me even though they didn't come right out and say it. They didn't have a going away party or anything like that. I think the softball team I was playing on was sorry to see me go because it would leave a hole in the infield."

Then we talked about the program and people at Berkeley:

"I was very impressed with the general educational level and eruditeness of the group. Well, you had a degree from the University of Chicago, there were some Berkeley graduates, and Harvard. So this really impressed me and I began to wonder—here's a little old guy from Kansas who graduated from Kansas Wesleyan and it's not like he's a hillbilly coming out of the piney woods but these people are talking on a different level than I'm used to. I'm not too used to getting up and saying anything anyway even though I had two years of teaching experience. I didn't feel like I couldn't do the work, that I couldn't make it. I was very interested in learning about Ghana. Of course, I didn't know anything about it. I did wonder about Nkrumah when he said, 'Seek ye first the political kingdom and then all things else shall be yours.' Taking that right out of the Bible and changing it like that—I thought this guy, something there is amiss.

"I remember the shrinks. I got in there with this young psychiatrist, I guess he was, and he said, 'Well, tell me about yourself. What kind of relationship do you have with your parents?' Well, I'm probably closer to my mother than I am to my father. 'AHH!' he said. 'Let's go into this a little deeper' and he woke up like he just sat on a tack. And I thought, man, what have I said? He said, 'What do you mean by that?' I said, 'Well, my dad works 14 hours a day at the drug store. I don't see too much of him. He works seven days a week, he gets half a day off every two weeks.' And I said, 'My mother is pretty much raising us, the family. My father is of the old school, wanting me to be strong and not be a panty-waist. He wants me to make my own decisions. So I feel closer to my mother, she's with me more. If you scrape your knee, she gives you sympathy. I never get any sympathy from my father … that's the way he was raised.' First time I've ever seen a psychiatrist and I'm trying to tell the truth and I'm wondering what he's making of it."

As a precautionary measure, all four of Bill's wisdom teeth were extracted. That experience was not as painful as the selection process, as Bill describes it:

"They called me into an office … there was a guy from Washington there [probably Nicholas Hobbs]. He said, 'You're not going to Ghana.' And I thought right away I had flunked the training and I asked. He said, 'Oh no, you didn't flunk the training. The Ghanaians didn't want you.' And I said, 'Well, I had a feeling they might not 'cause reading all the different subjects they wanted teachers for … I didn't fit into any of them, really.' He said, 'No, that wasn't it'. He said [Bill laughing] … I wish I'd kept a journal and written down exactly what he said … he said, 'The Ghanaians think that you might foment a revolution.' And I almost fainted; I was taken aback."

I just have to jump in here. I believe that Bill's recollection about 'foment a revolution' is accurate. I believe that in the confusion of preparing final selection materials and discussing them with Hobbs, someone on the staff made a mistake or that Hobbs, with the stress and tension of the selection procedure—he was the point man in telling trainees they were rejected—that Hobbs goofed and misdirected a piece of information he was given. There was a trainee who was deselected, about whom the comment, "foment a revolution," was accurate. He was a brash young man, quick of lip, a real self-promoting braggart. On at least one occasion, a talk on world affairs, he jumped into a role play, standing up and screaming at the group about how communism would bury decadent capitalism. I think Bill was rejected because of the obscurity (at least, in Ghanaian eyes) of Kansas Wesleyan and the fact that his only teachable subject was History. Finally, if Peace Corps truly felt that he had real potential for subversion, they would not have immediately enrolled him in the Philippines II project.

Bill finishes the selection story: "He mentioned the college from which I got my degree. Ghanaians rate colleges—Harvard, Yale, Princeton, Stanford, Chicago—and they said they couldn't find Kansas Wesleyan on the list. As I was walking out the door, the guy, almost as a second thought, said, 'Would you like to go to the Philippines?' I turned around and said, 'You know, I had no preference. Well sure, if the Philippines needed me, why I'm your man. I'll take a crack at that.'"

One last Austin story before he fades from the Ghana I scene—it has to do with the FBI background checks all trainees went through.

"One old farmer that I'd worked for, while we were in Berkeley, he was out plowing in the middle of a section on his farm. It was a beastly hot day and he says he's out there in the middle of this field plowing and he saw a car stop over on the road and somebody got out of it and start walking across the furrows. He said he stopped the tractor and he couldn't imagine, you know; he thought there might have been a death in his family or something because as the guy got closer he saw he was in a coat and tie and it was so hot. The guy came up to this tractor and showed him his FBI identification and wanted to know if he knew William R. Austin.

"This farmer said I didn't know whether you'd killed somebody or robbed a bank but I knew you were in bad trouble. I didn't know what to say. I said, Yeah, I know him. He's worked for me. It's still running through my mind that you robbed a bank. When he asked me some questions about you, I told him you were a good worker, and honest, and trustworthy and I went through all the qualifications of a Boy Scout on your behalf. I was hoping they'd give you a light sentence. He finally said he was investigating me as a result of your joining the Peace Corps."

When Charlie Peters had visited the program in late July, he showed us the newly developed organizational chart for the Peace Corps, giving substance to that vague entity whose banner we were about to carry to Africa. The chart had boxes of various sizes, connecting lines, both thick and thin, implying rank and accountability, with boldly named divisions of this new Crusaders army. Several of us gleefully pointed out a glaring omission—there was no box, line, or reference anywhere on the chart to "Peace Corps Volunteers." The oversight didn't surprise us. It confirmed our notion of Washington as remote, out of touch, and more concerned with bureaucratic niceties. We were not alone in being leery of "central headquarters." David Apter included the following comment in the University's Final Report on the training program, forwarded to Peace Corps/Washington in December, 1961:

"During the first weeks of the project, there was a constant stream of visitors from Washington who appeared without notice, who were not sure why they were sent, who were not clear about whom they were to see, and, perhaps more mystifying than anything else, did not seem to know very much what their colleagues in the Peace Corps were about here and elsewhere."

"Caught-in-the-headlights" mug book picture, Berkeley

Peter Dybwad

Valerie Deuel

Newell Flather

Ray Spriggs

Ken Baer

DeeDee Vellenga

Carol Waymire

Dave Hutchinson

Laura Damon

David Apter

Ruth and author (posing as skeptical New Yorker)

On lecture break outside Warren Hall. Author to left,
reading The New York Times.

In Warren Hall. 1st row: Dave; 2nd row: Meryl, Darleen,
Marian, Bob E., Tom P.; 3rd row: Newell.

4

HERE TODAY, GHANA TOMORROW

Meeting President Kennedy

After the discomfort of the selection process, we were glad that training had been shortened by one week, ending on August 21. We were to report to Washington on Monday, August 28, for a White House event and then board our Pan Am charter to Accra. As early as July 23, I had written home:

"Good news! Our training program is being shortened by one week and we are being given leave from August 21 to August 28." And added in a later letter, "We are being flown to Ghana by chartered plane from Washington and will be allowed up to 216 pounds of luggage [Why 216?]. We have to report to Washington by 11 a.m. on August 28.... There are rumors of a White House reception."

I remember envisioning a White House reception, based on earlier experiences at various bar mitzvah and wedding receptions. I expected a high class lawn party setting with gloved waiters in crisp white vests, circulating among us with canapés and drinks; we'd have an opportunity for casual 'cocktail party' chatter with the President, Shriver, maybe even Jackie. I was not alone in such thinking. Ruth Whitney said: "Georgianna and I wore our basic black dresses—now we kid about it all the time—and white gloves. She and I must have grown up with the same kind of mother who taught us what to wear for such occasions."

I think Peace Corps/Washington was content to reward us with a few days at home before the overseas adventure began. It could also serve other purposes: as of August, the Peace Corps legislation was working its way through Congress. Having us in our hometowns could and did generate local news stories such as: "Young Wilmette Man Leaves For Ghana"; "Graduate To Teach with Peace Corps in Ghana"; "Miss Vellenga In Ghana, West Africa" [in the Social News from a really local paper]; "Plainfield Teacher Chosen for Peace Corps in Ghana." We scattered from Berkeley for the brief leave to say goodbye to family and friends (and to buy our weight allowance of 216 pounds of clothing and supplies, trying to figure out how many handkerchiefs would be needed for two years).

Surely the most memorable of farewells was the one described by Alice O'Grady. She had continued through training to perform on weekends with a musical troupe, the Lamplighters, which was presenting Gilbert and Sullivan's 'The Mikado':

"We did a show that night I left for Chicago. The director, who was also in the cast, at the end of each performance would step forward and say, 'Thank you for being such a good audience; we would like you to join the cast in the lobby for coffee.' That night she said, 'We're not able to join you in the lobby because one of our members is going overseas with the Peace Corps' and I stepped forward and had my first and only solo bow with that company. Got a nice round of applause. Then, because the plane was leaving soon, I changed but none of the cast did. They all went to the airport as Japanese schoolgirls, etc.—in their costumes. When they called the plane and I was about to leave, they all went down on one knee and sang 'Hail Poetry.' It was just beautiful. It's a lovely kind of hymn; not from 'The Mikado.' They presented me with a hobby horse, a horse's head on a stick, for me to travel to Ghana on. It was a very touching sendoff." [1997]

The Peace Corps program of road surveyors for Tanganyika was completing phase one of its training in El Paso at about the same time. The second phase was to be field training at a special camp in Puerto Rico. In transit between the two sites, they joined the Ghana group for a day in Washington. The White House setting, remarks by Kennedy, and approximately 75 bright, young, newly minted Peace Corps Volunteers would attract useful press coverage. The White House reception was in the Rose Garden, a very crowded stand-up affair on the hottest day of the year, with reporters and photographers outnumbering guests, but we did get to meet President Kennedy. It must have been a heart-warming sight to those lobbying for passage of the Peace Corps bill. Kennedy appeared with Shriver hovering near and spoke to us. Many of the group best remember Kennedy's remark: "So I hope you realize—I know you do—that the future of the Peace Corps really rests with you." We were comfortable with that, thanks to Apter, Drake, and the others at Berkeley.

That the "future of the Peace Corps" really depended on us had been stressed by Shriver earlier in the day when he spoke to us at a perfunctory State Department "briefing" which seemed designed to reassure the briefers, not especially to inform us. He told us, "The President is counting on you. It's up to you to prove that the concepts and ideals of the American Revolution are still alive. Foreigners think we're fat, dumb and happy over here. They don't think we've got the stuff to make personal sacrifices for our way of life. You must show them. And if you don't, you'll be yanked out of the ball game." We had faced eerie psychiatrists, seven varieties of psychological tests, chilling stories of boa constrictor attacks, and the perils of partying in Strawberry Canyon above the Berkeley campus (I never knew they produced such large bottles of wine). Shriver could not daunt us. We were ready— to teach, if not to sacrifice.

I must have been mulling over Shriver's exhortation because at the Rose Garden I was interviewed by Tom Wicker of The New York Times (in my mind that made up for the hiding, bearded, in the back row of all those photos). He wrote:

"Robert Klein … made it clear, however, that he and his fellow corpsmen had not been trained as political missionaries or assigned to preach particular doctrines.

He said that David Apter, a political science professor who headed the four-man faculty for the Ghana group's two months of training at the University of California, had stressed that each volunteer was going abroad as an 'individual with his own ideas.'"

After the Rose Garden speech, President Kennedy, in a stage whisper, had asked an aide how busy his schedule was because he wanted to greet each of us individually. He retired to the Oval Office and we paraded through, single file. Everyone has some memory of that part of the occasion. Don Groff recalled, "I remember just being kind of dumbstruck, going through the line. I do remember that I shook Kennedy's hand; as I moved on, he said, 'Ghan-err or Tanganyika?' And I told him, 'Ghan-uh.'"

For Nate Gross, it was a storybook experience with this special history:

"I discovered the existence of Jack Kennedy in an interesting way. In 1958 at college I was trying to go to sleep after staying up late studying and had the radio on. The music changed over to a talk program. I was half asleep but it was someone interviewing a politician. I noticed a New England accent. I was about to turn it off and go to sleep but the guy was answering in such an intelligent way that I wound up listening for an hour. I wanted to find out who was this politician actually talking so intelligently. It turned out to be Jack Kennedy. Later in 1959 he came to a convocation at Beloit College. Jackie was with him with her classic A line dress and pill-box hat. He gave a great little talk there. I later got to shake his hand during the Wisconsin primary. So I had great feelings toward Kennedy before Peace Corps. It was really wonderful to be at the White House even though in the receiving line the exchange was perfunctory. We didn't have any conversation. He just said 'Good luck' and shook my hand. I think some people had a few sentences." I interjected: "Newell did." Kiddingly, Nate responded: "He probably mentioned family friends." [1997]

In fact Newell did just that. He was the last in the reception line and said to President Kennedy, "'I'm from Massachusetts too. And my brother was actually a roommate with your brother [Teddy] in college.' Then I said, 'I just want to say something myself. You've been under a lot of criticism, skepticism about Peace Corps. We're going to serve you well.'" As an aside, in our interview many years later, Newell said that he felt the comment was a bit 'saccharine.' [1997]

DeeDee Vellenga commented about the Rose Garden in her diary. DeeDee was a graduate of Monmouth College in Illinois and had taught for several years at Foxcroft, an exclusive school for girls in Virginia. We were not particularly close friends during training or in our early days in Ghana. We shared the common experience of being volunteers in Ghana I but little else. It was probably my New Yorker provincialism that exaggerated the distance between Junior High 136 in Harlem and Foxcroft and those who teach therein. DeeDee wrote:

"The Rose Garden reception was unbelievably hot and confused with reporters, cameramen, wires, tape recorders all over the place. When Kennedy did try to meet us informally after his brief message, he was swamped so it was decided to let us file through his oval office and shake hands with him—I couldn't think of a thing to say to him—all I noticed was his piercing blue eyes. He paused for a moment and looked hard at me and then said, 'Good luck'—didn't know quite how to take it! Meeting Shriver was very encouraging—he is down-to-earth and very dynamic in a gutsy sort of way. I think the Peace Corps has a real future if he continues to head it. Now it's up to us to see how things go in the field!"

The Washington whirl continued for us that evening with a party at the residence of the Ghanaian Ambassador, Mr. W. Q. Halm. Looking back it is remembered as a wonderful, hot and steamy introduction to Ghanaian hospitality. The Ambassador assured us that it never got as hot and humid in Ghana as it did in Washington D.C. We danced, ate, and drank for tomorrow we were, not to die, but to fly into the unknown of Ghana. After the Embassy party, Jim Kelly, Maureen Pyne, Ruth Whitney, and George Coyne (telling the story): "… went to a night club and then caught a taxi. We went to the Shrine of the Immaculate Conception. We wanted to say a prayer because we really didn't know what we were getting into and we wanted to light a candle. The cathedral was in complete darkness and we had to light matches to find the door but were able to get in."

It's reassuring that at least four of the group knew enough not to just curse the darkness but to light a candle. They were ready for whatever Ghana might bring.

Above the Trees and on the Ground, Ghana at Last

On August 29 we went to National Airport to board our Pan Am charter, a four-engine propjet, dubbed The Peace Corps Clipper. Before boarding there were some technical matters to be dealt with. Peace Corps wanted to ship all of our luggage with us on the flight, no doubt calculating that, like a security blanket, arriving with our newly purchased towels, sheets, and underwear, would bring us reassuring comfort in our early days in Ghana. I do not know the payload of the good old Clipper but full fuel tanks and an additional 10,800 pounds of baggage (if we each had packed our allocated weight allowance of 216 pounds, x 50) might be a problem. Some seats were removed from the plane and each of us was weighed on the luggage scale. Getting this project off the ground may have been more difficult than we were aware.

Sue Bartholomew remembered:

"We waited and waited and waited. Finally someone came to tell us they were taking seats out of the plane because we had all our luggage and that plane wasn't going to get off the ground. I thought it was funny. They even had to weigh us; then half the seats were gone. Howard [Ballwanz] had talked to the pilot and we joked about it. The pilot told Howard that there was something called Forest Airline, did a lot of charters. They got that name because with so many people on board they never got higher than the tops of the trees. The pilot said that's what we're doing. It'll take a couple of hours to make our altitude." [1997]

The flight took twenty-three hours, stopping in the Azores and at Dakar, Senegal, before arriving in Accra the next day, August 30, 1961. People recall the flight in different ways but all agree that there were two distinct groups—the singers and the card players.

Pat Kennedy was our escort officer, not out of fear that any of us would try to escape but to smooth the way in Ghana by assisting George Carter in getting us settled into our assignments. Pat had been involved with the development of the project from the very beginning. He had worked with the faculty to develop the training curriculum and then served as liaison between Berkeley and Washington, dealing with the nitty-gritty matters related to us becoming PCVs—documents, allowances, passports. His reward was a trip to Ghana.

The singers were people who, at Berkeley, would come together to sing madrigals for relaxation and their own enjoyment. Alice O'Grady, Tom Peterson, Valerie Deuel, Don Groff all had some musical training and sang beautifully. This was definitely not the Rathskeller Michael-Row-The-Boat-Ashore crowd. Thanks to the singers, Ghana I was able to rise to the challenge that Richard Thornell and the Ambassador had mentioned in a cable to Washington just before our departure:

"Planning high level reception PCVs at airport since this first group arrive abroad. Request most capable spokesman be selected make carefully prepared arrival statement. One other PCV might be interviewed Radio Ghana. Suggest group be prepared sing traditional Twi song learned Berkeley."

The challenge was that at Berkeley we had learned very little Twi and even fewer Twi songs but we did have great improvisational skills. The madrigal group, augmented, came to our rescue and not only learned the song, *Yen Ara Asase Ni*, but sounded good doing it. Someone, probably Pat Kennedy, had had the foresight to have copies of both words and music for this traditional Ashanti song. When the time came to sing at the airport after arrival, easily half of us stood in the back, moving our lips while the brave, strong voices of the true singers were being recorded by Radio Ghana. It was an instant hit with the Ghanaian radio audience as much for its novelty as for the quality of its performance. In our first few days of bus touring around Southern Ghana, several people commented, "Oh, you are the group that sang that Twi song. That was fine."

Back on the flight, the non-singers—the card players (Hearts)—had stormed through the transit lounge at the airport in the Azores during a refueling stop and stocked up on wine and cheese, which assured the continuance of the game and the avoidance of sleep, although, I'm sure most of us cat-napped during the flight. The flight also made a stop in Dakar, Senegal. This first step on the African continent was intoxicating. In the freshness of dawn, the air was warm and caressing, with the sweet fragrance of bougainvillea tantalizing the nose. We were touching the soil of Africa! We were giddy with anticipation and lack of sleep. I remember clumsily dancing around with frangipani flowers stuck behind each ear.

Nate Gross recalled: "Somewhere between Senegal and Ghana we were flying low enough to see the ground and some villages and huts and stuff. That's when I thought, 'Holy shoot, we're really going to Africa. Can I handle this? What's it really going to be like when we hit the ground?'" [1997]

We arrived in Accra and were met by a Ghanaian Ministry of Education welcoming committee. Ken Baer, an imposing figure and probably one of the few in the group comfortable wearing a seersucker suit, served as our solemn spokesman. Paraphrasing Shriver's remarks on his visit to Nkrumah in late April, Ken said, "We have come to Ghana to learn, to teach, to try to further the cause of world peace but above all, to serve Ghana now." We sang *Yen Ara Asase Ni* (some of us did, anyway) and then boarded buses to be taken out to the University of Ghana at Legon where we would have further training and orientation organized by the Ministry of Education. A lot had happened in the six busy months following President Kennedy's Executive Order of March 1st. The Peace Corps was now a reality.

Dancing the High Life

If there was any rite of passage hinted at in our Ghana training at Berkeley, it was to dance the High Life at the Lido nightclub in Accra. To do so would mean that you were becoming a participant in the "real" Ghana. The very first night after our arrival many of us did just that—dancers, non-dancers, drinkers, non-drinkers, the shy and the bold, those in culture shock and those too dazed from the journey to be shocked by anything. Valerie Deuel described the Lido:

"Sitting in a circle around the dance floor, everyone ordered beer; it was very hot, not air-conditioned, with an open roof, sweaty. People getting up and doing the High Life. Being shy and having a block against dancing all my life, I got up and did the High Life anyway. I think I felt it was required of me, so I danced. Back home I never even did the Twist but I was swept up by the feeling of that whole evening." [1997]

Our exuberance and joy at being there was capped by Laura Damon and John McGinn winning second place in a High Life contest, dancing an awkward but wildly enthusiastic combination of Jitterbug and the Twist with just a hint of High Life. The whole evening made me begin to feel that I was a part of Ghana. A sub-rite of passage followed—finding and then negotiating the fare for the taxi to drive us back out to the University and, in looking for our dormitory on the dimly lit campus, stumbling into an open storm drain.

Soon after our arrival, in the CPP party newspaper, the Evening News, the political columnist, identified only as 'Rambler,' wrote:

"You are welcome to Ghana, which, I understand, you have come to serve as teachers. I like the way you sang that Ghanaian hit on your arrival at the airport two days ago. Let that song make you non-aligned during your stay here, for though you came at our own invitation, you will terribly harm Ghana-American relations if you do not get yourselves acclamatized [sic] to the national climate of Africa. I wish you patient, understanding hearts—and a happy stay."

We might not have thought of ourselves as 'political missionaries,' as I had said at the Rose Garden, but others might be seeing us in a different light.

They're Taking Tom Away

George Carter arrived in Ghana a few days later. We had met him briefly at Berkeley in mid-August just after he was chosen by Shriver to become the Ghana Peace Corps Representative. For unknown reasons, the first designee, Ted Brown, was hastily 'un-designated' in early August. Carter told how he learned of his appointment:

"Chester Bowles was Undersecretary of State and had to go on a trip to Nigeria, to Cyprus, to Belgrade, Yugoslavia, and to New Delhi, India. I was completely disengaged from Peace Corps for this trip. Bowles had requested I go on this trip with him but now I do not recall why. En route between Belgrade and Delhi, I got called up to the front of the plane and the Undersecretary said, 'Sit down, George.' He handed me a cable from Washington he had just received and said, 'Read that.'

"I don't remember the exact language but it was from Shriver for Bowles asking him to release me from his party when we got to Delhi so that I could return to Washington at once. 'Carter will be offered the position of Peace Corps Representative to Ghana and run the first Peace Corps project. We plan to make him an FSR-2 [second highest level in the Foreign Service].'

"I read this and my face fell halfway down to my knees because I had been discussing with Bowles about an ambassadorship to a French-speaking, newly independent African country. I had some reason to believe that that was in the offing. So I asked the Undersecretary, 'Well, you know what I really want. What's your reaction to this?' He said, 'I think you ought to take it.' So, I did." [1997]

Carter was aware that being the first to serve as Peace Corps Representative in the field represented both opportunity and risk.

George Carter was in his early thirties, of medium height but imposing presence, neat and trim, handsome, dark-skinned, a bit remote but not intimidating. He was articulate but not effusive in language; you had to come to him, rather than his reaching out to you. The distance was reinforced by the constant presence of an unlit pipe that would seem to divert his attention at moments when he was thinking through a reply. He was the kind of person you would go to for a straight answer but not for verbal stroking. "Oh?" (voice tremulous, focused on pipe) was his frequent response to an awkward question or inappropriate remark. However, when he did respond it was clear and direct. His supervisory style, which emerged through our volunteer years, can be compared to that of a captain of a racing yacht. Manning a yacht in a race allows for little conversation; each person on the crew is expected to understand fully and be able to perform his or her duties without mishap and with scant direction. That is the captain's expectation of crew and that was Carter's expectation of us in our performance as Peace Corps Volunteers—we were judged competent and were expected to act accordingly. During our two years in Ghana, I don't think any of us were forced to walk the plank but some came mighty close.

Almost as soon as the fifty of us arrived in Accra, we ceased to be Ghana I. Although we came as a group, we were to serve as individuals. We had trained together for seven weeks in Berkeley; together we had been given a dizzying two-day Washington farewell; we had traveled together for 23 hours on the Pan Am charter flight to Accra. Now, after a brief stay at Legon, we were to be dispersed throughout the country to our teaching assignments, which we were told about soon after our arrival. Through July and August, we had come to be a group, if not united in purpose, at least united in circumstance (we were about to become the first ever Peace Corps Volunteers) and in mutual distrust of anyone, Shriver included, who tried to tell us how to be a PCV.

I can remember the exact moment I felt that we were no longer a group. We had just settled into our unfamiliar but pleasant dormitory accommodations at the

University. At the end of the first week there, a group of us were lounging just outside the residence hall when a Ghanaian walked up and said, "I'm here to pick up Mr. Livingston and take him to school. We're opening tomorrow."

And I experienced this sudden "panic" reaction, "Oh my God! They're taking Tom away!" The group had come this far and all of a sudden it was a shock to realize that the reality of being in Ghana was dispersal to schools all over the country. Others recalled that the abruptness of Tom's departure startled them too.

However, Tom recalls: "Mr. Addy, the Headmaster, arrives in his little Morris Minor. Dodowa's only twenty miles from Legon. It was a very short ride. I think I did get there four or five days before the students arrived. We did begin before all of the other schools. That first week at Legon we went off to Saltpond, Cape Coast, Elmina and there were still other excursions planned and I think I only had something like two or three hours' notice. We were going off to visit something else and I was planning to go on this visit too. Someone, I don't remember who, told me, 'Your Headmaster called and he's collecting you. His school is beginning early so get your things ready.' I didn't have any time to think about it. I didn't feel any distress at leaving the group. I just thought, Well, this is it. This is the beginning. All other stuff was just preliminary." [1997]

Off Tom went and the rest of us would soon follow.

Steve McWilliams recalled: "Assignments were being called out and our names.... That would break up all this togetherness. 'These are the three people who'll go off here. Here's the two at ——. And here's the one person who's going to LaBone. Well, I just—my heart came up to my throat and I was thinking, 'I'm going to be the only person at this school. I'm going to miss all these friends.' That kind of took me aback." [1997]

Because his college major had been Greek, Tom Peterson was expecting to be assigned to one of the prestige secondary schools on the coast, but, as he wrote home:

"I received my assignment the other night and was utterly shocked. However, after I removed the visions of rolling surf and palm trees etc. from my mind, I managed to work up some enthusiasm. I have been assigned to Navrongo, one of the most primitive areas of Ghana. It is approximately 420 miles north of Accra in the Northern Region. It is a few miles from the border of Upper Volta. I am about 100 miles from any large town (Tamale is the closest) … as I think about it, I am becoming more enthusiastic. It may turn out to be better than many others in terms of experiences. Accra is a nice town—it is the new Africa. I will be in the old Africa."

Ann and Richard Port were assigned to Sogakofe Secondary School, one of the newest of the G.E.T. schools. It was located east of Accra, near the Volta River in the Volta Region, on the other (eastern) side of the river, on the main road from Accra to Lome, Togo; but traffic depended on a ferry of historic vintage and pace (and forget trying to cross after 6:00 p.m.). The Ports arrived to find the school, the Headmaster, but no students. They spent their first several days crammed into the Headmaster's little red VW, traveling out to nearby small villages to find prospective students. Richard and Ann's presence on these forays was intended to lend weight and authenticity to the Headmaster's pleas: "These Americans have come all the way to our village to teach and we can not disappoint them."

We were busy checking the map of Ghana, translating strange names into actual locations and trying to envision the schools that would be our homes for the next two years. We also were absorbing the information about who in the group, if anyone, we might be teaching with. How did we fit into the system in 1961? Of the approximately sixty government-supported secondary schools, Ghana I was initially assigned to thirty (plus two teacher training colleges). Twenty of the schools were under the Ghana Educational Trust (G.E.T.), which was soon after absorbed by the Ministry of Education. Eleven of the assignments (postings in Ministry language) were to 'bush' schools—remote locations, on rough dirt roads, and usually the only secondary school in the district. Although at some schools someone might be the only Peace Corps Volunteer assigned, no one was really posted alone. Urban or bush, newly opened or established, every school had Ghanaian teachers and staff (and students); many had other non-Ghanaian expatriate teachers; most were secular but a few were church-affiliated, many Catholic—Opoku Ware, Holy Child, Bishop Herman; all were considered "public schools" in the American sense in that they received direct governmental financial support. A few of the urban locations were day schools—Ebenezer and West Africa in Accra, Fijai in Sekondi— but most were boarding schools and many were co-educational.

In our few days at Legon, we received settling-in allowances and began to arm ourselves with mosquito nets, Tilley lanterns, water filters, pots, dishes, and pans to go forth into the unknown (or at least the thoroughly unfamiliar) to live and work. Now we belonged to the Ghanaian Ministry of Education. To quote from the formal agreement:

"The volunteers shall be under the administration of the Ministry and shall serve under the direct supervision of the Headmasters of the schools to which they are assigned.

"The volunteers shall teach according to the syllabuses in their respective fields of instruction which teaching may include a regular, full-time schedule of courses and shall participate, as needed, in the after-school activities of the schools to which they are assigned.

"The Ministry shall provide housing and suitable accommodation for each volunteer.

"The Ministry shall pay each volunteer £G700 per annum."

For many years, the Ghana program was the only Peace Corps project anywhere in the world where the host country, rather than the Peace Corps, paid the basic monthly living allowance to the volunteer. I was told by my Ghanaian Headmaster that Ghana did this out of a sense of pride but even more importantly to show clearly for whom the volunteers were working. In 1961 a £G equaled $2.80 and £G700 was the basic pay for a Ghanaian graduate teacher in a secondary school.

Marion waiting to meet President Kennedy in Oval Office.

*President Kennedy speaking in Rose Garden August 28, 1961. Author to left, hiding his
beard. Seated in center Ruth and Georgianna "in proper black dress with gloves."*

*President greeting Darleen. Tom L.
behind, Valerie to right.*

Carol W. meeting President Kennedy.

5

LEARNING TO TEACH

But They Didn't Tell Us About That in Training

Teaching is an activity everyone is familiar with. Reduced to the bare essentials, it involves a teacher, students and a classroom. By the time each of us had completed college, we had been in such a setting thousands of times. The challenge now was to translate the generic experience of schools into live Ghanaian classrooms. Training at Berkeley had taught us some of the differences and similarities between teaching in the U.S. and in Ghana but the true test of what we had learned and what we had lived was now upon us. However, there were a few surprises along the way. Much of our initial reaction, as remembered in the interviews, was inward looking—seeing oneself in this new and often strange place, dealing with questions of personal comfort, accommodations, colleagues. It was only later that the focus shifted to the students and teaching—this transition time varied among us. I think there were even a few in Ghana I who may never have made that transition. In spite of Coach Shriver's rousing words to us just prior to our departure, we did not hit the ground running. We first had to learn to deal with the unexpected—those matters not really explained at Berkeley.

A good example is Carol Waymire's story. In 1961 Carol had lived most of her life in or near Santa Rosa, California. She attended elementary and high school there; did a degree at San Jose State College; was a 7th grade teacher from 1956 to 1961 in the Santa Rosa public schools. She was 27 years old and, as I remember her from then, the word, "modest" immediately pops into my head. She was modest in dress, speech, and demeanor—quiet, pleasant, approachable. Now at Yaa Asantewaa Girls Secondary School she faced Florette, the very model of a modern neo-colonialist:

"I was pleased my school was upcountry. It was outside Kumasi. I didn't want to be in a city. It seemed good but I was disappointed that there were so many volunteers together at one school. There were five of us.

"When we first arrived we all met the Headmistress, Florette, who was English and that went very badly. Within the first week she took us into Kumasi to a party with British soldiers [trainers for the Ghana Army]. For me that was just awful—so totally against whatever I was there for. Also she told us we'd have to buy a car or we'd be leeches on society; we had to have a house boy—none of us wanted a house boy. We really fought it.

"She took us into this party in her car and then said that we should find our own ride home. But, if we didn't, she and her boy friend could give us a ride. If I hadn't had Peace Corps training, I might have thought it very exciting to see a bunch of British soldiers and get to know them. But I was in Ghana to meet Ghanaians. Also it didn't take but a few sentences to know that they hated Ghana and didn't like Africans—had no respect for the people." [1997]

Another of the Yaa Asantewaa group was Sue Hastings. She was a slim, blonde, easy-going Californian from Malibu and a graduate of Stanford. Sue seemed to enjoy herself thoroughly, in her own way, on her own terms. In 1999 she wrote me from her home in Scotland:

"When I joined Peace Corps, my friends thought it was a radical idea; none of them had any interest in also joining—they still talk about it as if I had opted for space flight. It was different with my mother who had always wanted to go to Africa. Throughout my first year in Kumasi, she sent me supplies of Chubby Checkers records so I wouldn't lose touch and Crest toothpaste so I wouldn't lose my teeth."

Sue's adjustment to Kumasi differed from Carol's. She met and married Sam Bryson, a British expatriate working there for Texaco.

Steve McWilliams was assigned to a G.E.T. school in Accra, LaBone, and told about his settling in:

"I thoroughly enjoyed going to Kingsway Department Store. They had mosquito netting. Well, I thought, this is great—I am really in Africa; I have a mosquito net; where do I get the pith helmet? I was in sort of a daze with just the mechanics of getting established and trying to figure out what was expected of me. The people at the school took me by the hand and said—this is what you'll be doing and this is the book you'll be using.

"Finally reality set in. It took me about a month or so before I really settled into that kind of awareness that this is what it is. Now and then it hit me like a ton of bricks. My God, I don't have any transportation. I mean really that was the culture shock I experienced and it was about as American as you could get. I thought the solution was this. I'll have to write home and in some way have my car sent to me. It was a Volkswagen and I thought you could put a Volkswagen on a train and then on a boat to Africa. Soon other people start showing up in mammy lorries, tro-tros [local jitney-style buses or trucks], or whatever they were taking. It dawned on me that that's what you do. You don't have to take a taxi everywhere." [1997]

Another surprise was the "servant" question. In most school situations Ghanaian and expatriate headmasters and staff expected Peace Corps teachers to employ a servant—usually referred to as steward, house boy, or cook; usually male; usually, in urban areas, with previous domestic service experience. Part practicality, part pretension—it was just the way things were done (if things were to be done properly—a British and colonial point of view). It was also thought to be impractical for a graduate teacher to be concerned with day-to-day household chores. A teacher should be free to grade papers, tutor students, plan lessons, and perform non-class school duties such as Housemaster (dorm supervisor), Sports Mistress, school disciplinarian and the other roles needed, especially in a boarding school setting. Here we were, Peace Corps Volunteers, the antidote to the Ugly American, and our most immediate challenge in becoming a real part of Ghana was figuring out how to relate to a personal servant.

Laura Damon faced the question the instant she arrived at her new school, Opoku Ware:

"I was taken to my bungalow and on the porch—it was 5:30 or so, just beginning to get dark—were sitting nine African young men, all hoping that I would hire him as cook-steward. The Headmaster came over to welcome me. He had already hired somebody for me. I felt that was kind of an awkward beginning." [1997]

Ray Spriggs, one of two African-Americans in the group, was assigned to Fijai Secondary School in Sekondi and was living in town, not on the school compound. Sekondi-Takoradi, two towns that had merged into a single metropolitan area, was an industrial port city, a railroad and transport terminus. It was an urban center with a substantial blue collar working class. When the Ghana government announced an austerity budget in October 1961, there were strikes. Ray wrote to Professor St. Clair Drake:

"When I came, in my heart I was waving flags for glorious Nkrumah. Not now. He arrested about 50 people here. . . .

"Just before Nkrumah returned [from a visit to Russia], the strikes were at their peak. The problem over the budget, along with some other deep-founded gripes, is really genuine. The curfew lasted a few days in which everyone was to be off the streets between 6 p.m.–6 a.m. Armed ex-soldiers with machine guns, armored cars and some vehicle which resembled a WWI tank stalked the streets. The police, looking scared, traveled in herds about Takoradi … Enough politics."

However, in the same letter, Ray wrote, "The people, the sons and daughters of my great-great-great grandfather, are wonderful." [1961]

In looking through the many pictures of Ghana I, I don't see Ray Spriggs, except in the Warren Hall photo. I think his absence reflects Ray's ambivalence about being part of this Peace Corps group. He was positive about going to Ghana, as reflected in a newspaper interview in the Philadelphia Bulletin:

"Spriggs, an African-American, said he volunteered in April and asked to be sent to Africa. 'I want to help humanity and appreciate other people,' he explained. . . . He said his interest in the corps stems from his work with the American Friends Service Committee and The Ethical Culture Society." [Ray was also President of the Youth Council of the NAACP in West Chester, Pennsylvania.]

At the same time, in the West Chester newspaper, Ray was quoted on the question of explaining America to Ghanaians: "America is a land of change and freedom. Since Americans are free to believe what they want, no one can tell 'this is how' Americans feel about a particular subject."

Like most of us, Ray struggled with his role in being a Peace Corps Volunteer in Ghana, but he was also confronting personal questions of ethnic and cultural identity. In his interview with Rafe Ezekiel, Ray said:

"I've had this confusion and it hasn't been solved yet in my mind. I wrote an essay and the title of it was, 'Black American or African American.' I mean American African-American or African American, which came first—something which has not been worked out in my mind. It's difficult for an African-American in an all-white group. I have found out that the psychiatrists suggested that I would not be fit for Ghana because I had too many feelings, too strong feelings about African-American-white relationships."

Rafe asked: "Were you fit for Ghana?"

Ray: "Oh, yeah! And Ghana was fit for me also."

But this did not divert Ray from a strong involvement with his students and enjoyment of becoming part of life in Sekondi:

"I spend most of my time in the preparation of lessons, in correcting compositions and in teaching itself. These students want to learn and I want to teach them as much as I possibly can about as great a variety of things as I can—this is what I'm here for; this is essentially it.

"I love the students, I love the school, my job I love very much. I love the friends I've made. I'm not particularly in love with Sekondi, I'm not particularly in love with bathing in cold water but these are things which I have accustomed myself to.

"Ghanaians are very, very warm … now I have an idea in my mind that America is mine and Africa is mine, and I feel like rather a wealthy fellow.

"At school we had a tenth anniversary in November and they had dancing and speeches and plays and different kinds of activities. During one of the days—it lasted about four days—I was watching some tribal dancing and drumming. All of a sudden I found myself hoisted into the air, danced up and down the field to the beating of the drum. They set me down on a little stool, blew powder on my face and I poured libation. It was a real welcome home because this was in November and I had been here for two months. Oh, yes, I am an Asafohene [sub-chief of a traditional group; leader of the young men]." [1962]

Trying to Be a PCV

I had been assigned to Sefwi-Wiawso Secondary School (hereinafter referred to as SWSS), a new Ghana Educational Trust school scheduled to open for the first time in September. It was located 'out back of the beyond' in a forested area of western Ghana, 150 miles from the coast and 100 miles southwest of Kumasi, in the town of Wiawso. Wiawso is the headquarters of the Sefwi District of the Western Region which extends west from that town for 75–80 miles to the Ivory Coast border. It is an area of farm villages, with cocoa the main cash crop and timbering the main enterprise. The school was the first secondary school to open in the Sefwi District, under the benign sponsorship of its Member of Parliament, W. K. Aduhene, who was a staunch Nkrumahist.

Through the Ministry of Education, George Carter had found out that the opening of the school was delayed, so I moved from Legon into Accra to the Avenida Hotel, a modest colonial-era hotel. Here I could await word from the school as soon as a Headmaster had been appointed. My accommodations were a huge, high-ceilinged room, walls awash with flaking blue pastel paint, and a red wax-polished concrete floor. There was a ceiling fan, tall wood-shuttered windows, without glass or screens, and an enormous mosquito net and frame over the bed. A good anonymous room in which to have a quiet nervous breakdown. It felt alien and not the least bit comforting and reinforced my sense, at that moment, of isolation. I was bereft—having come all this way, eager, anxious, and ready to begin work as a teacher, seeing my Ghana I friends leave Legon to go off to their schools and here I was uncomfortably lounging on the veranda of a third-rate hotel, drinking beer and feeling sorry for myself. Here I was in the midst of strange, new territory but it wasn't going right and there was a sudden, nagging emptiness in my gut—a pain that meant maybe I had made a mistake. I missed The New York Times.

After an uncomfortable week, I finally got word that a Headmaster had been found, dragooned actually, and that he would momentarily collect me and take me to SWSS. As I was to find repeatedly while in Ghana, 'momentarily' is a culture-bound concept: a moment in New York City is a much shorter span of time than in Accra. Several days later, Mr. Amissah-Arthur, a short, finely featured, nervous man, appeared at the Avenida and we went in his car to Akim-Oda where he had been serving as Headmaster. The trip there was made mostly in silence since both of us were carrying a weight of unspoken personal woe. I was in a funk about the delays in getting to my assigned school and upset by my own inability to deal more positively with those delays. Mr. Amissah-Arthur, unbeknownst to me, was upset because he had been pressured, very much against his will, to become Headmaster in a completely new 'bush' school in a district with which he was totally unfamiliar. For him there were discomforts in going to a different traditional area since he was a Fante and the school was in the Sefwi district. It was as if, after ten years working in New York City, I was suddenly transferred to a job in a one-room school house in rural Georgia. Also Mr. Amissah-Arthur had worked hard at Akim-Oda to build the new G.E.T. secondary school and had been successful in getting it established.

The only joy for me was that I was out of Accra and on my way. I also looked forward to a visit with Peter Dybwad, who had been assigned to Akim-Oda. We had become friends during training as much for the differences between us as the similarities. At this point I was in need of a friendly face and a sympathetic ear. Pete filled the bill.

After two days at Akim-Oda, the Headmaster finally got ready to depart for SWSS. He would drive the six hours to Wiawso, taking his wife and children in his car. I would follow in the Akim-Oda school lorry which had been loosely packed with the Headmaster's household goods. Mr. Amissah-Arthur continued to seem gloomy about the whole proceeding and I picked up on that mood— hunkered in until I could see what really lay ahead. The school lorry driver spoke little English and I spoke even less Twi. In training I had memorized certain useful Twi phrases and could even haltingly speak them. Of course this did not prepare me for rapid-fire Twi responses from native speakers. With distinct articulation, totally inappropriate to a tonal language like Twi, I could say the opening greetings:

"Wo ho te den?" [How are you?]

"Me ho ye." [I am fine]

"Me ye Peace Kawni." [President Kennedy sends you his greetings.]

But worse yet I became convinced that even when I spoke Twi, the Ghanaian hearing me still thought I was speaking English and not very good English at that. Most Ghanaians were familiar with British, not American, accents.

In the absence of any meaningful communication, I couldn't ask the lorry driver why he was stopping so often, driving off the main road into villages, cramming people into the back of the lorry who would then alight at the next village, then repeating the on-and-off loading. What I didn't know was that the driver was using every spare inch of space to make extra money for himself, using the truck as a mammy lorry (a vehicle carrying goods and people on an improvised schedule; common throughout Ghana in 1961). The trip was slow, slow, slow—it eventually took twelve hours—and the closer we got to Wiawso the heavier the rain forest became and the thicker the dust. The last sixty miles is dirt road, constructed of laterite, a heavy, reddish soil that underlies the forest and can be graded into roadways. It gets deposited in and on everything and in the rainy season becomes like wet cement.

It was a long, frustrating day. At around 8:00 p.m., the driver finally dropped me at the government rest house in Wiawso, which is on one of Wiawso's three hills, up the road from the Lumumba Bar. I was feeling pretty low. I was hungry, thirsty, coated with laterite, and feeling totally isolated. I had a bath and then tea with bread, served by a smiling young Ghanaian man with whom I had no conversation. The rest house had the same gloomy and musty ambience as my room at the Avenida. I got into bed, snuggled the mosquito net around and above me, and tried to sleep. I couldn't. All I could hear was endless drumming echoing from down the hill— the Lumumba Bar? My mood hit bottom as I recalled something that had been emphasized at Berkeley. Ghanaians were upset at the death of Patrice Lumumba of the Congo in February. Many felt it was a result of CIA meddling in African affairs. We were advised to expect some hostility about this. Given all I'd been through that day, paranoia kicked in. My scalp tingled as the drumming seemed to swell into an ominous crescendo—I had been kidnapped and secluded in this godforsaken spot in the jungle to be executed in revenge for Lumumba's death! It was a wildly exaggerated but nonfatal case of culture shock induced by the sensory dysfunction of being in such an unfamiliar visual, aural, olfactory environment. I stared at the inside of the close, overhanging mosquito net; I heard the intensely polyrhythmic drums; I smelled the mustiness of the bedding.

I had to do something to shake off this gloom. I got out of bed and stepped outside onto the verandah, overlooking the village of Wiawso, on a hill, surrounded by dense rain forest vegetation and trees. The moon was out and the view was magical—a sight I had never seen—tall, silvery silk cotton trees, distant forested hills softened by the moonlight, as lush, dark and mystical as a Rousseau painting. With a deep sigh and renewed spirits, paranoia fled. I suddenly felt good about being where I was. It was bush, it was way out back of the beyond but it was real and here I was, a long way from West 91st Street in Manhattan. I slept soundly.

Early the next morning the lorry driver came to take me out to the school. SWSS is located about two miles outside of Wiawso. The lorry edged downhill from the hilltop, past the M.P.'s magnificent new residence, then onto a long dirt road through the forest to a small village, Anhwim. There in a clearing was the startling view of the school. The area around is covered with second growth rain forest, thick with undergrowth reaching up to the canopy of treetops, all encompassing, making the road seem almost like a laterite-tinted tunnel. In the midst of all this greenery stood a dirt clearing approximately the size of a football field, looking raw and unfinished with stores of construction materials strewn about and random piles of rubble. There were three two-story buildings situated around a cleared square area, the fourth side of which had a long, low-lying pavilion-like structure. These were classrooms, dormitories, offices, and dining hall. To one side of the compound was a line of three bungalows and opposite was a larger bungalow, off by itself. Everything was built of concrete block and painted with not very cheerful pastel tones—green, yellow, gray, pink.

As I got out of the lorry, I saw Mr. Amissah-Arthur standing in front of the larger bungalow. With him was a stocky, balding Ghanaian, Mr. Akoto, the School Bursar, to whom I was hastily introduced. Mr. Amissah-Arthur, looking even more disconsolate than the previous day, kept shaking his head from side to side as he spoke. "Oh, dear. Mr. Klein, this is terrible. What are we to do? Mr. Akoto says that we have only three students registered." I quickly interjected, "Well, I'm ready to start teaching as soon as possible." He proceeded to mention other problems we were facing. "The school has no water, no electricity. There are no desks or chairs for the classrooms." As the list lengthened Mr. Amissah-Arthur kept shaking his head, muttering, "Oh my goodness, how terrible. What shall we do?"

My new-found resolve—I am a PEACE CORPS VOLUNTEER, able to leap tall barriers, cultural or otherwise, at a single bound—began to erode. The Headmaster and the Bursar were in animated Twi conversation and I stood there feeling awkward. Were they trying to plan how to get the school open and running or was it what to do with this large, eager white man, standing there? Beginning to realize that for me life in Ghana was going to unfold on a timetable I could not control, I decided to at least free them from concern about what to do with or for me. I said to them, "Some of the Peace Corps teachers are at Yaa Asantewaa school in Kumasi. I will go and visit them. When the school is ready to open, send me a telegram there and I'll return." Mr. Arthur quickly agreed and I was delivered to Kumasi by the returning Akim-Oda school lorry driver. He did not charge me for the trip.

Through the years many Peace Corps legends have been recorded. Volunteers who climbed mountains, barefoot, in the snow, to dig latrines; others who, finding no school in which to teach, organized the community to build one; still others who, faced with no job, stayed in the village, learned the language, and created a world-class crafts industry. Looking back, I realize that I do not stand within that tradition. David Apter said I was going to Ghana to teach and, by God, I was going to teach, even if I had to wait the two years for the students to appear.

I didn't have to wait two years. By the end of October, SWSS was open. We had an ever-increasing student population and three faculty—me, the Headmaster, and G. Y. Adu, who was a nongraduate teacher. We had classrooms, some books, desks and chairs. I was assigned one of the new bungalows, a comfortable, screened six-room house with fluorescent fixtures, toilet, kitchen sink, faucets but with no running water or electricity. The school had to wait a year before it got its own electric generator and the water line from town never was built during my tour as a teacher.

Not Quite Tom Brown's School Days

Tom Brown's Schooldays would have been an ideal training text for us. Reading it, we'd have become familiar with the titles and systems common to most Ghanaian boarding schools which were patterned after British secondary schools. The principal was the Headmaster; a class was a Form, a teacher a Master or Mistress as in History Master or Maths Mistress. Class Prefect, Bursar, Matron were positions unknown to American school systems but were vital to the functioning of any school. Students normally attended secondary school for five years, Form I to Form V. Although there were subject exams, grades, and report cards, virtually all students were permitted to move through the five years. Completing secondary school was meaningless without successfully passing at least two of the "O" (Ordinary) Level Exams. These were rigorous standardized nationwide examinations in a multitude of subjects. Established schools also had a two-year Form VI which prepared students for the "A" (Advanced) Level Exams.

In mid-October, I wrote to New York friends, the Siegels:

"As yet, I have no real reason to regret my foolhardy gesture in joining the Peace Corps. I have not contracted malaria, dengue, or dysentery; I haven't been threatened by any blowgun-carrying hoods; I have neither been bitten by nor even seen any snakes [though if it were a boa constrictor, I'd been trained what to do]. The climate has been more pleasant than a New York summer; the insects, while not downright benevolent, have been controllable. Nkrumah and his dynamic African socialist non-aligners have not yet tried to detain me (as happened to 50 outstanding opposition and labor leaders)." [1961]

After exposure to David Apter and St. Clair Drake at Berkeley, I was ready to look with approval at Kwame Nkrumah's leadership both in Ghana and in Africa. Detention and the evolving one-party state did raise questions but events on the coast, in Accra, Cape Coast, Sekondi-Takoradi, seemed remote when viewed from the hills of Wiawso. That initially made it easier to dwell on Nkrumah's positive actions. The most obvious example, for me, was the very Ghana Educational Trust school in which I now taught. Also, in training we had been introduced to the idea of "suspending judgment" about Ghanaian politics as well as unfamiliar aspects of its society and cultures.

Back at SWSS through these first months, I was settling in; SWSS had a modest beginning. When I first arrived at the school in September 1961, it was far from ready to open—the compound looked like the construction site it had so recently been, debris-strewn and disorderly. As I wrote home, "The school compound looks raw and unfinished (because it is raw and unfinished)." Areas had been cleared for the buildings and an entry road but just 15 to 20 yards beyond the site was the rain forest, dense and, to me, foreboding. It was actually secondary rain forest which had been farmed for many years. It had large trees, undisturbed, mostly silk cotton, and crowded varied undergrowth. In the traditional "slash and burn" farming, an area was cleared and burned off. Then crops (cassava, plantain, banana, cocoyam, pepper, tomato) were sown in irregular plots. After several years, the area was left to lie fallow and the undergrowth regenerated. There was some remaining virgin rain forest in Ghana, in the remoter areas of the Sefwi district. That forest has a high canopy of large trees and little undergrowth.

I lived my life in suburb and city, and it certainly looked like jungle to me. I felt that if I were to wander off into the bush I would be totally lost, enveloped by vines, shrubs, small insects and large snakes. Despite assurances that there were paths, farms, and interesting flowers and birds, I stayed within the school compound, thanking my luck that I taught English and History and not botany, zoology, or biology, subjects which might obligate me to wander off into the forest to collect and identify "things." As it was, there was still an adjustment to the smaller, unexpected forms of local creepy things. No landscape was ever completely still—out of the corner of my eye I could always see at least one rainbow lizard, doing its primitive push-ups, casting a menacing (though minuscule) eye in my direction. Once safely inside my screened house, I would be startled by the geckos, clinging to the most unlikely surfaces of the ceiling or wall. At night, on a seasonal basis, with the Tilley lamp lit, there'd be a multitudinous gathering of insects—sausage flies, rhinoceros beetles, mosquitoes, 'itchy' moths.

The infrequently used dirt road at our entrance and the starkly limiting and encroaching forest made the school compound like an island to me—this was my world and within it I would live and teach and learn. The isolation was intensified by being two dusty and rutted road miles from the town of Wiawso, district headquarters, shopping area and market, seat of the Sefwi paramount chief, telephone and postal center (the school's phone number was Wiawso 4), and site of the only stretch of tarred road for miles and miles. Initially it was the physical environment that had an effect on me, not the predicted "culture shock." Through my thirty-two years I had lived with, taught, befriended, worked alongside lots of different people but I had never resided in the middle of a jungle (apologies to my training faculty—it is correctly referred to as rain forest but, on first encounter, it is emotionally, viscerally—a jungle).

And the people? My earliest friend, informant, and savior was Gabriel Yaw Adu. We were thrown together by circumstance. Under the hesitant leadership of the reluctant Headmaster, he and I were the teaching staff of SWSS in September 1961. Gabriel was probably the first Ghanaian who made the sincere effort to understand my form of spoken English—not so exotic a tongue but, to the Ghanaian ear, attuned to British speech, a strangely accented language with many unfamiliar vernacular expressions such as "How why ya?" "Whadja say?"

Gabriel was short, finely featured, ebony-skinned, with lively eyes and an expressive mouth, slightly crooked. He was the only Ghanaian male with whom

I could comfortably hold hands (a common Ghanaian practice). Our friendship became like two intersected circles in a Venn diagram, the overlapped area what we had in common. The major portion of each circle was our own personal life experience, Ghanaian and American. Within Gabriel's circle was 30 years of existence, strongly defined by traditions and customs of the Sefwi people (a distinct but small sub-group of Akans). He spoke four languages—Sefwi, Twi, English, French, and probably knew a smattering of Dutch since he had lived with and worked for some Dutch Catholic missionaries earlier in his life. He had studied Geography and Education, taught middle school (and now secondary), was a teacher, farmer, an incredibly insightful informant about his corner of Ghana, and bound by hundreds of ties to family, clan, village. Ambitious for himself and others, Adu was gregarious, easy to befriend, voluble and giggly after two beers.

I accepted my situation and that of the school based on my own understanding of it and with Adu's encouragement. Early on we were able to joke about the other assigned teacher—Biney. Biney was, like Adu, a non-graduate trained teacher. He appeared during our first week and received his teaching schedule. He announced that he had to return to Accra to collect his belongings and departed. He never returned. Week by week, as the number of students increased, either Adu or I would look at the other and say, "Well, Biney can teach that class." What was needed was simply day-to-day functioning—the appearance of regular schooling even in the face of our problems. In the absence of books, classroom desks and chairs, and anything like teaching aids, instruction could still proceed. We had a teaching schedule, students, a chalkboard (a smooth plaster area on the classroom wall coated with special blackboard paint).

There was much I didn't know about the political and subcultural undercurrents at play in and around the school and in the district. Adu and the Headmaster and the Bursar, Akoto, all tried to protect me from some of the harsher realities because I was a stranger who seemed content to work as a teacher there. This freed me to face the more obvious problems with enthusiasm since I am, by nature, an optimist. I had become a Peace Corps Volunteer because I wanted 'to help and to serve' where needed. SWSS in 1961 certainly seemed needful. Later in my career at SWSS I became involved with some of these other problems—often difficulties of local politicians interfering in the operations of the school.

I wrote home during October:

"This school is absolutely new but relatively isolated (it's not on the road to anywhere); we're considered a frontier or 'bush' school. As such, and because of the delays in getting it opened, we have had difficulty in getting students. The local District Commissioner is literally 'beating the bush' to find enough students to bring our roster to 70.

"My spirits, which were a little low during all the waiting, have picked up considerably now that I have arrived and have work to do. The teaching should be very exciting, particularly since I am told that none of the students will be able to understand my English. It will probably take at least a week or more [Ha!] for us to adjust to each other. The students appear bright, highly motivated, and well disciplined but, English being their second language, there is a problem of communication.

"The teaching is very challenging (none of my students understand a word that I say) and the extracurricular program should be lots of fun."

I do remember some early surprises. Unlike my classes at JHS 136 Manhattan, when I entered the Form IA classroom, all of the students stood up and said, "Good morning, sir." I responded, "Good morning, class" and for several months that may have been the only mutually understandable exchange I had with my classes. Another surprise was that almost every question, comment or statement I made was received with a "Yes, sir" response—polite but not much to build a class discussion on. Then, when I thought I was beginning to get through to the students, someone would stand up and say, "Please sir, I don't hear you." Speaking louder seemed to make no difference and I quickly realized that in Ghanaian English 'hear' meant 'understand.'

Bob Krisko had written about the language of students in an article in The Missouri State Teachers Association magazine, "School and Community," March, 1963:

"I had to learn a different language to communicate. They are used to British-style English and cannot comprehend good ol' American.

"One disconcerting thing is to ask one of our famous negative questions: 'You haven't done your assignment, have you?' 'Please, yes, sir' is the answer. 'Yes, you have, or yes, you haven't' is the next question. This runs on a few minutes, something like an Abbott and Costello vaudeville act. I half expected a student to say, 'Who's on first?'"

Thirty-five years later, in a Washington ceremony I was asked to speak to a group of Peace Corps Volunteers about to become teachers in Ghana. In explaining the historical importance of "legendary" Ghana I, I said, "Ghana I was important because we were the first group sent to the field and, looking back, we now realize that our real mission was to familiarize Ghanaian students with American English so that future generations of Peace Corps teachers could function more effectively."

Progress was gradual at SWSS as I reported to the family:

"October 17—Two weeks now at Sefwi-Wiawso and life is beginning to take shape. My bottled gas stove (which has been sitting in the kitchen since my arrival) was finally connected; I can now abandon the little one-burner kerosene stove. We have been promised electricity soon (I'm dreaming of a light Xmas) and the water should be turned on any day now [it never was]. My steward has been a godsend—without him to haul water, clean, and launder, I wouldn't be able to find time enough for my teaching and preparation.

"The adjustment to 'tropical' conditions has been a slow one and still continues. Day by day, I become more adapted to my surroundings and better able to provide for most of the needed amenities. I've been introducing Ghanaian food into my diet slowly—plantains, yams, local meat. All of it is safe, as it is thoroughly cooked. I can also get oranges (by the way they are really delicious but, unlike the Florida-dyed product, they are green), bananas, and grapefruit. Eggs, too, and bread. The only food I really miss is green, leafy vegetables [comment included for my mother's benefit], very few of which are grown here—I've had to depend on canned vegetables.

"My day starts at 6 a.m. with tea; breakfast break comes at 9:30 a.m. when I have hot cereal, eggs, toast, and tea. Lunch is at 2:00 p.m. and is usually my big meal of the day—meat, yam, and canned vegetable. Supper is usually soup and biscuits (crackers). I have been doing all of my own cooking since I prefer it that way and my steward, Donkor, is not an experienced cook [Donkor, fifteen-year old untrained innocent fresh from the village, was not an experienced anything but was the nephew of the school's Bursar; his tenure was brief]. In addition to tea, I drink beer, fruit juice, and gin and tonic.

"… At first, our problem was lack of students and now we are in danger of being inundated. We now have 70 students (35 per class) and government appeals for students have been so good that we are threatened with more. Since we are only 3 on the staff, have run out of desks and chairs, and are short on school funds, more would be a problem. The Headmaster is sending out an SOS to the Trust, telling them to stop. We are also awaiting another teacher who has not yet shown up [the elusive Biney]. He was here one day, saw the school, told the Headmaster he was going to Accra to collect his belongings, and disappeared!" [1961]

To former teaching colleagues at JHS 136 where I had taught for five years, I wrote a more complete description of the Ghana secondary school system:

"After fighting for so many years in NYC for a maximum class size of 30, I now find myself teaching classes of 42 and 44. Until we get more teachers, we will keep just two streams (classes).… Like most of the secondary schools in Ghana (which are also referred to as colleges; colleges U.S.–style are called Universities), we are a boarding school, located about three miles from Wiawso. School life is a 24 hour thing; I have become intimately concerned not only with the problems of teaching, but also with the students' personal lives, their social existence, their extra-curricular activities. I find myself developing a far greater interest and involvement than I was ever able to do at 136.

"As to the teaching itself—it is a problem. Although I am teaching the same groups both English and History, it would be unthinkable in this British-type system to attempt an integrated subject approach. English is divided into Literature and Language and the tendency is, as with all subjects, to keep the teaching and the materials rigidly separated. The entire system is focused on the School Certificate Exam.

"… all class work and home work is done in an exercise book (not looseleaf) and daily, as I return from class, I find myself confronted by huge stacks of them. It is convenient, in one way—there is no need to keep a marking book, since all of a student's work is available for inspection and evaluation at any time. There is no such thing as a formal report card (totally indifferent or incompetent students are merely expelled) and 'Open School Week' is unheard of. The teaching situation here is distinctly different than that at 136. I'm truly delighted to be here and think that it was a wise choice on my part. But I do miss 136, especially when you start to talk about the UFT [United Federation of Teachers]. There is a union of sorts here for teachers, but it is strictly a company union (the company in this case being the central government). Fortunately, teaching and the life of a boarding school keep me busy and, as a guest of the Ghanaian government, I wouldn't think of criticizing."

Becoming Teachers

Another experienced teacher, George Coyne, went to Sunyani Secondary School, about 75 miles northwest of Kumasi. It was a G.E.T. school with only two Forms and he was assigned to teach Agriculture, Health Science, and General Science to both Forms. In his Brewster Smith interview, George talked about settling in at Sunyani:

"Frankly, from what we were told at Berkeley, I expected a higher level of students ... and I came in delivering lectures geared to a higher level. The first couple of weeks, with my American accent and with these very flowery lectures that I was giving I am sure it was a complete waste of time. After a while I began—it's part of my teaching technique—to ask them questions and eventually to use these questions to lead us on to something else. After about a week or two, it became apparent that the boys really didn't have too rich a background—this came out in the questioning. I would ask one class what chemistry was and, Gee, they gave a terrific definition about analysis and synthesis and all of this and I thought, 'Boy, this is marvelous, really; we'll be able to do all sorts of things here.' Well, out of curiosity, I asked, 'What does analysis mean?' And not one kid knew—it was just a definition that they had memorized last year. They had been given these definitions and sure enough they could rattle them off but they couldn't tell what any of them meant. They didn't know what chemistry was; they didn't know what biology was. So, after about two weeks, why we just got down to basics." [1962]

Those who had never taught before seemed to have jumped right in, trusting that there was water in the pool. Pete Dybwad took a direct approach:

"We had these little books; so you just marched through them. You didn't really have a syllabus, you just had mandatory literature books—you went from page one to the end. All I had to do was stay awake. I once fell asleep standing at the blackboard." [2000]

Dick Maze reported: "I just boldly stepped out and took on my job. I had no laboratory equipment or things along this line so I started out with teaching botany—you see, there's this convenient tree standing outside, so I can just yank a limb off on the way to class." [2000]

Steve McWilliams struggled: "Here I am thrown into that high school situation and in subject matters about as foreign from my Conservation background as you can imagine. It was Ghanaian geography, Ghanaian and English literature ... and I didn't understand what it was all about. 'You can do it because you've gone to University and have a degree.' That's what the Ghanaians were saying." [1997]

Tom Peterson is a Classics scholar and he was assigned to Navrongo Secondary School, the most remote school location in Ghana, just a few miles from the northern border with Upper Volta. Jack Lord, who was at the same school, told of part of Tom's adjustment to teaching:

"Tom taught French but the Headmaster, Agyeman-Dixon, learned that he had been trained in the Classics—had a degree in the Classics. In the British style syllabus they offer Greek as an 'O' Level exam. The Headmaster thought this would be incredibly prestigious to be offering Ancient Greek here in the bush. So he insisted that Tom offer Greek.

"Tom was in despair because he couldn't figure out how Greek could possibly benefit any of the Navrongo students. His strategy was that he would just make it so difficult that they would all drop out after a week or two. To do that he just piled it on in terms of memorization—all these vocabulary words, declensions, conjugations. It became the most popular course in the school—the kids just loved it because it was so clear. You just memorize this and you write it down—chew and pour. It fit perfectly with the pedagogical paradigm of every student. So it was a self-defeating strategy."

Jack reported another problem at Navrongo that affected Marty Wallenstein, who was the science teacher: "When we were on vacation once, this is the first year, a thing comes from the Ministry, saying you have £G1000 to spend on science equipment. Marty isn't there, no other teachers are there, so the Headmaster takes down the science supply catalogue and starts ordering stuff with the result that Marty had things like Arsenic Determination Apparatus but the Headmaster didn't get as far as 'T' for Test Tubes before the money ran out. Flasks we had but I think he ended at the letter 'M.' We had this enormous thing for generating gas out of gasoline for running Bunsen Burners because it began with 'G.'" [2000]

John Buchanan was a trained geographer, employed in the preparation of aerial survey maps when he joined the Peace Corps, and he had never taught. John is a tall, laconic mid-Western type (even though he's from western Pennsylvania), part of a small, introspective circle of friends (John and Bob Krisko) with a specialized interest in cribbage and exotic travel. John told of his adjustment to Ghanaian education:

"... in the Fourth and Fifth Forms, much as I hate to admit it, the goal certainly is to get them through the certificate exams. It involves revision [review] of old certificate exams. Where understanding something was difficult, I just gave them definitions and told them, 'Memorize them, you may need them on the exam.' It's a brutal way to do it and it's not good teaching, and neither is it anything that is going to stick with them. But it is too late to start with people that you just get, only fourteen weeks before their cert exam, to start using any other approach. Their goal is to get through that exam.

"The students are so familiar with the syllabus that ... they can pretty much tell when you are teaching them something superfluous. They are not going to stand by and let you give them a lot of information. It's too late for the Fourth and Fifth Forms to start doing it any other way."

The lower Forms did offer more of a challenge and an opportunity to move beyond rote learning. John continues: "Now with the Second Form, I have taken a problem approach ... that teaches them how to think. I dispense with this memorizing scads of useless information. It's been hard; they're not used to class participation." [1962]

Laura Damon, graduate of Smith College in English, fluent in French, and a world traveler, had less difficulty. Laura is a slender, dark-haired woman of strong will and intellect, assertive and positive in thought and action. She's always been thin and appears somewhat vulnerable but she is tough. In her first few months in Ghana, she had malaria, tumble fly foot infection, stomach palaver, a tapeworm (which she named Archie), and was in a serious auto accident—and kept on teaching. She was assigned to Opoku Ware, an established, prestigious urban school in Kumasi, with a Sixth Form and a reputation for excellence—students admitted to this school had strong academic qualifications. Having a degree seemed sufficient for Laura to establish herself quickly as teacher. In letters home, she described her first few months:

"One class is Upper Sixth Form who take the exam November 16th. My work with them is practice in writing essays. Class work is choosing a topic and discussing various ways of presentation and occasionally giving them work to do under exam conditions. With the Lower Sixth, who take the exam in June, we are reading *The Old Man and The Sea* which they seem to enjoy. In Fourth Form we are reading *Animal Farm* as literature and have a textbook for English language. They are a very responsive group and so far make easy transitions from boyish silliness to serious work."

By October 12, when most of us were just figuring out where our classrooms were and what subjects we were supposed to be teaching any given group, Laura was writing home:

"*Old Man and The Sea*—today I tested them on the first 25 pages. It was an open book exam with a choice of questions: 1. Discuss Hemingway's method of description; give three examples; 2. What does the friendship between the old man and the boy tell us about either or both of them? 3. What is the significance of the old man's dream?

"In Upper Sixth essay writing I have been harping on the necessity for outlines from the beginning. Some of them are getting the idea but several feel that at the stroke of the bell they should start writing. They wrote 3-page essays for the last week and I spent an hour on correcting each one (30 papers). Some were really quite outstanding and others—well, they have too much to learn to get by the exam, I'm afraid.

"I gave the Fourth Form an exam on *Animal Farm*, sample question: How does Napoleon acquire power? Much fun to work with a book like that. There are only four weeks left in this term so I'm going to have the boys work on a research project." [1961]

We all had to deal with the students' view of the learning process. "Chew and Pour" is the way they described it. You "chew" your notes, committing them completely to memory; then, on an exam or when questioned, you "pour," repeating the material verbatim. Many Ghanaian teachers, themselves products of the system, had the same view. For them, teaching meant writing voluminous notes on the board, often taken directly from a textbook, having the students copy these notes, and then drilling the students until they could recite the material without mistakes. The ability to memorize is a valuable learning skill but, in the absence of other means of processing old and new information, it has its deficiencies. The closer a student was to the School Certificate Exams the less tolerant he was of teaching with a problem-solving bias. In the newer schools with only one or two Forms, like SWSS and Sunyani, we had less pressure and more freedom to integrate rote learning with problem-solving in our lessons. And, for the inexperienced educators in the group, more opportunity to stumble and fumble until a valid pedagogy emerged. At the older schools, it was often reported that students would stand up in class and say to a Peace Corps teacher, "Please, Miss, that is not on the syllabus." Or, "My senior brother passed his 'O' level exam and I have his notes. Can you please use them to teach us?"

At SWSS District Commissioner Fosu was a very successful recruiter. When enrollment reached 94, the Headmaster reshuffled the two Forms so that IA had the more capable students. Since I was then one-third of the teaching staff, an important measure of 'capability' was the individual level of comprehension of American English. The qualification for admission to secondary school was at least two years of middle school. Regulations stated that middle school instruction was to be solely in English but in a rural area like Sefwi it was not done. Use of the vernacular was common, depending on the teacher's level of comfort and familiarity with English. Also, the District Commissioner, in his political zeal to make SWSS a success, had convinced ill-qualified students (and their parents) that "Osagyefo, Dr. Kwame Nkrumah, President of the Republic of Ghana" personally wished to see them attending the new secondary school. Under such pressure, the Headmaster was obliged to be lenient in the admissions procedure, hoping that time (and lack of comprehension) would eventually encourage the non-academics to fade away. He was right. The age range was 12 to 25 (and perhaps older). Adu would characterize some students as "our seniors" and half jokingly swore that we had at least one father-son combination in Form IB. He would also say of some of the D.C.'s real bush recruits that they were "more comfortable with a cutlass [a farm machete] than a pen" and that SWSS was the first time in their lives that they had worn sandals.

By the end of October I began my involvement with what, in the long run, was my most satisfying teaching during my two years in Ghana—adult education. I wrote home:

"I was invited to address the local PEA (Peoples Education Association) in Wiawso and yesterday delivered a one hour lecture on the United States—government, economy, and social problems. There were about 30 adults present, teachers, civil servants, clerks, and they questioned me rather sharply for about a half-hour after the lecture.... They found it hard to believe that average incomes were as high as I said; they were fascinated by our 3 part system of government; they wanted more information about Negroes in America (Are they really American citizens? What is the Ku Klux Klan? Are white teachers in New York allowed to teach in the African-American schools?)."

And there were changes at SWSS. Mr. Amissah-Arthur, the Prisoner of Sefwi, who had been pressured into the assignment, was finally freed in November:

"The Headmaster just returned from Accra to announce that he is being transferred to the school that he just came from—Oda. You may recall my telling you what a raw deal he got, in being forced to come out here to a bush school with wife and 5 kids. Apparently the Oda community is not without influence in Accra and he has been recalled. The change may also be a result of an administrative switch that has been made. The Ghana Educational Trust ... has just been abolished and all schools are now under a single agency, the Ministry of Education. There had been confusion, jealousy, and competition between Trust and Ministry."

Mr. Amissah-Arthur's absence from Akim Oda Secondary School had led to a strange interlude for Peter Dybwad. Peter had never taught, was fresh out of college, and, in appearance, looked more like a secondary school student than a teacher. Before even reporting to Oda, Peter had been appointed Acting Headmaster. Then as now, he is self-effacing to a fault and, in a telephone interview in 2000, tried to remember some of the details of his unexpected introduction to Ghanaian secondary education:

"Akim-Oda was in a clearing in the forest. It was a school—it had dormitories, classrooms, and housing for the teachers and a big house on a hill for the Headmaster. The school was only in its second year and the staff was a couple of women and there was a man, Mr. Fouda, from the Cameroons. He was amazed at what was happening and a bit hostile. I think I was the Acting Headmaster because I was the only one with a degree. Since there was no teaching schedule I felt my job was to deploy classes and classrooms and teachers. When I arrived I moved into the Headmaster's house on the hill. I know I moved there because that's where I had all these little pieces of paper on the table—classrooms, sections, courses and teachers. I had to get the right piles in the right places. My doing that was an important way of my establishing whatever little authority I had. Fouda, for example, was a 'new' African; he didn't need no stinkin' colonialists to come and help students to learn, especially a short, skinny little person.

"[Enter the villain] The Bursar was a strong-willed man who quickly sized up the situation. He, the Bursar, would run the school. He held the purse strings and he made the school run. His name was Aidoo, a tall man, very stern, like a career soldier. He lived in town so the school truck went into town every evening whenever he wanted to go home. I had a sense that I couldn't commandeer that school lorry. The Bursar's view was, 'Whatever goes on in the classroom, you teachers can do; you can't have any money to do it with; you can't make any decisions; I'll run the school.'

"Whatever it was that came up that led to a battle between the Bursar and me—and there certainly was one—was a result of teachers saying, 'I need this,' and my deciding that what they needed made sense and that we could have it but for the Bursar. That was true and then I came to believe the Bursar was withholding information from me. When I asked for funds for school things, he would say, 'You can't have any; they don't need that; they're lying.' The image that comes to me is that of a brand-new lieutenant 'weenie' meeting a sergeant who's been doing this for 20 years; in fact, saying, 'Not only are you incompetent but you don't even want to be doing this—I'm doing this and moreover I want to do this. You're irrelevant here.'" [2000]

About this time, I visited Peter, on a trip from Sefwi to Accra. I remember this slim little whiff of a guy rattling around in the huge, barren two-story Headmaster's house, behaving like a character in a neo-gothic (or at least neo-colonial) mystery. In our 2000 interview, I added my part of the story:

"When you described your struggle with the Bursar, it really made me nervous. I didn't know if you'd become paranoid, delusional, or if some of the things you were relating were real. What triggered me was this—you insisted I drive you to Swedru or Winneba [at least 20 miles from Oda] so you could mail a letter. Do you remember? When I asked about it, you said, 'Well, if I mail it locally, the Bursar will get his hands on it.' It may have been the letter to the Ministry that said the Bursar was stealing."

When I got to Accra, I told George Carter of my visit with Peter and of my concerns about his health (physical, if not mental). George had just returned from a quick visit to Peace Corps/Washington. In Shriver's Weekly Report to the President, October 31, 1961, it stated: "Report from Ghana: One of our volunteers, 22-year old Peter Dybwad from Leonia, New Jersey, has been appointed by the Ghanaians as the Acting Headmaster of the secondary school in Oda (South Central Ghana) to which he is assigned." I am sure George heard my report with interest. Peter completed this part of his Peace Corps adventure:

"It all came together really quickly. George began to realize he ought to do something besides planning to give me a Jeep. At the Ministry they said, 'Don't worry. This is going to resolve itself in a couple of weeks.' And soon Amissah-Arthur came back and that was that. The Bursar was his problem, not mine. I went back to my little bungalow and became a teacher.... I may have felt some remorse in being reduced in rank. At the same time, I had a lot of responsibility lifted from me."

Pete did recall one accomplishment as Headmaster. We finished the interview with this exchange, starting with Peter:

"I remember going into Accra one weekend to buy a lawn mower for the school."

"[Laughing] Nobody in Ghana had a lawn mower!"

"They sure did. There was a lawn mower to be bought and I brought it back."

"In your role as Acting Headmaster?"

"Yes."

"Were you trying to ease the burden of the students who had to cut the grass?"

"No, I thought it was inefficient the way they took their machetes and just struck at these tender blades of grass." [2000]

Mr. Amissah-Arthur soon departed SWSS to return to Akim-Oda, rescuing Peter from future conflicts with the Bursar.

6

THE FIRST YEAR AT SWSS

Exit Mr. Amissah-Arthur; Enter the Banana Man

At SWSS, Mr. Amissah-Arthur was quickly replaced by Mr. J. O. S. Acquaye whom I remember as a friendly, soft-spoken middle-aged man with chubby cheeks and a ready smile. We never became close personal friends; we had good professional relations but he was content to maintain a proper headmaster–teacher distance. He was a solid, reassuring presence on the school compound, a welcome change from the nervous and ill-placed Mr. Amissah-Arthur. I wrote:

"The Ministry of Education was able to find a replacement very quickly. Our new Headmaster, a Ghanaian named Mr. Acquaye, will be arriving this weekend. He was here last week to look the place over and I met him; he seemed very friendly and not the least bit daunted by the pioneering aspect of life at Sefwi-Wiawso. The job is a good opportunity for advancement for him since, up until now, he has only been a teacher. Starting out as Headmaster at a new school, helping to build it into an established institution … can help him in his career."

Rereading my letters home during the first year at SWSS, I'm struck with how frequent the mentions of Adu are. In the realms of SWSS, Wiawso, and the Sefwi district, he certainly was a big part of my life. Our friendship was initially situational like the good friends I had when I was in the army. I can recall John Scarboro, Don Pickett, and Mike Manzo vividly but only in the context of the enlisted men's club at the 72nd Ordnance Depot Company of the U.S. Army in Korea. That is where our friendship existed, through endless hours of inconsequential, humorous and griping conversation while drinking at the makeshift bar. We shared little of our inner lives and only incidentally referred to our family, friends, and hometowns. It was the mutual experience of being in that place, at that time, under similar circumstances, that created the common ground on which friendship could grow. Seeing each other day by day over a period of months, sharing mess hall meals, work locations, the confines of the company compound—all provided the currency of personal exchanges.

I was in Korea almost as many days as I was at SWSS but, unlike my army buddies, Adu became a true friend. At the start, Adu and I were two-thirds of the staff of SWSS, lived in neighboring bungalows, twenty feet apart, taught in adjoining classrooms, and shared the same groups of students. All this helped overcome the distance between us—me, a bulky, bearded, pale New Yorker, with a friendly smile; Adu, a slender, wiry, ebony-skinned Sefwi, with a soft-spoken manner. Early on we each recognized in the other a sense of humor, a desire for friendship, and a common commitment to making a success of SWSS, though for different reasons: I, because I felt that Peace Corps deserved my best effort; Adu, because he was a Sefwi. Without knowing much, or even knowing how to go about learning much of each other's personal lives, we did have the common problems of the school to talk about and the common inconveniences of living on the unfinished school compound to complain about. Although I was older, more experienced, and with a graduate degree, Adu, in effect, became my mentor in leading me into a full and rich involvement with Sefwi and Ghanaian life. He illustrated perfectly the meaning of the Twi proverb, "The Stranger Is Like a Child," by patiently explaining unfamiliar things I encountered and by protecting me from things that might be disturbing or difficult for me to understand.

In February of 1962 I wrote about Adu introducing me to more of Sefwi. I remember my first road trips back into the interior where there was still virgin rain forest. It is starkly different from the overgrown, over-farmed and over-timbered 'bush' along most of the roads I had traveled around Wiawso. Original rain forest has a canopy formed by the high branches of the tall tropical trees which shades the area below from sunlight. Thus, the ground vegetation is fairly sparse and the impression is almost cavelike. Where the large trees have been cut and where slash and burn farming has been done, the heavy rains and ample sunlight promote thick, luxuriant-looking undergrowth.

"Sunday, the entire staff (the Headmaster, Mr. Adu and myself) took a drive into the interior of the Sefwi district to Juaboso. The trip was quite good. We visited several of the villages that our students come from and met many of the parents. In two villages, Asafo and Asawinso, we were formally greeted by the chief.

"The chief's house usually contains an inner courtyard in which there is a slightly raised platform, with the chief's stool and chairs for visitors. We entered the courtyard, shook hands with everyone there (up to 15 people—members and hangers-on of the chief's family), and sat down. Then, Mr. Adu would explain our visit. Then, they all got up and came around and shook hands with us. Next, beer was served and the chief would speak briefly in greeting. Then, we got up and shook everyone's hand again. Finally, as we were leaving and since we were unable to be the chief's guests for the night, the chief's spokesman gave us some money which represented a gift of the amount that would have been spent to provide for us. Of course we then had to return to the courtyard and shake hands around one more time. It was the same pretty much at both chiefs' houses.

"In visiting the families, we were also presented with small gifts such as yams, pineapples, eggs, etc. It was not the purpose for which we took the trip, but the offering can hardly be refused. I insisted that Mr. Adu keep all of the gifts. As a non-university graduate teacher, he is earning only about 350 pounds a year." [1962]

Week by week, I was feeling more established and relaxed at SWSS. I did travel out almost every other weekend to Kumasi to buy food but, more importantly, simply to enjoy the company of my Peace Corps friends. We were each adapting to Ghana in our own way and it helped, in dealing with the unfamiliar, to touch base occasionally with the familiar.

November was busy and I was beginning to shift my focus away from immediate personal concerns (food, housing, health) and toward being part of the world of SWSS and its students. The new Headmaster arrived, classes fell into a regular pattern, daily life settled into a routine. It was about this time that I gave up using the mosquito net, another transition. Even though my bedroom was screened and the door kept shut at all times, I had been following a nightly ritual. My bed had a huge, billowing mosquito net on a supporting framework. Each night, once I was in bed, I would very, very carefully tuck the net in tight, all the way around under the mattress, creating a gauzy cocoon, a psychological, if not physical, barrier against the terrors of the night—mosquitoes, sausage flies, rhinoceros beetles, snakes, lizards, and whatever other invasive creatures my mind could conjure up. It worked and I slept well but by the end of November, like the trapeze artist who has achieved complete self-confidence, I faced the world without a net.

Two further developments occurred in November—a car and a second job. As I told my folks:

"First, I was utterly amazed this afternoon to see the PC Ghana Director drive up to my cottage in a Jeep! (MY JEEP) ... Mr. Carter delivered my PC Jeep. He was accompanied by the PC doctor (Dr. Chin) who was driving the PC car. Carter, after 3 hours on the road from Kumasi to here, was really a sight. He was encrusted in a thick layer of red dust and his first words to me were, 'Klein, you're right, you do need a vehicle—my God, what roads!' Carter and the doctor were only able to stay an hour or so.... The doctor declared me to be healthy (and left a six months' supply of vitamin pills).

"Needless to say, almost the entire student body turned out to greet Carter (who is African-American, by the way) and to welcome Mr. Klein's VEHICLE. The students were amazed to find out that my 'leader' was an African-American. To confuse them further, Dr. Chin is Chinese-American. I've spent hours since they left explaining to the students some things about the U.S.

"Secondly, I have started my lecturing in Bibiani. Tuesday evening I went there by cab to deliver my first lecture on World Affairs and it was a success." [1961]

Both the Jeep and the adult ed classes enabled me to enjoy more than just the SWSS school compound and Kumasi weekends. There is an apocryphal story about the Jeeps. When George Carter first requested permission from Peace Corps/Washington to purchase them, the initial response was, "Are you forming the First Peace Corps Armored Division? Planning to invade Togo?"

One afternoon after class, as I was taking my siesta, I heard a light tapping at my front door. I shook off the half-napping fuzzy feeling, went to the main room and opened the door. There was a barefoot, roughly dressed, short, smiling Ghanaian of indeterminate age with a full stalk of green bananas on his head and a farm cutlass (machete) in his hand. His English was as bad as my Twi but fortunately one of the students, who'd been working on the school paper, was there and served as interpreter. My visitor was Mr. Asare who was from the nearby small village of Ahwiam. He put down the bananas and the cutlass and shyly shook my hand as the student introduced us. He was happy that I had come to teach at SWSS and the bananas were a gift. He absolutely refused my offer to pay for them and then departed. A full stalk has forty to sixty bananas, all of which will ripen within a three- or four-day period, and for several days thereafter I gorged on bananas and would not talk to any student who visited until he or she had eaten at least two bananas.

Mr. Asare became a regular but unscheduled visitor for the rest of my time at SWSS and, just between Adu and myself, earned the friendly title, "The Banana Man." He would bring bananas, oranges, mangoes, and an occasional pineapple. We eventually worked out a "payment" scheme by which I could give him two or three shillings each time, with the understanding that I was not paying for what he had brought but was simply giving something to help him pay his children's fees at the local primary school.

Pop's Death

From the time I was 17 years old, I was accustomed to living away from home—at college, in the Army, teaching in New York City. But it was comforting to know that Mom and Pop were around. The family home was there (on Long Island), a modest sanctuary against the major and minor outrages, bumps and bruises, along my way to maturity. To the folks, my joining the Peace Corps and going to Africa was no more exotic than my serving in the Army in Korea or teaching junior high school in Harlem. By letter or visit, I always stayed in touch.

I remember Mom and Pop taking me to LaGuardia airport to catch the Eastern shuttle to Washington in late August 1961 on my way to Ghana. My visual memory of Pop gets mixed up with family album photos of him. I picture him with a stern visage, wearing a gray fedora with the brim down, shadowing his eyes, and in a heavy wool overcoat, his hands plunged deeply into the side pockets—fixed, stolid, unmoving, like a massive ceremonial statue—in the photo, as in life, a strong presence. My memory is inaccurate since it was a warm August day and Pop was likely wearing a sports shirt and slacks. Even though he had suffered two heart attacks, my feelings, in saying goodbye to him and Mom, were the same as when I went off to Chicago, Korea, or Manhattan—it felt good to know that they were there, were part of my life, were pleased with the things I chose to do, and would be there when I returned.

During the first Christmas vacation in Ghana in December 1961, I joined George Coyne, Laura Damon, and a few others in the group on a borrowed car trip through northern Ghana. When I finally returned to Sefwi-Wiawso at the end of the month, there was a telegram waiting for me at the school. It was from my brother and the message was that my father had died. It was dated about seven days earlier. I suddenly felt terribly alone. I spent that day and the next crying and sleeping and crying, in a numb, formless, forgetful state. I didn't recall images or events of being with my father; I didn't think of how Mom, my brother, or my sister were feeling. I avoided Adu and the Headmaster; the school compound was virtually empty since school vacation was still on. Time didn't matter.

Adu later told me that he was extremely upset in not being able to console me at this time but the overlapping circles of our friendship did not include death and mourning. By the second day, I had recovered some composure and more than anything else wanted to speak with Mom, just to hear her voice, and be reassured. The limitations of life in Ghana were such that I could only make a Ghana–U.S. phone call from Accra. I sent a telegram home from Wiawso, saying that I had received the news about Pop, and that I would try to arrange a call to speak to Mom. I then phoned George Carter in Accra and asked him to help me arrange a trans-Atlantic call. He readily agreed and off I went in my newly assigned Jeep on the ten hour trip to Accra.

Within a short time of my arrival there, I was able to make the call and speak to Mom; it was now almost two weeks since Pop's death and the funeral had been held even before I had had news of his death. George Carter gave me the privacy of his office to talk. I don't remember the exact conversation with Mom but I know I came away from it feeling that she, strong woman that she was, was all right. She said that her thoughts were very much with me and that I should not try to come home at this time but continue my work in Ghana. She said that was what Pop would have wanted. George had informed me that the Peace Corps had a policy of compassionate leave and that I could go home for a week or two if I wanted. Mom ended the conversation with the idea that maybe we could find a way to meet in Europe during my summer break from SWSS.

When I returned to SWSS in early January when school reopened, I no longer felt that loneliness. The brief contact with Mom and a flood of memories about Pop somehow renewed me and I began a term that included new and ambitious projects and a deepening of my friendship with Adu and the circles of his fellow Sefwis. I was teaching at school and at two adult ed locations; we started a school newspaper, a farm, a stamp club, a library, and a huge mural map project. This was what being a Peace Corps Volunteer was all about and I was reveling in it.

The Juaboso Connection

I have known Kwaku Armah since 1961 and, although he is now in his sixties, when I visit him I still think of him as a "young man." Kwaku and several other Ghanaians, who became like family to me, all came from an area deep into Sefwi, centered on the village of Juaboso. Like many Sefwi, Kwaku is small-boned, of medium height, with fine, almost delicate, features, and dark ebony skin. He is very soft-spoken and I have to strain to catch every word. When I first met him, he went by the name, Barnabas K. Armah. Many young Ghanaians of that era adopted English first names, initializing their traditional day name in the middle, and using the mother's family surname. I'm uncertain what it meant in terms of changing cultural patterns and so-called westernization—by the time he came to the U.S. in 1970, he had totally abandoned Barnabas and from then on was simply, Kwaku

Armah. I have no middle name and at SWSS adopted Kwabena (a boy born on Tuesday and I was) as mine.

My interviews with Kwaku in 1999 were conversational as we both recalled life at SWSS with fondness and frequent laughter. Kwaku tells his own story and, in doing so, speaks often of Gabriel Adu who was then very much part of his life and, for two years, of mine.

"In January 1961 I was what we call in Ghana a head teacher. I had finished ten years of elementary school in 1958 and then joined the teaching force. At that time called pupil teachers, we were a cadre of folks who had just finished elementary school; without any real formal training, we were distributed to the villages to do teaching in the elementary schools. The school where I went had K–6. At the end of my first year, the head teacher, who was also a pupil teacher, had served as a pupil teacher for seven years and that was the limit you could serve without formal training. He did not go to training college and therefore he had to be dismissed. So I became head teacher. It was at Densamosie in Sefwi, about 12 miles from Juaboso. It was very small, in a rural farming area, the village had about fifteen houses. I finished my fourth year of Middle School at Asafo where Gabriel was. I knew my family couldn't pay for secondary school fees so my goal was to go to teacher training college. While you're there, you're on study leave and continue to receive pupil teacher's pay. After completion I would be bonded to teach for four years. So, in 1961 I had taken the training college entry exam and had passed for St. Mary's in Apowa, near Takoradi. I was going to start in September."

I then asked Kwaku how he learned about the new secondary school in Sefwi and how he came to attend.

"I heard that they were building a secondary school at Wiawso. It was out of my mind at the time because I had written off the idea of attending secondary school. My pursuit was training college. Some time in 1961 I came to Wiawso to visit Gabriel. He was still teaching at the Catholic Middle School. He took me to the site of SWSS and mentioned that, if it was possible, he would want to teach there. The site had been cleared. I remember the classroom building looked so big to me—it was three stories. Then I saw portions of the bungalows—the masters' quarters. There was no road there but the contractor constructed one.

"When the school opened in September, Gabriel was teaching there on the staff. He sent me a message—it was October, a Sunday early in October; we had a football match at Juaboso; we were getting ready. Luke Mensah, who had been my junior at middle school, appeared out of nowhere. He said he had been sent by Gabriel—Luke was at SWSS—and Gabriel was not feeling well and had asked Luke to come and get me. We spent the night since there was no lorry out in the evening. Monday morning we took the next available lorry. When we were coming Luke was telling me about the secondary school—it was nice but my mind was elsewhere.

"When we got to Wiawso, I wanted to go to the hospital to look for Gabriel. Luke said, 'Oh no, he's not at the hospital, he's at the school.' We walked to SWSS and Luke took me to Gabriel's house and he wasn't there; he was in the classroom, teaching. Luke went to tell him I was here. After the class was over, Gabriel appeared, smiling, all happy. I said, 'I thought you were sick.' He said, 'Yeah, I was sick but I'm better now.' We sat and we talked. He said, 'You know I'm teaching here and I think you should come to the secondary school.' I said, 'Gabriel, why are you suggesting secondary school again? You know I went to Opoku Ware; nobody had any money to pay for me. Nobody can pay for me to be here. Meanwhile, I have admission to Apowa and I'm leaving in two weeks.'

"He talked and talked but, in my mind, I had cut him off. Then, he said, 'By the way, let's go see my friend.' So we walked down and came to your house and he introduced you and I remember shaking your hand. You started talking and asking some questions and I kept saying, 'Yes.' I could hardly understand your accent but I responded. Then the conversation ended.

"As we walked out of your house, I said to Gabriel, 'What was he saying?' Gabriel answered me, 'What do you mean, what was he saying? He was asking you if you were coming to the school and you said, Yes.'

"I said, 'Gabriel, that's not what I said.'

"He said, 'Oh, you said, Yes, and remember, you can't lie to the white man.'

"I still didn't see how I could get someone to pay for it. So, Gabriel said, 'Let's go to the Headmaster's house.' We went—it was Mr. Amissah-Arthur—and he said, 'Your brother said you want to come to the secondary school.' I looked at him, hesitated, and said, 'Yes, I want to come but I can't pay for it.' He said, 'Well, are you a good student, are you clever?'—that's the Ghanaian term. I said, 'Yes. I can hold my own. In fact, I passed for Opoku Ware.' And I gave him the story. He said, 'Then, you don't have to worry. You come—the Cocoa Marketing Board is going to conduct an exam and the bright students will get scholarships. There are other scholarships too.' So, I said, 'OK, I will come.'"

I had always known that Gabriel was Kwaku's "senior brother" but, given the complexities of family, clan, village, and traditional group relationships and connections, I was never quite sure what that meant. During my first year at SWSS, when Gabriel and I wandered about the Sefwi district meeting people, attending adult ed functions, collecting eggs, pineapples, and bottles of beer, he introduced me to many of his "brothers and sisters." When that number exceeded twenty, I asked Gabriel exactly how large his family was. I don't remember his answer but I do know that in future introductions he would distinguish between "brother— same father, same mother [as Gabriel]" and "brother—same village, or fellow Sefwi, or same class at Winneba Training College."

Although he arrived a few weeks after school opened, Kwaku quickly stood out as a student in my classes—perhaps because he had been a teacher, definitely because he is extremely smart, probably because he was quick to understand my version of the English language. By the end of the first term, he had been chosen to be Senior Prefect of SWSS. In the Ghanaian system, it is a highly responsible position; working with class and house prefects, the Senior Prefect (SP) is expected to oversee student behavior and be an exemplar in his own studies and activities. Like Gabriel, Kwaku had begun to serve as mentor to some of his "brothers and sisters" from the Juaboso area. Just as through Gabriel, I had met Kwaku, it was through Kwaku that I befriended Ernest K. Bennie and Grace Esi Daniels, also students at

SWSS. When Bennie was given a half scholarship by the Cocoa Marketing Board, Gabriel and Kwaku convinced me to help pay the rest of his fees—it was about this time that Bennie, unofficially, was helping me with household chores.

Kwaku recalled: "Somewhere in the second term—I was Senior Prefect then—Chief Quartson, head of the school board, came and asked everybody who owed fees to go home and get money. Grace, at that time, thought she wouldn't be able to come back because she knew that nobody at home could afford to pay for her. At that point you had been helping Ernest. You had adopted him; you were paying his fees. He became a day student, living at your house in the steward's quarters. Gabriel may have intervened for Grace and you began to help her too. You had asked me and I told you her situation and somehow you made a decision that you would pay the difference since Cocoa Marketing Board was paying half her fees."

The Invisible Man Meets the Prisoner of Zenda

During the first year at SWSS, teaching was easy with just two classes to face, Form IA and IB. The rosters and configurations kept changing, the "O" level exams were five years away, and we all, staff and students, were happy just to be in existence. Each term completed made it seem more possible that the school would continue to exist and even to prosper. Each project started—farm, library, stamp club, flag pole, excursions, school paper—was further proof of our viability.

I taught History (about which I remember nothing) and English, language and literature. After a term without books, we finally got Reader's Edition copies of *The Invisible Man, The Prisoner of Zenda*, and Shakespeare's plays, as well as grammar books. In the early weeks I did a lot of improvising. I started with lessons in alphabetizing, writing simple sentences, and punctuation. The only color slide I have of me in the classroom shows a lesson on the chalkboard, "Active and Passive," changing ten sentences from one voice to another, an oral and written exercise. I dictated sentences (to help with spelling and to encourage students to tune in to my speech) and even did oral drills to try to move their pronunciation toward a more neutral, less vernacular English. I still remember two drills:

"Put the pepper in the paper."

"Where's the waiter with the water?"

Repeat those quickly ten times, in a lively cadence, and silly laughter will probably overwhelm you (just as it did with me and Form I). We also had lots of fun reading portions of *Zenda* and *Invisible Man* out loud. 'Rudolf Rassendyll, Princess Flavia, the King of Ruritania'—such exotic names invite irreverent instruction. All these activities made it easier early on for all of us to become comfortable with each other. I remember that some of the students came to call me 'Invisible Man,' a reference to my lack of dark, rich skin pigmentation.

Kwaku talked about my role as teacher:

"We enjoyed your class. We thought you were a hard marker because you corrected as well as graded our work. For me, it didn't take long to catch up with the accent. I had experience with the Dutch priests in Asafo. Most students—it didn't take long. We had been raised under the impression that Americans didn't know English. Even though Americans spoke English, they didn't know English. But you were speaking perfect English and not American English.

"Thinking back, I think we were glad that you were there and you were a graduate. One of the things I still remember—you would come in the afternoon after classes and you would sit on the porch of your bungalow. We would come and talk. You know, strange enough, masters' bungalows were out of bounds; we couldn't go to the masters' bungalows without special permission. Students were also coming to carry water to the house from the stream [to be rewarded from my abundant supply of fruit from the Banana Man].

"Another impression—and for us it was significant—the closeness you had to students was unusual for us. You were an expatriate professor and we expected that after the classroom you would not have any interaction with us. That's why sitting on the porch and our stopping by and talking was such a big deal to us." [1999]

Adult Ed—Outside the Walls with the Extra-Mural Department

The adult ed lecturing I did was sponsored by a Ministry of Education program that was constantly changing names—The Extra-Mural Department, The Peoples' Education Association, The Institute of Public Education. In the remote fastness of Sefwi, I was not affected by the changes and my enjoyment in lecturing adults on world affairs was a constant throughout the two years at SWSS. Given the political tensions and apparent crises in U.S.–Ghana relations during that time, I was remarkably free from any local political pressures as I lectured on topics such as: Communism, Capitalism, and Socialism; The Cold War; Pan-Africanism. George Carter would probably have had a fit if he knew the substance of my world affairs lecture program but I never found it necessary to tell him any more than, "I'm doing adult ed lecturing in the bush and getting a wonderful reception." Two things in my background made it easy to present these lectures—an M.A. in History and five years' teaching experience in Social Studies.

The lecturing was a grand adventure in getting to know Ghanaians in what was for me very comfortable settings—a classroom and the local bar—and there were some comical bumps along the way. Throughout my first year at SWSS, I reported in letters both to my folks and to my sister, Betsy, who was attending Skidmore College.

November 17: "I have accepted the lectureship at Bibiani. The head of the Extra-Mural Department was out here to see me and we agreed on arrangements. Until I get my Jeep, they will pay the expense of taxis for me to get to Bibiani two evenings a week."

November 22: "I have started my lecturing in Bibiani. Tuesday evening I went there by cab to deliver my first lecture on World Affairs and, as far as I can judge, it was a huge success. There are about 25 adults in the class (which meets at 6:00 p.m. in a local primary school, by the light of a kerosene lantern) and the expectation is that 10 or 15 more will be joining [not much to do in Bibiani on a Tuesday night].

The first night was a comedy of errors. The cab driver who was to take me to Bibiani was late in getting to school here; we then had to go collect my Ghanaian liaison man in Wiawso (but wait 15 minutes while he changed into suitable clothes); next, the cab driver had to tell his mother he would not be home for supper (another ten minutes); next, the cab did not have enough gas to get to Bibiani, so to the petrol station; finally (by now we were more than 40 minutes late in leaving) off to Bibiani. I arrived only one hour late, just as the class was dispersing because of my failure to show. However, once I arrived and began to lecture (on the Berlin Crisis), everything was OK."

December 1 [by now I have the Jeep]: "I've completed my 4th lecture at Bibiani (the drive takes about 1½ hours each way—45 miles). The class has held to a register of 25. My best talk to date has been on the United Nations (I think that Eleanor Roosevelt and Adlai Stevenson would have been proud of me). I can tell from the questioning after the lectures how much my 'students' have benefited.... I try to make my lectures factual and non-political but, it being the nature of World Affairs, I conclude with several minutes of opinions, West and East, right and left, on any given topic and then open the lecture to questions. Although most of the group seem to favor a western point of view, they also seem to be quite anxious to develop their own neutralist point of view. I both agree and disagree with the neutralist attitude, depending on the issue. I argued strongly against the neutrals' weak stand at Belgrade on Russia's resumption of nuclear testing.... Next Colonialism and The Congo."

December 7: "Saturday, I gave a lecture to the Wiawso group (a repeat of one of my Bibiani lectures—the UN). Most of the question period was taken up with a discussion of admission of Red China. I am scheduled to give 3 or 4 more lectures here at Wiawso after the holidays. Tuesday night's lecture on colonialism was a big success—had the largest crowd to date, 32—and the most stimulating question period." [1961]

January 27 [after Christmas break]: "I'm back lecturing twice a week in Bibiani and have been discussing Communism, Capitalism, and Socialism. I really have to do my homework to answer all the questions I've been getting. There is much talk here about a new form of 'African Socialism' and my evening students are very eager to get clear definitions and some understanding of what it is all about. Much to my delight, the attendance has been regularly 25 plus (which I am told is quite good for classes out 'in the bush'). I'm also doing repeats of these lectures for the adult group here in Wiawso."

February 15: "I lectured in Bibiani last night, accompanied by Mr. Adu who had to stop at the Catholic Mission there to get some prayer books for our kids. During the lecture, there was a terrible windstorm, followed by heavy rain (none of which is supposed to happen—this is the dry season). By 7:45 p.m. we started to drive back to Wiawso, Mr. Adu joking about the rainy season when all sorts of trees fall across the road—lo and behold, there was a 6 foot thick mahogany tree, lying smack across our path. We stopped and were soon joined by 2 mammy lorries and the comedy began. Heavy rain, crowds milling about, the 2 drivers attempting to saw through the tree with a 2 hand saw. I agreed to drive a man back to Bibiani to get a large axe. He and another man got in my vehicle (the second man was a mystery all night) and we drove back to town.

"Stop 1 - dropped man #2 (Why? No one says.)

"Stop 2 - a mile the other side of Bibiani at a noisy bar. Man #1 disappears. 20 minute wait (during which I meet an old taxi driver friend from Bibiani—adult ed student—who listens to our sad story, smiles, and leaves).

"Stop 3 - Man #1 reappears with new man, #3; drives with us to a private house (who knows where—road sign reads, Boston 115 Mi). #1 and #3 disappear, returning with man #4 (I'm beginning to worry about man #2—forgot where we left him).

"Stop 4 - Mr. Adu stops at Mission, briefly prays, confesses, father agrees to put us up for night if necessary.

"Stop 5 - (By now have almost forgotten why I am driving around; heavy rain.)

"Stop 6 - Find man #2 by roadside with loaf of bread under arm and bottle of beer (was tempted to ask him about axe, but thought better of it).

"Stop 7 - Men #1, #3, #4 disappear into small village, return with axe (we stood and sang 3 verses of "Raise High the Flag of Ghana," except #2 who was too busy with beer and bread).

"Stop 8 - to talk to another taxi driver; man #3 departs (a spy?).

"Stop 9 - back at tree, all hands have stopped sawing in anticipation of arrival of axe (now 10:00 p.m.). Men #'s 1, 2, 4 start chopping.

"Mr. Adu and I return to the Mission, spend the night. Up at 5:00 a.m., back to Wiawso. Road clear where tree was (only evidence of any incident—one small crust of bread)."

March 4: "I lectured at Wiawso on Saturday evening. It was only a small group, but very enthusiastic; the topic was 'Pan-Africanism.' I also met the man from Juaboso who wants me to come there to lecture. We have both written to the administrative head of PEA [Peoples' Education Association] to see if we can get approval."

March 17: "I had another Bibiani adventure last week (or the week before, I think). I had picked up some people on the way; toward the end of my lecture it began to rain very heavily which tends to make the road hazardous. As I left to return to Wiawso, the same people appeared and asked for a lift back to Bekwai. We got as far as Bekwai and couldn't drive further because of the rain. There I was stranded at 9:00 at night. One of my passengers turned out to be the Headmaster of the Bekwai middle school. He insisted I come home with him and wait until the rain stopped. I did so and was entertained with beer, cake, and most friendly conversation for more than an hour. I also had an opportunity to help start a PEA branch, as that was what we discussed! By 10:30 the rain had stopped and I proceeded on to Wiawso."

March 24: "I'm the talk of Wiawso [population: under 2000] this week. Wednesday evening, the local PEA branch, whom I've been lecturing informally, had a social to close out the academic year. I was invited. As part of the festivities, various members of the group were called upon for recitations, songs, riddles, etc. After hearing more than half the group perform (all on an informal basis, between dances), I finally was brave enough to rise to the occasion. I sang! After the first, there was no stopping me. I did three folk songs [I am sure that one was Michael, Row the Boat Ashore] and received an enthusiastic response. I even got up enough courage to dance at least one High Life."

April 16: "I expect to make a few short trips over the long weekend to visit some people in the Sefwi area at Juaboso and Asawinso about organizing some new PEA branches."

May 2: "I started an extra series of adult ed lectures at Asawinso on Friday and really had a wonderful time. Asawinso is even more 'bush' than Wiawso (30 miles to the interior from here) and the young adults of the town have been more than eager to have someone come and speak to them about current affairs. I have been deeply touched by their open and very heartfelt welcome to me (in their eyes, I am sort of doubly blessed—not only have I traveled thousands of miles from the U.S. to come to Ghana to teach, I've also been willing to come further into the 'bush' to speak to them).... At the request of the group I spoke on 'Nuclear Testing and Disarmament'... I tried to explain nuclear bombs but refused to defend our resumption of the tests. I think it is completely wrong.... After the lecture, the group insisted that we adjourn to the local pub to relax. We must have spent another two hours, talking more personally about the PC, the U.S., and Ghana." [1962]

At the end of my first year at SWSS in June, the peripatetic Brewster Smith and his sidekick, Rafe Ezekiel, appeared to conduct their research interview. I invited them to join me and go to Bibiani for my lecture.

In his personal diary, Brewster described the evening:

"We met in the Catholic primary school—an old, miserable building—essentially a shed-like building divided into rooms opening on a roofed porch along one side; old fixed wooden chairs and desks. Hanging from a nail at the front of the room was a sign (to be hung around the neck of a misbehaving or poorly performing child) labeled 'Shame.' About 30 casually western-dressed people, mostly young, including one pretty woman, gradually assembled. After Bob K. introduced us to the group, he proceeded with his lecture on the Common Market and its relevance for Ghana— an amazingly competent, straight forward, uncondescending presentation, very well organized and full of references to Ghanaian parallels or implications. Both Rafe and I learned a lot about the common market and were impressed by Bob, but wondered if he hadn't pitched the level too high. But then came the question and comment period, and the response, in the Ghanaian English ... showed a keen and intelligent appreciation of the issues. Here were the westernized elite of the village—primary and middle school teachers, petty clerks, the owner of a service station (a former school teacher)—eager to keep alive to what was going on in the world, beyond the meager contents of the Ghanaian press.

"Bob K's lecture was a thoroughly objective and Ghana-oriented presentation, not in the least a presentation of U.S. positions.... Afterwards there was a vote of thanks, we left and waited, and then the leaders of the group, including the Pres. (principal of the Middle School), the Secy. (chief teacher of the Catholic Primary School) and the pretty woman (an elementary teacher from Ashanti) came with us to the local cafe for beer. This was a little hole-in-the-wall lorry rest station at the Mobil gas station (owned by one of the group) outside of which we sat at a mahogany table after the rain. Our hosts kept uncapping bottles (the big near-quart ones prevalent in Ghana) and pouring beer; one's glass was always full. Rafe was quizzing someone on various things African; I was chatting with Mr. Adu, Bob's colleague, with the pretty Ashanti girl, and with Bob. Altogether it was a very warm occasion.

"One of the group quoted a Twi proverb to the effect, 'We drink, and then we talk,' which Rafe copied out for use at Berkeley. The lecture was 5–6 and we broke up what was clearly good for an evening's party by 7:30; Bob glided furiously along the bumpy road back." [1962]

The Farm Disaster—Blame it on George

Caught up in the zeal of Peace-Corps-ness, I began to think that, by the great Shriver, all things were possible. The farm disaster story unfolds during my first year at SWSS, more comedy than tragedy, told through letters home.

December 21: "Three of us [including George Coyne] drove to Mpraeso to visit with an American couple here at an agricultural mission. We are seeking information on plants, crops, soil, seeds so that we can start small gardening and farming back at our schools." [1961]

January 10 [After a Christmas trip with George Coyne, whose plans for a farm at Sunyani Secondary School seemed imaginative and replicable]: "With the help of one of the U.S. agricultural advisers here in Ghana, I'm going to try to establish a small farm here at school. Most of the students come from farming families—it would be great to teach new methods and new crops."

February 11: "I'll have more to say about our farm after this week. An agricultural expert from a USAID Mission is coming here at my invitation. He is going to survey our area and advise us on what we can do. The dry season will last until early April, so there isn't much planting that can be done before then. If he selects a plot, we'll spend the next few months preparing the soil and fencing off the area to protect against the roaming goats from the nearby village."

February 15: "I got more than 200 mango seeds from Kumasi.... So I, being a New York City boy who always believed that vegetables grow in cans, am now the SWSS Agricultural Science master. I most innocently invited the agricultural adviser to help us plan a small vegetable garden. He was here last week—we now plan to put in 5 acres of oil palm, 200 mango trees, 3 acres of coffee (4 varieties), 4 acres of rubber, pineapple, marijuana, and cocoa (we were much too busy to talk about a vegetable patch)."

February 19: "On Sunday, I worked with about 15 of the boys here, preparing beds, planting the seeds and watering them. So we've made a start on our farm. We formed volunteer 'work' crews to rotate weekly in caring for the seed beds. Next project is pineapple, then I am hoping to get 200–300 packets of vegetable seeds from one of the other PCVs who received over 1000 packets gratis from a U.S. seed company."

March 4: "We planted pineapple in our farm this week but sustained a serious loss in the mango patch. Apparently, we did something wrong in planting the mango seeds and they are not germinating properly, just rotting away—our first serious setback. We are also working at clearing more bush to plant oil palm trees and a vegetable garden."

March 7: "In spite of all the advice that we received, we find that we made many errors in our farming and have to start all over. We did not prepare the soil properly and many of our seeds have failed to germinate; we didn't shade the seeds. All these things are a mystery to me but I hope that the next year and a half will see some successes."

March 17: "I'm here at Wiawso this weekend and we'll all be working on the farm. I was able to get vegetable seeds and we'll be planting them, hoping they don't suffer the same fate as the mango seeds which have now become a standing joke with us."

March 24: "We are gradually recovering from the mango seed disaster and are forging ahead full steam with a vegetable garden. I was able to get several packets of seeds and now every available box is being used to nurse tomato, lettuce, etc. seedlings. What we lack in agricultural skills and knowledge, we make up in zeal."

April 16: "The farm is not prospering but we are all praying that the rainy season begins soon. We are due to get heavy rains any day now. Until we show better results, I'll delay planning a menu based on foods from my garden. As if to mock us, all the mango trees in Wiawso are in full fruit now, each tree bearing several hundred mangoes."

May 28 (last mention of the word farm, garden or mango in any correspondence): "My farm has produced its first crop! Two string beans and a half-rotten cucumber were all—but food never tasted better. We are now investing in insecticide…" [1962]

June 24, 1963 (excerpt from the Farewell Address to Messrs. Klein and Hutchinson by the Senior Prefect of SWSS):

"The Mango Project: Mr. Klein brought 250 mango seeds to help establish a mango plantation but very unfortunately all died. However, the project has not been a failure. The idea of starting an orchard for the school is operative in our subconscious minds and owes its origin to Mr. Klein [I blush]."

Sefwi-Wiawso Secondary School

Mr. Asare, The Banana Man.

Gabriel Yaw Adu, my Sefwi mentor.

Teaching Form IA.

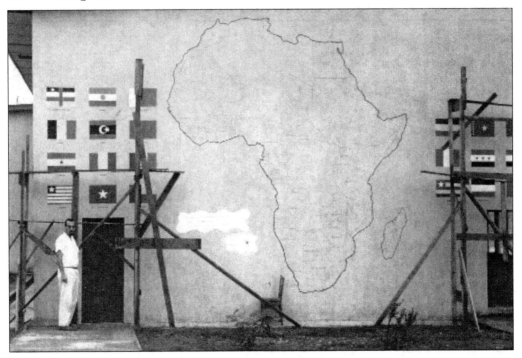

The almost-completed Africa map.

My Sefwi "family" — Barnabas (aka Kwaku), Grace, and Bennie.

My house on the SWSS compound, enfolded in the rain forest.

The "Girls' Sports Mistress" with happy volleyball team.

The Ghana map.

Preparing to paint the Africa map.

Working on the Africa map.

Adu

7

WE HAVE COME TO TEACH

The Ur-Ghana I

After settling in, we faced the full cycle of the year as teachers in secondary schools in Ghana. Kennedy, Peace Corps, Berkeley, Legon, Ghana I all faded and in our immediate view were classrooms and students and books and subjects to be taught. How did we deal with it? We really were fairly ordinary people, caught up in these extraordinary events. But now the glamour and glare were gone. A serious-minded John Buchanan became a serious-minded teacher; a quirky and mercurial Sue Bartholomew dealt impatiently but, at times, brilliantly with teaching; a high-minded Newell Flather worked tirelessly to broaden the intellectual horizons of his students. We were assigned from Accra on the coast to Navrongo at the northern border. After dispersing from Legon, each of us went through a period of adjustment, facing the realities of assignment, grouping, and the personal challenge of becoming one's own Peace Corps Volunteer. We all came to Ghana with the mandate to be teachers but echoing within that mandate were both our own motivations in having joined the Peace Corps and the expectations of others—Headmasters, other teachers, Peace Corps/Accra and Washington.

We saw ourselves as teachers first and Peace Corps Volunteers second (or, in some cases, third, fourth, or fifth) but at the same time we were also aware of the Peace Corps Catch 22—although we felt ourselves to be nonpolitical in doing our jobs, our success had political dimensions. His students might like George Coyne because of what he did as a teacher but they were also aware that he was an American and part of the Peace Corps. So be it. But we resented anyone who tried to mandate or shape our non-teaching lives with the intent of broadening our benign influence.

George Coyne was the Ur-Ghana I. His activities and achievements, in the role of teacher, represented our Peace Corps ideal. His acknowledged success was the best refutation of the Peace Corps/Washington viewpoint that we should be in the villages, speaking vernacular, meeting the natives. George is an unpretentious person, comforting and easy to be with. I remember traveling with George and some others in the group during the first Christmas vacation. We went through northern Ghana. With George along it seemed that any crisis could be dealt with, under his steady hand. On his 1962 visit to Sunyani, Brewster Smith had described George:

"Modest but self-confident ... imbued with relevant Peace Corps motivation, in a way like the best sort of Eagle Scout type. The school is his entire life and he is devoted to the students ... is full of projects accomplished and planned."

It's impressive to listen to George describing his work at Sunyani in his first interview with Brewster. With a degree in Forestry from Rutgers University, George introduced a course in Agricultural Science to the school. Modestly using the editorial "we," he said:

"It's something new which we have started. We would like eventually to offer Agric as one of their certificate subjects. We have a whole section of land here and we would like to put it to use. Rather than just let it remain in bush, we'd like to plant some orchards and to show the boys new scientific techniques as far as farming is concerned. It's not usual to have Agric as a regular course in these academically oriented G.E.T. schools. This is how it happened. I've had a background in agriculture. The school has this section of land. The Headmaster is interested and the Board of Governors has supported it. Also the Chief in town [whose land had been given for construction of the school] has gone along with this. He has let us use the land for orchards.

"We have to set up farms that eventually must be inspected and approved by the West African Exams Council. Then our boys may sit the exam in Agric. Our idea is to offer Agric as well as General Science and Health Science for the First and Second Forms—our boys lack a background in practical applications of science so we want them to take these three basic courses before starting to specialize in biology, chemistry, physics."

George also served as Assistant Housemaster (supervising a dormitory) and Form Master (responsible for school reports on students). And School Dispenser: "... as a matter of fact I have quite a large practice here. So far I've treated everything from a compound fracture of the big toe to malaria and stomach palaver—the two main things—various cuts and bruises and fungus diseases and itches. The hospital in town supplies us.

"I take care of the school farms; a lot of this is all afternoon work where we go out and plant and weed and so on. Besides that I'm chairman of the Entertainment Committee, which is an interesting chore to say the least. We try to provide a varied entertainment program for weekends and holidays.

"We took twenty boys on an excursion to the south, down to the coast—there were boys who had never seen the sea before. We did this on the school lorry and the school subsidized the trip. This was during Easter holidays.

"Then there's the Science Club. I tried it the first term but there was lack of interest but by third term a group of boys started a petition for a science club. I told them about first term and they assured me that wouldn't happen; they were wondering if we could give it another try. We held a meeting and more than 60 signed up. We had to restrict it to Second Form. The First Form would have to wait until this club became established. Now we have thirty boys and it's really been a terrific experience—they've stayed with it. We hold our meetings once every two weeks on a Saturday afternoon in the science lab. The students run it themselves and they have agreed to put on a science exhibit for Speech Day. We expect to have 25 or 30 different exhibits.

"My roommate and I have tried to encourage the boys to beautify their school a bit. As a part-time thing we are trying to seek out volunteers to work on Saturday mornings to plant shrubbery and grass." [1962]

From Accra to Navrongo (with a Stop in Kumasi)

The PCVs who had the greatest number of overnight visitors were at opposite ends of Ghana in Accra and Navrongo, and in Kumasi which was the center of the Ashanti Region with seven or eight outlying schools. Everyone had reason to visit Accra—shopping, socializing, stopping at PC headquarters—and it was convenient (and economical) to find a place to sleep at Steve McWilliams' in Christiansborg or at DeeDee Vellenga's in Accra New Town. The same for Kumasi at Yaa Asantewaa and Opoku Ware. Almost everyone made at least one visit to northern Ghana, which is culturally and geographically different from the rest of the country. Other than the Government Rest House at the regional capital of Tamale, the place to stay in the north was Navrongo Secondary School. Navrongo was an easy way station on the road to Ouagadougou in Upper Volta, and, for the most adventurous and foolhardy, a port of departure for Timbuktu.

Assigned to Navrongo were Jack Lord, Tom Peterson, and Marty Wallenstein —unique individuals with separate interests and no special experience in working as part of a team. It was probably this that enabled them to function effectively in what was a very isolated post.

Tom Peterson was a student of classical Greek and Latin: introspective, tall, gawky with a shock of yellowish hair, and ever curious about languages.

Marty Wallenstein was born in Brooklyn, attended Brooklyn College, and taught science in a Brooklyn junior high school—he has a sardonic, urban-provincial wit, an impatience with authority, and looks like Harold Lloyd—horn-rimmed glasses and a toothy grin. At Navrongo he became the environmentalist in a government-sponsored forestation project, trying to improve the stark landscape of the dry savanna by planting dozens of trees to provide shade on the school compound—to me, an incredible act of faith and belief in the future. It fit with his role as school disciplinarian. Since there was little or no weedy grasses for the students to cut as punishment, Marty had them haul X number of buckets of water from the nearby catchment dam to water the trees. I have heard from people who visited Navrongo Secondary School twenty-five years later that some of the trees, in fact, did flourish.

Jack Lord was a Harvard graduate with an interest in film-making, and served as the mediator, when necessary, between Tom and Marty. He is an even-tempered, serious-minded person with an insatiable curiosity about whatever people and places he encounters. Jack tells some of the Navrongo story:

"I was assigned to Navrongo to teach Geography and I protested to Carter. Carter thought it was because I didn't want to go to Navrongo because it was so far and bush. That had nothing to do with it. Fact is I didn't know anything about Geography. The reason they posted me there was that I had taught Geography in Connecticut to seventh graders. I'd been able to do that because there was a guy on staff who was working on his Ph.D. in Geography. He said, 'Yeah, you go ahead and keep a few pages ahead of the kids. I'll coach you.' That was how I taught Geography for a year.

"But I was in no way qualified to teach British Geography. It is a very serious subject, much more rigorous than anything they teach here. What I found when I got up to Navrongo was that Second and Third Form Geography was all Earth Science and that I could deal with. So, it worked out. My degree was in English but they wouldn't allow us to teach it—we didn't speak it properly.

"When they announced the assignments at Legon, I protested to George. I said, 'This is crazy, I can't teach Geography.' George said, 'Off you go.' What had happened was that Larry Abavanna was the Minister of Agriculture and the school in Navrongo was there because of him. He had apparently said he wanted Peace Corps people. The situation at the school was we had one teacher who was a Ghanaian without a degree, a Nigerian expatriate, a Ghanaian who taught Bible Studies. The southern teachers did not want to come up to Navrongo. The school was desperate for teachers. The Headmaster was Agyeman-Dixon, a Ghanaian from a well-connected, wealthy southern family who claimed to have gotten a degree in the States. Maybe he didn't. I think he was assigned up there as a way of getting rid of him. He was a very interesting guy, tremendously energetic, but not the kind of person you need to be a principal of a school. His problem was not his degree; it was getting along with the Northern Councils and things like that. He was an Ashanti. Only one staff member was a northerner and the rest southerners.

"The north is, of course, different—it's more related to the Sahel but it really wasn't a problem. One of the advantages our group had was that the job was so clearly defined. We were trying to prepare these kids to get through the 'O' level exams; it's not like doing community development in South America.

"It was a newly constructed G.E.T. school with bungalows for the staff, electricity, once in a while. The big problem was water; there's almost no rain. We had a pond for when the tap water [from wells] dried up—six weeks or longer. Then students were then assigned to get one bucket per teacher per day from the pond. It was artificial; it had been dammed as part of the school construction; it was less than an acre; it collected water in the short rainy season. The three of us shared a house. We hired a cook and a steward because otherwise we wouldn't have been able to teach. We had no transportation, no way to get food. The cook's name was Salifu and the steward's name was Charles who was just a prince of a guy—one of the best people you'd ever want to meet. Salifu took sugar and things like that from us but he was OK—the food was not wonderful. Dr. Chin was convinced we all had tuberculosis because of weight loss. At the end when he did the termination physicals, I'd lost fifty pounds; Marty, who couldn't hardly afford to lose any, and Tom had lost all this weight. Chin said, 'They've all got tuberculosis.' Then he did the patch test and was amazed we didn't have TB. It was just the food; there was nothing to eat.

"The school was about four miles from town. To start we had no vehicle and I bought a bicycle. We were pretty much confined to the compound for two years basically—we hardly ever left the compound. Once in a while on a weekend we'd go into Bolgatanga—there's nothing to go into in Navrongo. People go to the one local store which was of the nature that one week they'd get a shipment of marmalade and that was all that was on the shelves. Then the next week it would be, you know, corned beef from Argentina or something like that. That was the kind of store but Bolgatanga had real stores, a bank—less than an hour away. The school lorry would take us when it had to make trips for school needs. Our diet was yam [large fibrous tuber, not sweet potato], meat, damn Guinea fowl. The thing that drove us, Marty particularly, was fried tomatoes and boiled yam every day. Beef—we're not talking steak here.

"There were about 200 students; first of all they were northerners; there was a small group of southerners that couldn't get in anywhere in the south and so they had connections that got them in Navrongo; some bright students. There was a hospital in Navrongo, run by the government, not a mission. Dr. Chin came up and toured it. It was very embarrassing. You know how the dispensary is—everybody waiting. I was with him and he went down the line—he's a doctor, right? These people sitting on the bench, he'd take their prescriptions away from them and read them and just blanch. You could see he was really upset. He'd give it back and go down the line and take somebody else's. When we got back to the school, he told us never to go to the hospital under any circumstances.

"About my teaching? It was only Geography. I had a syllabus to guide me and the kids had books. We had maps, some wall maps, but remember I was teaching Earth Science. I wasn't teaching them where the Carpathians are. I was teaching how do rivers meander and why. If it had been the Carpathians, I would have been doomed. For me it was more important you go out and look at rock piles and things outside and ask, 'How did they get here?' That kind of stuff. But it made some local people very nervous because some rocks were sacred.

"We took a poll at one point of languages in the school—I think Tom did it and he came up with close to 200. The language used in Navrongo is not the language system in the surrounding area. In fact, it's as different as Hungarian and English—Kassim and Nankanni. Navrongo is kind of out there isolated; the school was totally to itself. It didn't have much interaction with its surrounding farmers or anything like that. The language in the school was English. Agyeman-Dixon would get after kids for speaking anything other than English, including outside the classroom.

"You know, Marty has a strong Brooklyn accent. When we were in training and all that, we thought how are these kids going to cope with Marty's Brooklynese. So after we'd been there a couple of months, we did a poll and asked the kids, 'Can you understand us?' What resulted was they could understand Marty perfectly but they were having a lot of trouble with Tom and me. Marty, anticipating that there was going to be a problem, was taking care to speak slowly. There's probably a generation of northerners who speak with a Brooklyn accent." [2000]

An African Student Asks His Science Mistress

> Please Miss,
> How can I make my eyes to see this thing?
> I cannot hear you when you say that this is so.
> And yet—you have a key to where I want to go.
> Please—may I know?
>> by Dorothy Dee Vellenga, Accra, 1962
>> (after teaching the first lesson in using the microscope)

DeeDee was an attractive blonde with a ready and toothy smile; though somewhat reticent, she was warm but not effusive, always neatly dressed. Soon after joining Peace Corps, DeeDee was quoted in a newspaper interview, "I think it is an exciting venture and only time will tell how effective it will be—but it certainly is an opportunity for those of us participating in it." That remark echoed a feeling many of us had after some time in Ghana—we were getting as much as we were giving.

In 1961 DeeDee had just completed two years' science teaching at Foxcroft. She had graduated cum laude from Monmouth College in Ohio. While there, she was a member of two honorary scientific scholastic fraternities; an officer in the local of the sorority, Alpha Xi Delta; secretary of the senior class, active in the school newspaper, college orchestra, and student religious organization. She spent a semester junior year as a selected student at American University in Washington and a summer with Experiment in International Living in Turkey. DeeDee was not one of the group with whom I initially became friends—our backgrounds were different. In college I picketed barbershops, attended Henry Wallace rallies, and served as a poll watcher for the Progressive Party.

In Ghana DeeDee was assigned to West Africa Secondary School in Accra. It was an established urban day school with a run-down physical facility but a lively teaching staff, augmented in 1961 by DeeDee and Don Groff. Those who taught in urban day schools did not have the built-in Peace Corps opportunities that people in the new, bush G.E.T. schools had. George Coyne at Sunyani, the trio at Navrongo, Alice O'Grady at Dormaa, myself at Wiawso—we all had the chance to become involved well beyond the classroom because our schools were new, boarding, and in rural village environments. DeeDee talked about the school in her interview with Rafe Ezekiel:

"The first time I saw this school I was very discouraged, not having met any of the people connected with it, but as soon as I met the Headmaster then I felt much better. As far as my relationship with the Headmaster is concerned, I feel I have a good rapport with him. I used to ride to school with him when I lived over in the other part of town and Mr. Amar picked me up every morning. So, I had a chance to talk to him and I really appreciated the thought that he—I somehow got the feeling that he felt that I was somebody he could talk to about a lot of things. Our working relationship is very smooth. He wants to improve the science facilities a great deal so that I've had a lot of cooperation from him on that—equipment and that sort of thing. He really appreciates that we have come there—because we were without a science teacher and a lot of these boys were going to be disappointed in their science work. He really feels that the Peace Corps is one of Kennedy's best ideas. He's quite strict and demands the respect of the rest of the staff. He's done quite a lot for the school....

"There is a very good feeling among the staff and this is what several of the staff members have mentioned to me, appreciating this school in comparison to other schools where they have taught, that there is none of this pettiness or rank-consciousness or things like that. It's such a blessed relief from what I went through the last few years at this girls' school."

DeeDee mentioned that her time and energy went into her teaching but that she was not involved in extra-curricular activities. These were more difficult to organize and run at a place like West Africa Secondary School since many of the children were day students and, lacking a proper school compound, others stayed at a nearby boarding house, not a school dormitory. DeeDee taught Form I General Science, Form III Biology, and Forms IV and V Biology and Chemistry. All five of her Fifth Form students successfully passed the "O" level exams the first year. DeeDee also talked about life in Accra:

"Well, as far as the creature comforts are concerned, Accra is definitely better than someplace like Akropong—we don't have to boil our water here, for instance; we don't have to fuss about electricity. It's just not that much different from the States and I'm able to get the food that I'm used to. I'm at school usually at 6:30 a.m. and home by 2:15 p.m. I often go out to the University of Legon and visit friends, or friends come here; we go out to dinner, a film; I stay home and read. Also, this last month I've been having company every weekend, people coming in from outside Accra. They are doing their shopping, usually Saturday morning and Saturday night we go to the Lido, go dancing, or to a movie.... This is kind of a city life and so I really wish that I could get out to see more of the real Ghana—which I did over the Easter vacation when I went to one of my student's homes and got to see a bit more of village life."

Early Peace Corps brochures and news stories contained photos of the Accra PCVs—DeeDee, Ken Baer, Don Groff—because of their ready accessibility to visiting Peace Corps photographers. It was easier to taxi around Accra to take pictures, than to wander off on dusty and uncomfortable roads to the more remote locations. DeeDee mentioned this:

"There have been times when I sort of wished I were really on my own and I didn't have the Peace Corps image to live up to. I've been a little bit annoyed by all the publicity because I've been getting in on it, being here in Accra, and, I mean, my picture in different magazines and quoted, usually wrongly, about different things." [1962]

During her two years, DeeDee carved out a role for herself that matched most Ghana I's definition of what it meant to be a Peace Corps Volunteer in Ghana—primarily teachers. What else we did depended on personal interests, adventurousness, and personality. DeeDee became involved with a group of college students at the University of Legon—African and American. Out of curiosity she ventured into a rural village to live for a week as the guest of one of her students. During the summer break, she worked with the Women's Division of the Social Welfare Department in the area around Kumasi, visiting and meeting women's groups in many small villages. This experience strongly influenced her career after Peace Corps. She also played violin in the Ghana National Orchestra (a touch-and-bow institution at the time).

Teaching at a Catholic School

Bob Scheuerman, from Bison, Kansas, was a U.S. Navy veteran and experienced teacher when he became a PCV. He's a big "teddy bear" of a person with a very expressive face that breaks out in a sly grin, a mock grimace, a broad smile—punctuated by pudgy cheeks. He's easy to befriend and voluble in talking about anything and everything. He joined the Peace Corps because of his friend and fellow Kansan, Bill Austin. Bill thought Peace Corps was a worthwhile endeavor and welcomed the opportunity to get out of WaKeeney, Kansas. He thought it would be fun to do so in the company of a good buddy and that's where Bob came in. Bill cajoled Bob into completing the application; they took the test together and were both selected for training at Berkeley. Bob made it through but Bill was deselected for Ghana and then was assigned to Philippines II.

Bob was assigned to teach French at Bishop Herman Secondary School in Kpandu. Unlike most of the other schools, it was an established Catholic boys school with no G.E.T. affiliation; it was in the distinct, almost separate Volta Region of Ghana—the traditional culture was Ewe and it was once part of German Togoland. Bishop Herman was a well-run school under a strong Headmaster, Father Premis, a Dutch missionary priest, and Mr. Manti. Bob described them in his interview with Brewster:

"Mr. Manti is the senior African staff member who has been here for ten years—he was the first teacher hired and he's still here. He's a non-graduate but they call him the senior Ghanaian staff member and his advice is taken quite seriously by the Headmaster because of his experience. Father Premis has been here since he founded the school ten years ago but he relies heavily on Mr. Manti—they have worked together all those years."

Non-classroom and informal contact with students was not part of the fabric of school life at Bishop Herman. As a Protestant in a Catholic school, Bob didn't participate in morning prayers and assembly or Sunday Mass or Wednesday Mass or evening benediction. Bob spoke about this:

"The students are very respectful of the staff members, very friendly, outgoing, although regulations of this school put a bit of a damper on relationships between staff and students because the Headmaster does not want the students to come to the staff bungalows. For me, contact with the students is in the classroom or at the formal social functions like debates or films or lectures."

He defined his role as a Peace Corps Volunteer: "Here you're assigned to do a job of teaching school and, if you do that job well, and you know how to do it, what more can they ask?" [1962]

In his trip diary Brewster Smith commented about this in writing about Maureen Pyne who was assigned to Holy Child in Cape Coast, an all-girls Catholic school, equivalent to Opoku Ware in Kumasi:

"Great difference in school situations with respect to opportunity for informal contact with either students or other Ghanaians. In Klein's new Trust school in a remote village, easy, indeed unavoidable. In the Catholic school in Cape Coast where Maureen Pyne teaches, hard. She said to Sisters, would like to have some students to my bungalow; they said, fine idea but virtually marched them in and out."

Three's a Crowd—Five's a Party

Swedru Secondary School was a specially favored school. It was the prime G.E.T. location, politically favored, first to open, with an abundance of buildings, facilities, students, staff, and Peace Corps Volunteers. Five were assigned there—Howard Ballwanz, Sue Bartholomew, Sue Glowacki, Nate Gross, Loretto Lescher. It was neither bush nor urban, but readily accessible to the coast and to Accra (about an hour and a half away). The staffing situation was, in a perverse way, more challenging than the teaching. It was described by Brewster Smith in his diary:

"The problems of assimilating this large cluster of Peace Corps into the school were complicated by the presence of two additional expatriate teachers—an Englishman and an American. Altogether, the 'European' contingent at the school was large indeed and the two teachers just mentioned catalyzed a situation that both kept the staff in turmoil and effectively ruled out any real integration of its Ghanaian and 'European' components."

The Englishman was a stridently outspoken political leftist who delighted in trying to find ways to discomfit the PCVs and expose American neo-colonialism. He succeeded in polluting the social and educational atmosphere and thoroughly puzzling most of the Ghanaian students and staff. The other American was an AID contract teacher who seemed to be constantly disgruntled and resented the favorable attention that Peace Corps occasionally attracted. The malaise was compounded by the Ghanaian Headmaster who seemed unable to integrate the faculty and whose style was characterized years later by one of the group:

"… enormous amounts of huff and puff but no sense of how to run a school. He would have been a lot happier if he had not gotten so many of us. We were left out a great deal. The important stuff happened before and after staff meetings."

In mitigation, another said of him:

"[He] had studied at a small college in South Carolina in 1948. I think he had some bad experiences. He had very ambivalent feelings about Americans. We didn't always know where we stood with him. We didn't see him that much. Staff meetings were tedious." [2000]

But, there were students and teaching schedules. Occasional unfriendly fire from the British left flank led only to minor flesh wounds; whatever the undercurrents, the volunteers had the opportunity to establish some sanity and stability in the classroom and on the playing fields. And they did.

Nate Gross is a solid, sincere, and modest person. He has a way of tipping his head slightly forward and smiling when in conversation; it makes the contact more intimate and friendly. Originally assigned elsewhere, he was then reassigned to Swedru with the explanation from George Carter that he was being sent to add stability to the group. Knowing that five in one school was a burden, George more likely chose him because Nate is calm, easy-going and self-assured. He was interested in a career in Foreign Service and, having spent time in France with the Experiment in International Living, was happy to be in Ghana. He felt well able to adjust to the demands of teaching even though he had not taught before.

In our interview, Nate talked more about the incidental pleasures of life in Swedru and some of the missteps of a beginning teacher: "In English class I put a long sentence on the board to outline and started outlining and explaining it myself. A student piped up and said, 'No, Mr. Gross, that's not a gerund, that's a participial phrase.' After that, I learned why teachers often say, 'Kofi, go to the blackboard.' Or just say, 'What is this word—that's the subject, very good—now, what's this—Kofi, isn't that correct?'

"For the first three months, we lived in town at the house of a former cocoa executive; kind of a plantation house, large window shutters, wide verandahs. We had one party there, you may remember."

I wasn't at the party but did remember we used to joke about 'Swinging Swedru' and asked Nate about it:

"That reputation came from that one monster party we had that was while we were still living in town. I just remember an awful lot of volunteers and other people. We must have had forty people in that big house. Everybody slept on the floor and it was a great party. I think everybody was new in country and it was great to get together, probably the first such since Legon. Everybody had a good time.... We worked hard and partied hard. Practically every Saturday night the five of us would go into town to the Saturday night High Life dance in Swedru [at the Happy Corner Bar per Howard Ballwanz]; 50, 75, 100 people on the dance floor at a time and good bands." [2000]

But Nate taught French, English, and History to Forms I, II, and III; organized a basketball team and intramural play, was the track coach.

Even sitting still, Sue Bartholomew seems to be in motion; she has the taut body of a dancer but in conversation she explodes with ideas half-stated, partly explained, moving rapidly from one to another, expecting the listener to fill in the missing words and phrases. The summer before joining Peace Corps, Sue had been part of a Crossroads Africa project in Guinea. About joining Peace Corps, Sue said:

"I knew what I didn't want to do. I was in a Ph.D. program at Harvard and I knew I wanted to get out of there—I wanted a break from it; I wasn't ready to go on. I really did like the idea of the Peace Corps. I had done Crossroads—that was too short—Peace Corps was just perfect."

In Ghana, she was disappointed at being assigned in a group but unhesitatingly made the best of it, pursuing and utilizing personal interests in dance and theater at the school and in Accra. At Swedru she taught Forms I, II, and V in English, Music Theory and, for a short time, Religious Studies.

"Religion—I thought well let's start with Genesis; it's a good opening for interpretations—wrong—I was supposed to get up and just read the Bible. That was soon dropped from my schedule. Music Theory—we had one copy of 'Jesu, Joy of Man's Desire' [humming the hymn]. I never want to hear that music again as long as I live. There were 550 students. Of course, three-fourths were men and they knew their Sol-Fa's beautifully. I'd teach this from one sheet of music and the women—remember they had this strident 'Eeee' sound [demonstrating]. Poor Bach.

"We got into small productions. We did some stuff from 'West Side Story' and then some African dance.... Our world was the compound and when we did shows we never thought to invite people from town. That compound was big enough, there was enough going on with over 500 students. We did a Christmas pageant, 'Little Drummer Boy.' I didn't have the words so I made them up. To this day I think—talk about rights—someone'll come up and say where the hell did this version come from. There was this thing about the doll—nobody had a black doll so Jesus was a white baby, all bundled in straw. So right in the middle of the show— some of it was impromptu—Mary picks this baby up—the straw scatters—the audience loved it. Talk about looking like the Wise Men—these gorgeous Kente cloths—they brought nothing but their best to be Wise Men. Their carriage was beautiful and they were elegant. I staged the whole production, with an unusual version of 'Little Drummer Boy' but with real drums." [2000]

Like a sheltered harbor on a storm-swept coast, Loretto Lescher was a calm point in chaotic Swedru; maybe because she was from a large family, the youngest of eleven children. In 1961 she was a teacher with two and a half years' experience and a love of travel. I didn't know Loretto well but recall her as a pleasant-looking, well-dressed, friendly woman. To me she seemed somewhat remote because our circles within the group were different. Through training and in Ghana, we had little interaction. Reading her interviews with Brewster, I get a picture of a highly competent, private person and a no-nonsense teacher. She taught French to Forms II, IV and V and described how she started with her classes in Ghana:

"Well, what I do when I first start a year, especially in a new school, is to give a quiz—what I think a person should know after one year. I looked through the books and thought, well, if they have gone this far, they should know this. I gave them a little quiz with grammar and a little vocabulary, and told them to write a short composition about 'my family'—this is basic vocabulary. Well, I was positively astounded when I received the papers. They couldn't put two words together that made any sense whatsoever. So I knew right away—I had to start right from the beginning. In the Fourth Form, they had a little bit, not much, so actually I started from scratch in every class.... Since I was a woman and since I was new and came in and told them they were doing things not quite the right way—until I could prove myself as a capable teacher, they were just willing to study on their own. But after about three or four days they realized that I meant business and that I knew my subject, that I had taught before, and then they were willing to accept whatever I told them. So, it's all right."

Loretto also talked about her motivation for joining the Peace Corps and what she felt was the role of the PCV:

"We were asked often enough in Berkeley, 'Why did you join the Peace Corps?'

to make it sufficiently frustrating—I felt, like other people, that I like to travel and I was so sick and tired of what I was doing and I wanted to do something. If I could do something, then fine; I would like to do it.... I've traveled quite a bit and, you know, I've gotten around and met a lot of people. I find that they have tremendous misconceptions. I don't know if I consider myself a model American but I don't consider myself an American tourist—walking around with three cameras flung around your shoulders, in a loud suit, a loud person. I just feel that if I could do anything to destroy what they think of a typical American, then this is what I would like to do, even out here.

"Well, when we were in California we were told that our main job over here was teaching, and it was not to go around and publicize the Peace Corps, the fact that we were Americans, the fact that we were suffering in any way. So that's what I take it as. My main job out here is teaching. I don't have to go out and wear a big sign on my back, 'I am Peace Corps' or anything like that." [1962]

Loretto was a successful teacher—thirteen of twenty-five Fifth Formers passed in French the first year, "actually an astounding number [for Swedru]"—and a successful traveler. During her tour she visited: northern Ghana, Ivory Coast, The Canaries, Morocco, Spain, Italy, Germany, France, Libya, Tunisia, Togo, Dahomey, Niger, Upper Volta, the Cameroons, and the Congo. And I'll bet she didn't have three cameras slung over her shoulder.

George Carter, with pipe and that "Oh?" look.

Outside the hostel in Accra, Howard, George, Ken, Richard P.,
Dave, and (backs) Carol W. and Darleen.

Frank, with monkey, at Asankragwa S. S.

Alice and fellow teacher at Dormaa-Ahenkro S. S.

A gathering at Swedru S. S. with Sue G., Nate, Tom L., Steve, Mike, and Sue B.

April 1963 visiting the Akosombo Dam site, George, Shriver, Don, and Sal.

July 1963 Ghana I meets Kwame Nkrumah, standing, third from left.

8

THE VIEW FROM ACCRA

The Lumumba Thing

The view from Accra was not the same as the view from Wiawso or Navrongo or Kpandu. The Ghana PCVs were like satellites circling a planet, each in its own orbit, linked by unseen forces to a center. That center was Peace Corps/Ghana in the person of George Carter. However individual our efforts at our schools, our group identity continued to exist, manifested by the Peace Corps office in Accra. Throughout the two years there were many internal and international political tensions which barely impinged on our lives at the schools; nor were we aware of them as crises in relation to our roles in Ghana. But in Accra it was different. George Carter was obligated to stay informed about the Ghanaian political scene since it could affect our functioning in the schools or even the very existence of the program. George's official position was Peace Corps Representative, a job which had never before existed and for which there was no official guide. First of all, he was our leader, mentor, counselor, even though each of us was responsible to individual Headmasters and worked under their direct supervision (or lack thereof). Secondly, he represented the Peace Corps in its relation to the government of Ghana for present and future programs and reported directly back to Peace Corps/ Washington. Thirdly, as with any U.S. agency operating in another country, he was responsible to the U.S. Ambassador.

George Carter had arrived in Accra a few days after we did and had moved quickly to establish himself in relation to the group since we'd met him only briefly at Berkeley. He described his early days in Ghana:

"You were at Legon. I got to Ghana and Jim Green [U.S. Deputy Chief of the Mission] met me and took us to the Embassy to introduce us. I was with my son, Eddy. I indicated I was anxious to get with my crowd and see them. I mentioned to Ambassador Russell that I did not know this group very well—I had just met them once before. I was anxious to get out to Legon to see the troops.

"The assignment list was not complete. B. A. Brown [Permanent Secretary,

Ministry of Education], Thornell and Drake had walked through this but there were some problems. Pat Kennedy had come over with you guys. I sent him in that little green Studebaker—go and look at the countryside, get back here and tell me what we're going to find. And he took off.

"I stayed with the group until we left Legon. I spent my time at Legon, and wherever I was in contact with them, getting to know people, putting names with faces. I wasn't interviewing people but I was very conscious of being face-to-face. I was aware that assignments were not perfect—Dybwad as Acting Headmaster instead of an experienced teacher like Klein. I was loath to come in there at the last minute and start changing a lot of things around. I didn't know Brown. I didn't know what those guys [Brown, Thornell, Drake] had been through. I didn't yet know what the real problems were. I guess just out of the caution that builds in you over the years—don't come in here and screw up the table, old boy; you don't know what you're going to eat.

"I did learn very quickly over those opening days that Drake was a fountainhead of information of all sorts, about the school system, about individuals, which guys to be careful of, who were the jerks, who were the guys you could really work with. I vaguely remember a biographical rundown on B. A. Brown. It was very helpful; I used that three- or four-minute description of Brown for the rest of the time. Brown was my contact. I had had a couple of conversations with him before that morning of departure from Legon. I didn't yet know anything about the bureaucracy—how the thing works and who's boss of who and my theory in places like that is, speak to as few people as you can get away with speaking to and use one as a source of information until you find out that's the wrong guy, then get somebody else."

I asked George if he was worried in sending us all off to our assignments. He said:

"The kinds of things I was nervous about—had been nervous about—Pat Kennedy answered most of those questions. That's why I was anxious to get him out in the field; Thornell would have been able to give me that information but Thornell was in the hospital. Pat went out and he was as enthusiastic as a little boy at his first Christmas. He saw enough of these new schools to have a general idea of what they looked like and what was there and what wasn't—what the problems were. Pat was worth a gold mine." [2000]

Pat Kennedy also spoke about these early days. When he returned to PC/Washington, he was like Lincoln Steffens returning from a visit to the Soviet Union in the 1920s, proclaiming, 'I have seen the future and it works':

"I remember going back and reporting at the Senior Staff Meeting. I was the first person back to report about the volunteers in the field. I remember talking about the Lido and the High Life contest and the 'We've come to learn' speech and the song at the airport—I didn't give such a good presentation but the material was so rich and the audience was so thirsty to hear it. You were coming back to people who had worked for five, six months to land a man on the moon in a sense and someone comes back and says, 'Well, I've just come back from the moon and the man is doing quite well.' It was a great feeling." [1997]

Given the complex political environment in which we were expected to be living, we'd been cautioned in training to 'suspend judgment and walk on eggshells' as we settled into our teaching assignments throughout the country. The training faculty had been encouraged to emphasize that outlook in a lengthy cable to PC/ Washington from Richard Thornell in Accra, June 1961. In his message, he wrote:

"The day after Prime Minister Patrice Lumumba of the Congo was killed an American walked into his classroom and was confronted with remarks on the blackboard suggesting that the U.S. and Western powers had conspired to kill Mr. Lumumba. All during the period questions were fired at him asking him to explain American policies in the Congo. (These policies have been roundly condemned by most Ghanaians and particularly the government press here.) … To be respected an American does not have to agree with the Ghanaian on every issue, but must at least be aware of the factors and interests upon which the Ghanaian's viewpoints are based as well as those of his own and his fellow Americans'."

So, we were primed to expect accusations of U.S. complicity in Lumumba's death although we were not given pat responses to use—the training faculty was too sophisticated to do that. We did have separate lectures and discussions on The Congo Crisis, The Cold War in Africa, and American Foreign Policy. Even though I have not encountered any Ghana PCV who was ever asked about Patrice Lumumba's death, The Lumumba Thing is just a reminder that during the period 1961–63, the Cold War was raging and Nkrumah's ideas and actions were constantly being scrutinized by official Americans in Ghana in East–vs.–West terms, seeking hints as to present and future courses of action vis-à-vis the U.S. This led to constant tension and encouraged crisis mentality. George Carter was able to insulate us against most of this. Also, thanks to Ghanaian friendliness and our generally non-political view, we did not become Cold Warriors. If anything we made light of the political ups and downs. A reminder is one of the folk song parodies we sang, in the privacy of our parties, to the tune of "O, Tannenbaum":

Osagyefo, Osagyefo,
Where did the opposition go?
They did not go to Timbuktu,
They're still around and so are you …

Desist

In late March of our first year, we received a notice from the Peace Corps/Ghana office about a special meeting to be held in Accra on April 12: "A set of circumstances have arisen which makes it imperative to assemble the entire Peace Corps group at the earliest possible opportunity." The notice ended: "Please desist from discussing, speculating about or spreading rumors about this meeting."

Well! Talk about an invitation to discussion, speculation, and rumor! We had no idea what was going on. Out of respect for George and from a vague sense that things did happen in Accra about which we knew very little, we muttered amongst ourselves but said little else. I know I took the opportunity to chide George, saying, "Desist? From what? How can we desist when we know absolutely nothing?" Desist did become a useful word and was the closest we ever came to having a

Peace Corps secret code. After this crisis, it was agreed that, if the information in a Peace Corps/Ghana notice had sensitive political ramifications, the word, desist, would appear somewhere in the text. It was used on two occasions during the next twelve months when internal political problems led to curfews, roadblocks and restricted travel.

What led to the calling of the April meeting? In March, skirting protocol, President Nkrumah had called George Carter directly to Flagstaff House for a meeting, an invitation George could not refuse. All George could do was to inform Ambassador Mahoney that he had been summoned by Nkrumah and then go. George had met Kwame Nkrumah once in the mid–'50s on a visit to Accra when Nkrumah was Chief Minister in the pre-independence government under the British. It was a dinner with Bayard Rustin, Nkrumah, and Carter during which the three talked into the early morning hours about the future country and the historical origins of Nkrumah's choice of Ghana as its name. George described the March 1962 meeting:

"When I got in Nkrumah's office, the first thing was to make him remember me and that dinner. And he did. So that immediately changed the flavor of our meeting. We talked about that earlier dinner for a little while. Then he got very serious and said, 'I was not aware that your people were teaching courses other than Science and Math.' I said, 'Yes, I guess I'd become aware of that, Mr. President, but I was not aware of the fact that you did not know this.'

"He gave me no direct orders nor more importantly did he tell me that he was going to take any action. He brought up the History thing, saying that he did not know they were teaching History. He said, 'My understanding was that they were teaching French, Math, and Science. I did not know they were teaching History and Literature.'

"My great fear was that he was going to tell either me or Mahoney, 'Get all of those non-science types out of here.' He didn't. For me that was—uhh, hold your breath once. The next question was, now what was he going to say to Mahoney because it's a little touchy for him as Chief of State, unless he's really angry and wants to go kicking tables over, to give me an order of what to do and what not to do rather than to the Ambassador who is my boss. Never, never that I was aware of did he order me or Mahoney to get the teachers out."

I asked George if Mahoney, who had only recently become Ambassador, was angry about the breach of protocol: "No, no. I had not seen nor made any contact with Nkrumah until the day he called me up there."

"At the meeting Nkrumah made it very clear to me that, 'I want you to keep those kids in line' (he didn't use the word, kids, but that's the thrust of what he was telling me). I don't recall exactly but I had the sense that Nkrumah must have told me that day that he wanted all of the teachers to meet with Dowuona-Hammond, the Minister of Education, to tell them how we want to run our schools."

I asked if Nkrumah ever told George that we were to stop teaching History. George replied: "You were employees of the Ministry of Education. You taught what they told you to teach. It was the Ministry of Education that made these assignments, not me."

So, in early April all of Ghana I reported to Legon. The first night we gathered at George Carter's house, ostensibly for a party. When we were all gathered, the blinds were drawn, the doors closed, and George spoke to us. Most of the group now are hard pressed to recall any of the specifics of the meeting—maybe George's "Desist" message has become embedded in our subconscious. George recalled:

"What I did with you guys was to tell you that the damn thing was hot; that they were concerned about the History, etc. We've got no instructions to do anything except I've been told to keep you guys in line." [2000]

The next day the Minister of Education addressed us. His speech was reported by Peace Corps/Washington, in its Weekly Summary to the President, May 8, 1962:

> Ghana Education Minister Addresses Volunteers
> Reflecting Nkrumah's increasing awareness of Peace Corps presence in Ghana, his Minister of Education addressed the volunteers during their Easter recess. He called the Peace Corps scheme a 'godsend' and 'a bold experiment.' He also admonished the candidates [*sic*] to bring an open mind to Ghana's socialist program (probably responding to party pressure to have the Minister orient the volunteers to the political realities in the country).

That was about it. Dowuona-Hammond didn't threaten or cajole. He was polite and gracious and he did suggest that we be sensitive to Ghana's struggle to realize its destiny through African socialism.

From the minutes of the Peace Corps Director's Staff Meeting, April 26, 1962:

> 1. Report from West Africa (Nan McEvoy): Ghana: political situation very tense. The Volunteers all realize the importance of staying out of domestic controversies and realize that a 'postcard incident' in Ghana would have drastic consequences.

George Carter was on a visit to Washington and reported to the Director's Staff Meeting May 15, 1962:

> 1. Report from Ghana: Mr. Carter stressed that the Peace Corps is doing an excellent job in Ghana but that sensitivities are such that one significant mistake will mean the end of the Peace Corps in Ghana. Our Volunteers know this—but this doesn't change the basic situation.

Our perceptions of the "crisis" were a lot less dramatic, as we commented to Brewster Smith in the interviews in June 1962, following the April meeting.

George Coyne: "It was all very humorous as far as I'm concerned. I didn't see it as quite the dark and complicated crisis that they made it out to be down there in Accra. It just looked like a great deal of cloak and dagger work as far as I am concerned; I didn't take it quite as seriously as they did."

Alice O'Grady: "I thought it was kind of exciting [laughing], you know. The way there was all the tension that was built up. We never had a crisis where we felt that we're so intimately involved in real diplomatic relations and I found it kind of exciting from that point of view. I thought George was very wise in being cautious because there was a lot at stake."

Brewster had commented in his diary about the April meeting:

"G.C.'s taking the group into his confidence at this point may have considerably undercut the feeling, especially voiced by Klein, as to the uselessness of the Accra staff."

In my interview with Brewster I had reflected some of my anti-establishment bias; I still held to my labor unionist values that defined worker-supervisor relations in adversarial terms. I described the "crisis" to Brewster:

"Well, we came together and I believe George and Ray [Parrot, Carter's Deputy] had a sense of crisis about it, which is very hard to explain, but they had it. And they somehow transmitted it to most of the group so there was a certain amount of tension. Then when it turned out that there was no crisis and there was no real cause for worry, well, just complete release.

"You see, I don't know if it was an error of judgment on the part of the staff in Accra or if there was a crisis that somehow disappeared. It's very difficult to say and there's the feeling again of the distance between Wiawso and Accra; as I say, I wish they'd get out of Accra more. It's very annoying when you're going along quite well and everything to suddenly get a letter from down there, saying that, you know, everything is in jeopardy." [1962]

Looking back, I think that I was being every bit as parochial as I accused the staff in Accra of being. When I talked with George Carter about the April crisis, he asked me:

"Why wasn't there more resistance?... I mean you people were being directly attacked; something bad about you, can't let you teach History because you're contaminated. I had no sense of rebellion against me or against what we were doing."

I replied: "We had a strong feeling about Ghana, so I think we were willing to accept that. If we were being attacked, we certainly weren't being attacked where we live which is up at the schools; so that, if anything we could sort of say, 'Well, that's George's problem.' People were puzzled but it wasn't a big shock. They went back to their schools and went ahead and continued to do what they were doing. Nobody said, 'Well, that pretty much knocked it out for me—I wasn't going to put out for Ghana.'" [2000]

Paris or Bust; We Vote with Our Feet

After the April crisis, the next threat to our happy existence as Peace Corps Volunteer teachers in Ghana came from Peace Corps/Washington. It emerged from the ongoing but never resolved question of what was the proper role of a Peace Corps Volunteer working in the developing world. The issue for us centered on "the long vac." Ghanaian secondary schools closed from early July to mid-September for the long vacation, approximately 8 to 10 weeks, during which time teachers were free of any school responsibilities. Through the spring of 1962, we received several notices from George Carter about the Peace Corps' summer vacation policy:

1. Vacation was to be only four weeks.
2. We were expected to engage in worthwhile projects during the rest of the vacation.
3. There was to be no vacation travel back to the U.S. nor to Europe.

We gradually became aware that these policies represented a defeat for George in his struggle to preserve our autonomy and to avoid imposing Peace Corps image-enhancing activities on us. George talked about it:

"[The policy] was the final result of several heavy duty rounds I fought out with Washington and lost on. I was against this—all the other teachers in the system have off; I don't think we should treat our people differently. My concern was this—this is another 'let 'em live in the trees' kind of policy; you guys did not come here to have fun and enjoy life and get to see the continent; you came here as [Peace Corps] missionaries. My attitude was—nonsense—but I flatly lost that battle. The 'soft-headed' guys won that flat out and Shriver bought it. I had to play ball." [2000]

Our group probably split three ways on this but most of the outspoken members were in the oppositional third. They muttered, protested, circulated a petition (never finalized) and went ahead with their European travel plans. The opposite third felt that the policy was sound. People expressed their opinions to Brewster and Rafe.

DeeDee Vellenga: "I feel that I was just lucky to be in Africa and my way paid over to Africa. While I'm here I might as well see as much of Africa as I can. The only reason I would have wanted a longer vacation would have been to go to Europe and that, right now, to me seems sort of foolish. Once you are here in Africa—you're probably not going to come back to Africa to see Africa—the chances are you'd have more opportunity to go to Europe.... [My project] is working with the community development program up in Ashanti, stationed at a rural training center about 36 miles from Kumasi."

Alice O'Grady: "I think the policy is fine. It would be nice to have a two months' holiday but I certainly think that if we could get something useful done—I'm more pragmatic—I guess, I say, 'Well, let's try it and see if we turn up anything useful during our project month.' I think it's a very good thing."

Bob Krisko: "I thought that we should only get thirty days, because when I signed the contract it said thirty days.... We get this vacation at Easter, we got a vacation at Christmas; we're living in luxury. Why should anybody gripe about not being able to spend two months."

The "Paris or Bust" point of view was fully and a bit over-dramatically expressed by Newell Flather, though there were many who agreed with him:

"Well, I'm still deliberating whether to write Shriver and tell him what I'd like to do with my summer; explain to him that when they say, 'Do something to benefit your community'—really, if I walk in to Winneba and start building a dam or a sewer, I'd be on my way home for sure. My community is my school. If they ask me what I can do to help my community, I'll say, 'I've done a good hard year's work and I think that's quite a bit and I plan to do another one.' Over the summer there is a lot I can do to make my second year a better one. I think the best way is to do something that would capture my enthusiasm, such as a trip to France to study in a French university.... I may get caught, I may be yanked out of the ball game but I think I'm going to take those extra two weeks to make sure I get a good course in France." [1962]

Newell did and they didn't.

I went to Europe and Israel to see my mother and sister, whom I had not seen since the death of my father at the end of 1961. George Carter gave me a sort of 'papal dispensation' for the trip since I had not taken the opportunity the Peace Corps offered to go home for three weeks in December. Some of the group traveled with parents, starting with a visit to Ghana. Many traveled in West Africa, with a few making it as far as fabled Timbuktu—the fables ain't true and getting there is an achievement more to be celebrated than experienced. I commented to George Carter about that summer and the travel policy:

"People worked it out—their disagreement with you—by going to Europe and saying, 'Hey, let him deal with it.' That's kind of appropriate—it's a nice reflection of the relationship, I think. You trusted us to do a job and we trusted you to deal with what wasn't a terribly complicated issue. It didn't affect our role as volunteers; it didn't affect the work we were doing.... People said, 'I went; I'm coming back; I'm going to do my job; I'm going to be as good a volunteer second year as first, probably even better. Let George explain to Shriver what we were doing running all around Europe.' We trusted you to take care of it in the long run. I don't think anyone chose to challenge Washington—it was unthinkable—that's George's job. It also means we had come to accept the role you were playing—whether we accepted every policy you put out is another matter. You were the man on the spot as far as the shape and direction of Peace Corps in Ghana." [2000]

Sal Tedesco came to Ghana at the start of our second year to become George Carter's Deputy. Sal had been City Manager of Santa Cruz, California, and after a brief stint in Ghana, went on to direct the Peace Corps program in Somalia. He is a craggy-faced, warm and friendly person, a good coach who advised and supported us with open ear and gentle persuasion. When I spoke to him, he had vivid memories of coming to work for George Carter. During Sal's orientation in Washington, he had heard horror stories about ill-conceived and ill-managed Peace Corps projects but Ghana and George Carter had unique reputations:

"The Ghana program was so well structured and organized. The government of Ghana played a very important role. It was more than a partner. The government controlled things like placement [and paid us]. One thing I remember distinctly and this is the George Carter touch. I remember George in dark suit and tie—no one else was wearing a dark suit and tie—stepping into the Peace Corps car and going to the Ministry. He knew exactly how to wheel and deal—he'd get right in and see the Permanent Secretary or the Minister of Education. That made a tremendous difference. If someone had stayed with the presumed Peace Corps image and had shown up wearing a pair of dungarees and saying, 'Hi, I'm the American Peace Corps,' he'd have been shown the door.

"The Peace Corps pretty much left him alone because it was George's program and it was a success." [2002]

9

THE SECOND YEAR

Changes

Changes occurred as we began our second year of service in Ghana. The program expanded with the arrival of Ghana II in September; it was a second contingent of teachers (Math, Science, French, English, no History). The project now totaled 114 Peace Corps Volunteers. Within our group, Carol and Roger Hamilton had been married the first Christmas and by June Carol was pregnant. Although they wanted to continue teaching at Half Assini, George Carter, with Washington's concurrence, decided that it would be prudent to ask them to return to the U.S., given the isolation and lack of medical services in the area where they were assigned. Sue Hastings had married Sam Bryson, a British employee of Texaco in Kumasi, and had moved off the school compound at Yaa Asantewaa into company-provided housing in town. Sue wanted to continue teaching as a Peace Corps Volunteer but was not allowed to. She was forced to resign from the Peace Corps because her new living conditions did not seem appropriate to volunteer service, according to those who were more conscious of appearance than substance. Sue continued teaching at Yaa Asantewaa for a second year. Lucy Carmichael had married Tom Miller, an African American Institute contract teacher whose tour ended in July 1962. She left Ghana after her first year.

There were transfers. Bob Krisko, who had wanted a more remote and challenging assignment, was sent to Pusiga Training College, far, far away in the northeast corner of Ghana, near the border with Upper Volta and Togo. Jim Kelly and John Demos were assigned to Adisadel in Cape Coast, one of the prestige secondary schools, ranked among the top ten in the country. Now that we had established our reliability (or viability?) as teachers within the Ghanaian system, George Carter wanted to go a step further and demonstrate that our academic credentials were legitimate enough to meet the standards of the best of Ghana's schools. John and Jim filled the bill and each was replaced at their original schools by a Ghana II teacher.

Dave Hutchinson was transferred to Sefwi-Wiawso Secondary School. I was less than enthused. I knew Dave only casually, having had some contact with him in Tarkwa where he was assigned the first year; I had heard that he had had some personality conflicts with the Headmaster. Dave was an intense, but immature, young man who had the chunky, bull-necked build of a college wrestler. He was a graduate of Berea College in Kentucky, self-reliant, eager to do well but not always knowing how to do so, not responsive to supervision or suggestion. When I heard of the transfer, I went immediately to George to complain. Being possessive about SWSS, what I wanted, going into the second year, was for a Ghana II Science teacher, preferably female, to be assigned. Such a person could provide some continuity of Peace Corps presence at the school beyond my second year. We desperately needed a Science Master (and the equipment that would accompany a Peace Corps teacher), and I felt there was a need for a female staff member to be working with the girls, who were a distinct and unrepresented minority within the student body. In light of this, I said to George, "Why send Dave to SWSS?" He answered, "Well, I think it would be good for him to be assigned with a mature volunteer such as you." My only response was, "Hey, what about me?" End of discussion.

SWSS—The Second Year

At SWSS Dave Hutchinson taught French and was considered a stern disciplinarian by the students. He took on additional duties, primarily leading student crews in beautifying the campus with various plantings and shrubs, and he took over one of the adult ed classes in Bibiani, teaching Political Science. We shared a house but related to each other tentatively. My main problem with Dave was that he was the world's worst driver and we shared the one assigned vehicle. Ghanaians generally were tolerant of poor driving; poorly maintained vehicles and roads, absence of police supervision, inadequate training, all of which led to a steady stream of highway mishaps. People depended on whatever transportation they could get access to. However, after several outings with Dave, Adu, the very soul of tolerance and understanding, refused to drive with him for fear of his life. Each time Dave left in the Jeep for his Bibiani lecture or to visit friends in Tarkwa, I said a quiet prayer. Dave never received an injury more serious than a bruised knee and a mild cut on the forehead and the Jeep, true to its military origins, kept running with dented fenders, misaligned wheels, and assorted nicks and scratches. This situation was not the basis for a deep and lasting friendship between Dave and me but, like the Jeep, we survived.

My second year at SWSS was a continuation of the teaching and projects of the first year. Things felt familiar. I wrote home early that year:

"I really feel at home—the old banana man just came out of the bush with a full stalk of them on his head. I introduced Dave, my roommate, as my new cook-steward; poor banana man is confused."

There were other familiar things as well. In her travels in Europe, my mother the matchmaker had met a family, the Gellers, who were close friends of Meryl Blau's parents. Mom asked if I knew Meryl and if we "socialized." I wrote:

"Yes, I know Meryl Blau very well; she's teaching in Cape Coast and traveled to Israel during the holiday with her folks. Our dates were different, so I didn't see her there. She's a real fine gal, but, as yet, I haven't asked her to marry me." (In Cape Coast, Meryl met the man who was to become her husband, Raman Menon, a fellow teacher at Ghana National College. Besides, Cape Coast was many dusty and rutted road miles from Wiawso.)

Even with the addition of a roommate, living conditions were still quite modest— sporadic electricity, water hauled from the nearby creek, bare bones furnishings— but it was of little consequence. In his 1963 trip diary, Brewster commented on his visit to Sefwi:

"Found Bob Klein in the same squalor [I think that's a bit harsh] as a year ago. Still no running water, still the appearance of camping rather than living in the bungalow."

My involvements on the school compound and in Bekwai and Asawinso adult ed classes were still fulfilling. The only dark cloud was an escalating controversy over the Bursar that was complicated by the internecine struggle between the Sefwihene (the Sefwi Paramount Chief) and the Sefwi Member of Parliament (W. K. Aduhene). The bright spots were a deepening friendship with Adu, my ever-present companion on school excursions and adult ed nights, as well as a growing avuncular relation with three of the students—Barnabas, Bennie, and Grace. My most offbeat school duty was that of Girls' Sports Mistress. I had felt that the girls tended to get short shrift at the school and tried several approaches to getting them more involved. Sports was one area; the school newspaper and the library were others, as well as including them on a school excursion to the north (thanks to Laura Damon serving as girls' chaperone).

I was one of the six Ghana I volunteers that George Carter had picked to participate in the orientation of Ghana II in early September 1962. The new group was housed at Legon for about a week; their schedule, arranged by the Ministry of Education, included occasional brief lectures and extensive day trips by tour bus through southern Ghana—the usual suspects: the Volta Dam Site, Tema Harbor, Makola Market in Accra, Elmina Castle and Cape Coast. The six of us—Jack Lord, Peter Dybwad, Marion Morrison, Alice O'Grady, Jim Kelly, and myself—served as guides and guardians against some of the culture shock, answering the newcomers' questions and informally discussing with them what to expect at assigned schools and in teaching. Having been exposed in training at Berkeley to semi-mythic stories about the sterling qualities of Ghana I, Ghana II was reassured to discover that we were neither paragons nor SuperVols, but, like themselves, curious and somewhat committed adventurers, no more nor less competent than they were.

The participation in the orientation reinforced my growing interest in working as field staff in Ghana for the Peace Corps once my volunteer service was completed in July. I liked the idea because it would give me an opportunity to continue to live in Ghana and to work at a supervisory level that I felt well suited me. On September 18, 1962, I wrote home:

"Carter was very pleased with my part in the orientation and is trying to get me into an administrative position. It seems fairly certain now that at the end of my PCV service I'll be taking a field position with the Peace Corps."

And on November 7, 1962: "Carter and I had a very long discussion about the Peace Corps, myself, and my future with Peace Corps. Knowing my interest in staying on, Carter told me that he had been contacting the Peace Corps/Washington office about me, with very strong recommendations to be employed as field officer."

And, by January 22, 1963: "Carter very much wants me to stay on in Ghana as a field officer. He's going to Washington this month and that will be one of the topics he'll discuss with Sarge [now that I'm almost part of the Peace Corps staff family, I call him 'Sarge']. I want to be assured, before I sign a contract, that I'll definitely be getting a field position and not an office, administrative job."

At SWSS my favorite project was the mural map of Ghana. Throughout the first year, I had often looked at the bare three-story end wall of the classroom block, painted a fading pale yellow. It was one of four sides of the inner school compound. The second side was the dining-assembly hall; opposite was the back of the administration block; the fourth side was the two-story science block, a pale sickly pink. One day the thought popped into my mind—bare wall = mural; mural = map; map = Ghana (to be topped with the flag of Ghana). With no artistic training and scant knowledge of cartography, what then? It seemed easy enough to get a good map of Ghana and draw a grid on it, 10 squares by 15. Next, build a scaffold next to the wall, draw an enlarged grid on the wall 10 x 15, and transfer map data grid-square by grid-square. It worked and because I was figuring it out as I went along with the advice and cooperation of a work crew of eight students, it was a real learning experience for all of us and a great opportunity to explore the English language in a practical context. By January 20, 1963, I wrote home:

"The Ghana map work is progressing steadily. Every student that stops to watch the work is now insisting that we include his town or village on the map. Every day now the Headmaster comes out to admire the wall. As soon as the school can purchase lumber for a new scaffold, we are going to begin work on another mural map. This one will be of Africa."

Our delight with the appearance of the Ghana map and a growing sense of artistic power led us to a very ambitious proposal for the science block wall. It was to be not just an outline map of Africa with country boundaries and capitals shown; the map was to be framed on both sides by the flags of each country in full color AND in a specially outlined section at the base of the map was to be printed: "The independence of Ghana is meaningless unless it is linked up with the total liberation of the continent of Africa. Osagyefo, Dr. Kwame Nkrumah." How's that for ambitious?

What I liked about the various projects we had at SWSS was that each gave me an opportunity for personal, informal involvement with many of the students. The map crew was one group; the librarians another; so too, the newspaper staff; and, of course, the girls' sports teams. In each I was learning how to do something and there was a group of students with whom I could share the process. Although I had spent many hours in libraries, I had never been a librarian or library aide. Schools and family friends in the U.S. kept sending me books. So, what do you need to start a library? Books, bookcases, a card catalog, lots of 3 x 5 index cards, a date stamp, and librarians; plus some chairs, some maps and pictures on the wall, and whatever magazines you can find. The Headmaster placed the library in an unused room on the second floor of the administration block and had the school carpenter build us some bookcases and chairs. The October, 1962 edition of the school newspaper had an article with the headline, "What A Tremendous Gift" and went on:

> On June 28, the Headmaster received a letter from the Principal of Harriet Beecher Stowe Junior High School in the United States. The letter contained a cheque for $185, which amounts to 65 pounds in Ghanaian currency.... In his letter to our Headmaster, the Principal tells what happened—'An entertainment was planned to raise funds. This proved to be a success, not only from the financial point of view, but also because it enabled us to learn about life in Ghana and the work of the Peace Corps. This cheque is presented in the spirit of friendship and cooperation that is based on the common interest that all students and educators share.'

Behind that letter and check was a story that I shared with Brewster in our interview:

"My old school is having a teacher-student show ... they hope to collect about two hundred dollars which they are going to forward to me and the money will be used for the school library to buy books. It's a controversy—an old division in the staff. The argument is that the money should be used for some worthwhile project in Harlem where it's needed and let the State Department worry about Ghana.... It was decided that the money would be divided equally, half would go here and half would stay at the school for a neighborhood project." [1962]

I reported home in November: "SWSS may be able to reach its goal of 1000 books in the library by July. The new library has been a rousing success—we now have a corps of 3 Librarians-In-Charge, 8 Librarians, and 8 Librarians-In-Training."

Adu was very much part of my life at SWSS, a wonderful informant about all matters Sefwi, a professional colleague, a drinking buddy, and a good neighbor. One weekend when Dave and I had traveled, Alice O'Grady showed up at SWSS, unannounced, for a friendly visit. Without any hesitation, Adu took over the role of host, provided meals and accommodations, and introduced Alice to the social life of the bars in Wiawso. Comfortable wearing African dress and going to local bars, Alice cut quite a swath with Adu's friends and with the peripatetic beer-drinking population of the small town of Wiawso.

One of the word games we played was initiated by Adu, who loved to play with languages (Sefwi, Twi, French, English, and a smattering of Latin). He would pick up on a phrase he had read in the paper or heard on radio and construct elaborate stories that would always end with that phrase as the tag line. The only such phrase I can remember was from a news article about a discredited Ghanaian political figure which ended with, "And rendered him impotent and ineffective." I could feel the laughter bubbling up inside me, as Adu would tell a story, even in Twi (bits of which I could understand) and end dramatically in precisely enunciated English with, "And it rendered him im-po-tent and in-e-ffective." It helps to be on the second round of beers.

On our excursion to northern Ghana, we had planned a day trip, in-and-out, to

Ouagadougou in Upper Volta. Returning in the late afternoon, we got lost and did not get back to the Upper Volta border checkpoint until after dark, when it had closed. Adu jumped out of the lorry and immediately engaged the border guards in an extended discussion in French about the poor students on the lorry who were hungry and trying to get to Navrongo Secondary School to rest and eat before our hosts ate up all the food. We were permitted to exit and Adu repeated the performance at the Ghana side of the border in a mixture of Twi and English, managing to get the otherwise unresponsive guards smiling and laughing and even forgetting to ask us for a bribe. We got to Navrongo Secondary School in time to eat.

Adu also encouraged me to become mentor to several of the students he knew well who were from the Juaboso area of Sefwi (the westernmost area next to the Ivory Coast border). It was the same role that he was playing with several "nephews and nieces" (not same family but same village or traditional area, often referred to as trans-Tano, the part of Sefwi west of the Tano River). So it did not feel at all awkward as I began to befriend Barnabas, Bennie, and Grace, and help them with school fees.

In our interview, Kwaku (who was then Barnabas) spoke about my "Ghanaian" family:

"It came together beginning from the second year when Grace had been sent out [for fees]. I remember you and I and Gabriel talking about it—when Bennie was sent out the first year, you had 'adopted' him. You were going to pay his fees and he was going to become a day student, living at your house in the steward's quarters. And you did so. But Grace could not do that because she's a female. So we talked about it and I told you her situation. You made the decision that Grace should come back to campus and you would pay the half of her fees not paid by the Cocoa Marketing Board scholarship.

"Prior to that I used to come to your house on Saturdays and then we were doing the newspaper and several of us were learning to use the typewriter. Bennie and I traveled together on excursions and other trips. Then Grace became part of that. I think the first holiday in the second year we traveled together to Sunyani or Dormaa. We could come down to your house and go quite freely; we were beginning to be your nephews and niece.

"Grace was smart, the only girl in IA. At Middle School, she was wonderful, always among the first three. Of all the women—we started with eleven—we ended up at 'O' levels with only three. On the exam she did better than the two others. With Grace, it was sad that it was in Ghana—she had these constant painful headaches—because if it was here [the U.S.] it would have been diagnosed properly. She probably would have done much better—the headaches had to do with her eyes [she was half convinced that she had been bewitched by a jealous aunt]. It only appeared when she was studying—it was later that I realized it may have been her eyes. Now she wears glasses and the headaches are gone." [1999]

From the second year's teaching I have only two artifacts. Both were sources of amusement at the time and were the kinds of errors that made it easy for me to open the door to corrections with humor and gentle persuasion. The first is a list of answers students gave on a Shakespeare exam:

"He was shot by Hamlet's sword."

"Edmund—he appears on the last page of Shakespeare."

"Macduff killed Macbeth because he was not born actually."

"The contract between Shylock and Antonio was that they were unfriendly."

The second selection, to me, is so perfect that I never could bring myself to correct it—it is sheer poetry. It was submitted by Francis Kwayie to the SWSS Journal:

> The hunter with the bravely heart shot the lion. It roared with a terrible cry and mounted to the hunter and devoured him into pieces. In fact it was a sad sight to see the blood soaking into his hunting coat and dropping from his side and flowing on the ground here and there. In fact it was awful to see a human being scattered on the ground like this cruel animal had done.

My work as Girls' Sports Mistress introduced me to games I had never heard of—netball and rounders. Netball seemed to me like basketball before they had agreed to a consistent set of rules; rounders was a combination of cricket, kickball and baseball. However, volleyball became the most popular sport because the rules were simple and to make a "pitch" for the game was relatively easy once we had acquired a net and some tall bamboo. But my finest hour came with track and field (about which I knew even less than netball and rounders), thanks to a robust young lady, Nancy Boateng. I trained her in the javelin; to wit: "Pick up the darn thing, run a few steps, and fling it with all your might." We were to compete in a regional meet with five other schools, all of which had been established years before SWSS.

The meet was reported in the school newspaper:

> The games began on Friday; SWSS competitors were nowhere. We were down completely at all levels, both boys and girls. This was a good attempt for a young school like ours. How can we withstand our uncles and fathers from Bogoso Training College? At one point we nearly withdrew from the games. Mr. Klein, who took an active part in our few days there, encouraged us to go on. We would have lost our sole cup if we had withdrawn.... Not despairing, we did our best and, as a result, Nancy Boateng won a trophy for first in the Javelin Throw. In fact, I can not describe our joy. We are very proud of that trophy.

All Politics Is Local (So Maybe George Carter Won't Hear About It)

One of the aspects of being a Peace Corps Volunteer for a two-year tour is the limited scope of your influence once you leave. Although you may perform at an excellent level during your assignment, whatever your achievements and influence, they become hostage to other forces and people the instant you depart. This should and often does lead to caution against getting involved in local struggles which have deep-seated roots and which may play out on a time scale measured in decades not months. Also, as an invited guest, it could be considered proper to withhold judgment as well as comment. I ignored all of this when it came to the struggle with the Bursar, partly because of my strong feeling about SWSS and even more so because of my friendship with Adu.

I briefly described the background of this struggle to Brewster:

"Our member of parliament has been barred from coming into Sefwi even though this is his constituency because last year he misappropriated—you may remember my talking about it last year—something up to £G40,000. He's a strong person and still wants to keep control in the district and this is his school as far as he's concerned. The paramount chief's people have said that if he comes here, he'll be killed. But he's still the M.P. and he's been trying to run the school from Accra without a good intimate knowledge of what's going on. He runs the school through the Board of Governors which is made up of people on his side."

About the Bursar, first in a letter home: "The Bursar's a very petty person and has tried to use his position to threaten and intimidate students, disciplining them without our knowledge, playing favorites, and more.... The Headmaster, with our support, called the Bursar to appear and we were present to support the Headmaster. The Bursar was drunk and abusive."

In talking to Brewster: "The masters would give orders and then later the Bursar would rescind them. He would get drunk and walk into the dining hall and shout at students who hadn't paid their fees. He would try to withhold food from students. Most of the members of the staff agreed that this was serious and he should go. The Headmaster began to take action to move him off the compound. The Bursar immediately left the school and went down to the M.P. with a long story about the Headmaster being on the paramount's side and accusing Adu of fomenting the trouble.

"There was a Board of Governors meeting in Accra. The Headmaster attended and I went as Secretary of the Board and also the Headmaster asked if I would be there to back him up on the charges. Just about everything had been agreed to in advance by the M.P. and the Board (which I did not know). The Bursar was there and we questioned him and he denied everything and I lost my temper. The Bursar was sent away and the Board came up with a very elaborate plan that the Bursar would not be sacked but the M.P. would monitor his behavior and decide if he should be sent away. At this point I stood up and told the Board that, if they were not going to take action against the Bursar, I had to withdraw from the meeting. The M.P. immediately said, 'Wait; let's have an adjournment for five minutes.' He took me aside and said, 'Don't worry. It's all been worked out. We're just doing this so we can get him to go back to the school, finish the accounts, the books, and then he's going to be sacked.' I really felt like a fool with egg all over my face."

They took up Adu's case and the M.P. was saying that he had been causing trouble and would be sacked from the school and immediately sent away. I continued with Brewster:

"I again spoke up and said, 'Look, he came there when the school opened. He's from Sefwi. He's worked hard. He's as much part of the school as anyone and it doesn't seem reasonable to send him away.' So the M.P. considered this and said, 'Well, all right. But he must move off the compound. He may stay as a teacher." [1963]

The longer the meeting went on, the more tangled the issues and actions became. I left saddened and confused and feeling powerless to do anything further in the situation. For the rest of my time at SWSS, the Bursar was still around and Adu continued to live on the compound.

However, there must be some kind of cosmic justice in the world. Soon after I left SWSS and returned to the U.S., I had a letter from Barnabas:

"Friday, July 5th the M.P. came to the school. On his departure he told the Bursar to leave the compound before six o'clock that day. Very unfortunately for him, it was raining very heavily and he had arranged no truck. All of his belongings were taken out of his rooms. I wish you had seen him walking to and fro on the compound. He was asked to pay £G10 for the school truck. He did reluctantly and packed in the rain. He left before the last stroke of five."

Not Quite Ready to Leave

In her interview with Rafe Ezekiel in June of the second year, DeeDee talked about coming to the end of her Peace Corps Volunteer service in Ghana:

"I sort of feel [it's] one place where I'm not quite ready to leave.... Other places where I've been, college, Foxcroft, I've been ready to leave but I don't quite feel that way about here, about having been here, or about Africa in general. I'm just not quite ready to leave." [1963]

That sentiment was probably shared by a good number of Ghana I. Four or five people wanted to do a third year of teaching but the Peace Corps policy then did not allow it—volunteer service was not to be a career and two years was the tour of duty. For some the second year was the payoff. As Jack Lord said, "You get better at teaching the more that you do. I had a much better idea of how to teach than I had back at the beginning." Newell Flather described it: "It took me a full year to leave America and enter Ghana. It's like flying, breaking the sound barrier, and once you're on the other side, you're there." Not everyone felt that way. One of the group commented, "It just got to the point where I said, 'I just have to get through this next year.'" And Carol Waymire, living through a difficult school situation, kiddingly told George Carter that when she returned to the U.S. she was planning to join the John Birch Society. If things really got bad, we had a running joke about our safety valve—Pan Am had a flight that left Accra 9:15 a.m. Sunday morning and arrived in New York City by 6:00 p.m. (New York time) that evening—instant escape.

By the second year people had made peace with the issue of the proper role of a PCV teaching in Ghana. With a year's experience behind us, we knew how we were behaving and what we were comfortable with. We were a diverse lot in our social and personal responses to the environments in which we worked. However, overwhelmingly, we saw our roles primarily as teachers and the rest was a matter of choice and preference. An occasional newsletter from Peace Corps/Washington that emphasized "image" and the primacy of "meeting people" might tweak our consciences, but we had made our individual adjustments.

In his second-year interview with Brewster, Bob Krisko talked about this somewhat philosophically:

"Well, [Ghanaians] are just like people anywhere. I like some of them and I don't like others. You meet phony people everywhere that you don't like. Other people are very natural. I hitchhiked today with a fellow. I thought he was a nice guy. The fellow next door I don't particularly care for."

Brewster asked how PCVs 'ought' to relate to Ghanaians and Bob replied:

"Just like any other friend. I don't think you should go out of your way. I think you should be natural; I mean, if you like the person, you just treat him as you would anybody else at home—not to force it, because a forced relationship is kind of strained. They might feel it and then they wouldn't respect it."

Bob Krisko is basketball-player tall, reticent in manner, very bright, and perpetrator of the humorous aside. The second year he was assigned to Pusiga Training College, located in a remote corner of Northern Ghana in the hot and dry savanna grasslands. He taught only 21 periods a week, had few extracurricular opportunities, and in the constant heat of the region struggled with lassitude. He said: "It seems strange having so much time.... You lose your interest. I've read somewhere that when the temperature gets about 80 degrees people tend to become lackadaisical. I've found that's very true. I don't feel like doing anything—just reading something where I don't have to think. I find I tend to read escapist literature—mysteries, science fiction."

Bob traveled to see the PCVs at Navrongo and even went into northern Togo to visit a pair of volunteers stationed there. Ever curious, he sought out people, Ghanaian and expatriate, who could lead him to areas where game might be seen—lions, antelope, baboons, elephant. He was keenly aware of the physical environment of the savanna, writing home about it:

"It's nice to think that I have less than two months to go. I get a little nostalgic, at times, when I go out in the evening and gaze out over the surrounding plains. There is a freshness that isn't found in the city; it is just so unspoiled. I don't know if I ever will enjoy a pure city life again; somehow living close to nature one comes to appreciate it much more than the artificiality of the urban environment.... There is that atmosphere of Africa that lends added enchantment." [1963]

However, enchantment has its limits and Bob sustained himself through this second year with thinking about, planning, studying brochures, and writing to his family about his intended purchase of a Jaguar XKE automobile on his way home from Ghana. In letters home to his parents, Bob wrote lovingly about the soon-to-be-realized fantasy. Unlike some of his Ghana I peers, Bob was quite ready to leave when July came. Writing in late July from England, Bob related: "I got the train and reached Coventry at 3:30 and was grinning from ear to ear by 5 o'clock. The car is everything I always hoped for."

Newell Flather's second year was filled with highs and lows, fueled by self-doubt and periodic outrage at indifferent colleagues and callous students, but tempered by growing personal maturity and a more sophisticated understanding of his role at Winneba Secondary School. Many other Ghana I's went through similar experiences, but Newell, in his contemporary Brewster Smith interviews and in our oral history 'conversations' in 2000, was and is very articulate. He is willing to relive the ups and downs, without being driven by the need to make alibis. The Brewster interviews present an informative contrast to my interviews with Newell and illustrate the sentimental character of oral history (at least as practiced by this author).

Winneba's School Certificate Exam results from 1962 were dismal, the lowest scores in the entire country. At the same time, the school was relocated to a newly constructed compound on the edge of Winneba (provided by the G.E.T.), potentially a much sounder educational environment than the old location in an abandoned warehouse in the middle of the crowded center of town. The Headmaster and staff were trying to improve student discipline and performance. The students, in turn, were resistant to enforcement of stricter regulations such as longer study hours and fewer privileges. In 1963 Newell was troubled about his second year. He related incidents where his good intentions had unsettling and unexpected consequences, even going so far as to say to Brewster:

"Coming to Ghana, I have found that I have a very unique ability for making enemies; well, I've been slapped in the face by the wife of the Englishman on the staff because somehow I had insulted her. She felt I had done something to her husband. I took some students to the (European) club pool and taught them how to swim. The Club Director thought that her husband was to blame for this.

"One night I invited some African members of staff to dinner, and a few students. They were very insulted to have been invited to the same dinner with students— that is not done. They were also very insulted that I had taken students swimming."

Then Newell added: "If I was really going to accomplish something here, I should stay for five or ten years. I did feel, even throughout this low period, that I was making contact with a few very good students. Last year I realized things weren't so good here but when I first came I felt that perhaps they weren't so good because they'd never had an enthusiastic and interested teacher. I was quite sure that a remedy to the situation would be an enthusiastic and interested teacher who was willing to devote all his time to the problem.... I found that devotion wasn't the solution." [1963]

After thirty-seven years our memories acquire a patina of nostalgia. Like many others I interviewed, when Newell spoke in 2000, the story is softer and gentler. He recalled some of his achievements during his two years at Winneba: the establishment of a 5000-volume library; a school production of the musical, "The King and I," the introduction of the African History syllabus to the school curriculum; a nurturing relationship with one particular student, Margaret Quist-Therson; a stimulating friendship with a carpenter on Ghana Railways, Kofi Hagen, who was a self-educated literacy advocate and a devout nationalist. Newell had returned to Ghana in 1999 at the invitation of some of his former students to join in the celebration of the fiftieth anniversary of the founding of Winneba Secondary School. The sentimental glow of that visit illuminated our interview almost a year later. Newell spoke about it:

"On the last night of my 1999 visit we all gathered on a rooftop [verandah]— maybe fifteen, eighteen former students, spouses, some kids. One of the students who was a First Former when I was there—he's now a High Court Justice—was with his young wife; she was being very polite and pleasant to these older women [the Margarets]. They began to sing from 'The King and I'—the judge's wife was astounded. I was in tears."

The Margarets: "I was teaching Third Form first year. I remember there were three students. As I started heading toward the classroom, I would see these three girls running to the room. Boys tended to dominate discussions and sort of put down the girls. I remember these three were not to be put down. They banded together and were known as the Three Margarets ... incredibly energetic, very enthusiastic, very bright. A student-teacher friendship developed and I came to think of Margaret [Quist-Therson] as a special member of that special group."

In 1962 Margaret Quist-Therson had become Galatea to Newell's Pygmalion—every teacher's fantasy. However, Newell's inborn sense of propriety kept the relationship within proper bounds. Margaret stood out as an articulate, eager learner, warm and friendly. Newell responded to that and an unconventional intimacy grew between them [they are still friends]. When others in the class began to spread unfair rumors of favoritism and perhaps more, Newell settled the problem by helping Margaret to gain admission to Achimota, one of the top-ranked secondary schools in Ghana.

More astounding to me was the fact that Newell took an advocate's role in the second year in introducing and teaching the West African Exams Council syllabus in African History, with the active support of the Headmaster. I think to myself, "Did George Carter know about this? More important, did Kwame Nkrumah know?" But Newell's enthusiasm and self-confidence carried the day and also led him into involvement with Louie Williams and "The King and I." Louie was an African American Institute contract teacher with a background in theater:

"That was more obsessive than any library project—it was Louie's idea. Looking back at the politics of the time, 'The King and I' was quite risky—the story of how a colonial came to a developing country and defies an imperious leader. It was Louie's show and Louie was the genius behind it but it was very useful for him to have me as a worker bee who was as passionate about it as he was." [2000]

The performers were mostly students and the audience was the rest of the student body plus all those whom Newell was able to cajole into attending—the Minister of Arts and Culture, Ghanaian friends from the University and Winneba Training College, some of the American Embassy people, and fellow Peace Corps Volunteers. They were all rewarded with a very polished performance; such a dramatic musical presentation was unique at the time among all the schools in Ghana. "The King and I" helped to boost student morale and pride in the school. And, although there is absolutely no cause-and-effect evidence, the School Certificate Exam results improved greatly the second year from 38th to 15th in the country. Newell and Louie, Anna and The King, Rodgers and Hammerstein, the 5000-book library, the African History course—all can claim some credit.

All Days Are Not Equal

There were hazards associated with teaching in Ghana—illness and accidents but, fortunately, no fatalities. People in the group contracted malaria, hepatitis, dysentery, as well as flu and the common cold. Urban, bush, or in between, the occurrences were not predictable. The same was true of vehicle accidents; the risk was the same whether in a PCV-driven Jeep, as passenger in a lorry or taxi, or in a friend's private car. The injuries and illnesses were curable with medication and occasional hospitalization so they were less devastating than school strikes and riots (and struggles with thieving Bursars), which undermined the very ground on which we stood—the schools and classrooms. The causes of the student protests were often not easily understood but the immediate effects were obvious. Brewster had written about these issues in his travel diary:

"… [problems] must be seen in the general context of Ghanaian secondary education of the time, in which a mixture of authoritarianism and chaos raised serious disciplinary crises in many schools, which American Peace Corps volunteers were by background and personal inclination likely to be ill equipped to handle."

On a few occasions the protests became inadvertently personal. The resilient but sensitive Alice O'Grady experienced one such incident that happened late in the second term of her first year at Dormaa Ahenkro Secondary School. It was still fresh in her memory when she was interviewed by Brewster:

"The students rioted a few months ago and broke the windows of the Headmaster's office and refused to go to their classes. They really upset the whole school routine for a number of weeks right through term examinations. As a result of this twenty-one boys were sacked from the school and we decided that something needed to be done to teach the boys discipline so this wouldn't happen again."

What was done was to establish an elaborate disciplinary system that listed demerits given and punishments meted out, with each student having a personal record. Alice became the reluctant secretary and record keeper as the new system was imposed on the students:

"… the boys were ready to believe anything … I'm the one who signs the summons to come to punishment, I sign the summons to appear at a disciplinary committee meeting, I have been announcing suspensions, of which there have been many this term, to the whole school in assembly hall—their assumption is that I am the one who is responsible for all this strict discipline … so they really, a lot of them, do think that I am the ogre and on occasion they have treated me with a lot of disrespect and made life miserable for me.

"One day I had the job of supervising punishment … a large group of 25 to 30, I think. I hadn't been feeling well, had been too busy, and was short-tempered. I had to keep after them and tell them to keep working, shouting, 'You there, stop loafing around and get to work.' I noticed that clumps of dirt kept flying and hitting me—they weed with cutlasses [machetes] and if it hits the ground sometimes dirt flies. At first I thought it was accidental and then there was so much of it that I knew they were doing it on purpose but I just ignored it. I sent some boys to weed near the cinder track … so stones were really flying in my direction … and on purpose. I really got angry, so I made a remark about why don't they stand and throw stones at me.

"They all looked up and looked innocent … somebody started making a noise, a hissing noise. I turned around and saw this sea of faces and knew how futile it was to try to find out who did it and I just broke down, started crying, and walked away."

Alice said that the stoning incident made her want to leave the school, immediately, and not teach there any longer. However, living in the bush has some advantages; some simple, and unexpected, amenities can brighten the darkest mood. Alice continued:

"That evening I went over to Asante's house [another teacher at Dormaa]. I didn't come home to my house; but he wasn't there. I just stayed there and cried for a while. Then Asante came home. He was driving me to my house and I was telling him my troubles. We got here and I still didn't know what I was going to do.

"We had never had electricity here before and, just as we arrived, for the first time—they had just completed the wiring—the lights went on and it was a beautiful sight. It was so wonderful that I completely forgot all my problems, pulled some beer out of the kerosene fridge and we had a little impromptu party.... The fact that I could come out of it so easily showed me the way that this really wasn't the end of the world and so the next morning I decided I certainly wasn't going to leave." [1962]

In spite of a series of illnesses, Alice continued her teaching the second year and enjoyed it well enough to consider staying a third year but Peace Corps policy prevented that. What happened to the school discipline system? In her second interview with Brewster, Alice said:

"It's fallen apart almost completely this year. We tend to handle discipline problems individually." [1963]

There were no further strikes, riots or 'stoning' incidents at Dormaa-Ahenkro.

John Buchanan and Mike Shea went through two strikes at Akim-Abuakwa State College in Kibi in their second year. John had not taught before joining the Peace Corps. He worked hard to become an effective teacher in a school system unlike any he had previously experienced. John developed a creative system of feedback about his classroom instruction:

"I have students coming down for special help [to the house]. It's a good indication of how they find the lesson. Perhaps some weeks nobody will come down; perhaps I'll give a class on Monday and in the afternoon, I'll have five, six, seven, or eight students come down for help. That's an indication to me that something has not gotten through, because these will generally be my brighter students. I know if they haven't understood it, the rest are just afraid to come down. If the material is more obtuse to them, the visits are more frequent." [1962]

But things fall apart. The inadequate boarding conditions for the students at this old, rundown school (a former military camp) created an undercurrent of dissatisfaction which could easily flare up and lead to a strike or riot. One strike was precipitated by a faculty attempt to tighten up on students' work habits, in which punishments were given for failure to complete homework assignments; the second was caused by a breakdown of the school electric generator and a general mishandling of attempts to restore order and calm to the school. John described some of the worst of it in talking to Brewster at the end of the second year:

"We had many problems. Students went on strike on two different occasions. One time we lost control of the discipline completely. The Ministry was forced to step in and close the school and we even had to call in a platoon of police to escort the students off the compound. School was closed for about eight weeks. During that time the staff tried to reorganize and tried to get rid of the troublemakers. We listed eighteen students who had been actively involved in the strike.... We were assured that they would not be back to the school.

"School reopened and these people were not recalled. The rest of the students were asked to pledge that they would obey the orders of the Headmaster and all authority on the compound. Some of the people who were dismissed had contacts with influential men in the government and the Ministry of Education was pressured into having them readmitted. We found ourselves with the eighteen strike leaders back on the compound two weeks after.

"I'm not embittered about it. The only word I can think to use is just 'disillusioning.' The fact that you come out here, travel 8000 miles for the specific purpose of teaching and you find so little opportunity to actually teach. It's sort of a waste, that's the point that's disillusioning, not the people themselves. I am certainly not disillusioned with the students but just this whole thing that has taken place. The teaching part of the job I've really enjoyed." [1963]

Then there was the mystery strike at Swedru Secondary School that Sue Bartholomew told me about in our interview:

"We did not finish the second year. Classes ended abruptly. There was some huge rebellion between the students and Mr. Appiah [the Headmaster]. We didn't know what. So we left never having said goodbye to our students. The last three weeks we sat around. The students were there; there was this uncanny feeling of unrest and all classes were canceled. Nobody gave us an explanation." [2000]

Thanks to some detective work by Howard Ballwanz, who was also assigned to Swedru, I found out what happened. In April 2001 Howard spoke to a former student, an old friend of his, who finally explained the 1963 strike. Howard wrote to me:

"The SWESCO student rebellion was a protest at the end of the 1963 school year. Students wanted to force Headmaster Appiah to sack two Ghanaian teachers who students felt were poor instructors in terms of preparing them for the West Africa Exams. They got their way since one of the teachers was transferred to Apam and the second was fired. It was not a demand for the Peace Corps teachers to remain for a third year."

Not everyone encountered strikes or riots and for many the second year was a payoff—less exotic but more steady day-to-day productive teaching. Dick Maze taught at Bogoso Teacher Training College which was academically less rigorous than the secondary schools. Training College students had been described by my SWSS friend, Gabriel Adu, as 'our uncles and fathers' and many of Dick's students were older than him. In his interview with Brewster, Dick Maze spoke reflectively about the two years:

"I think when I first came, of course, why all the information that we received from the Peace Corps, we were really going to step into a topnotch school program [laughing]. When I started out, I was completely over their heads. It took me a while to realize this; actually I realized right away but it took me a long time to find out exactly how far over their heads I was and what they understood. It was disappointing not knowing exactly where to start.

"I'd like to use more of my knowledge but I feel I'm not. But I do find I like the students in terms of general classroom behavior. They are much more respectful than they are in the States. In terms of everyday routine, you don't run into all this wisecracking and belligerent activity and so on in the classroom. Of course, I have to admit that most of the students are quite old; they should be over that stage anyway.

"Last year I think I approached Ghanaians more or less as—well, I'm an American and you're a Ghanaian and I'm very interested in what you are doing and let me see this and let me do that and so forth. This year I look on it more and more as— they've got problems and I've got problems and we're people instead of nationalities represented." [1963]

Laura Damon entered her second year of teaching at as full a tilt as her first. She wrote home September 1962:

"Originally I was to teach Geography again but when the School Certificate results came and 26 failed in English, Leo [the Headmaster] decided to increase the number of English periods for both Fourth and Fifth Forms with the result that I am teaching only English and have a Saturday class!! The rest of my time is with the Sixth Form—one section for *Emma* and *Murder in the Cathedral*, the other preparation in the general paper–essay writing.

"Our new PCV is fun to watch since his worries about first classes, etc. are so directly parallel to mine last year and I find myself as helpful as others were to me—'Oh, don't worry about it … you'll get the knack.'"

George Coyne summed up his second year:

"We've just sort of continued where we left off last year. We finally got a lab going and started on their biology syllabus but it's been a very, very quiet year … things went along fairly well; sometimes the kids would disappoint us in some ways but they'd make it up in other ways. I'd say it was not as good as the first year. The first year was filled with all sorts of new experiences and the second year was pretty much a repetition. I sort of got the feeling this year that Sunyani, Ghana, is really not a great deal different from Clark, New Jersey, where I was before as far as the job was concerned. We expanded our farms—the oil palms—we have a new plantation. The others are coming along quite well. It's a pleasure to go out there and walk around." [1963]

In our interview, Peter Dybwad gave a quick capsule description of the two years. Peter had begun his Peace Corps career as Acting Headmaster of Akim-Oda Secondary School, and had immediately become entangled in a titanic struggle against the evil Bursar. The regular Headmaster returned after two months and Peter, bloodied but unbowed, resumed his teaching position:

"The rest of the first year, I taught. I was happy to be the only westerner around. I mingled with the young Ghanaians on staff and drank Star Beer. That summer I toured with a band. During my project I met somebody at the library in Accra where I was working. I had my saxophone with me. These guys had a band and I went on the road with them, playing my saxophone in a High Life band—here's this skinny little white kid—an unlikely band member. The second year was kind of disappointing for me; a lot of westerners arrived—three Peace Corps Volunteers, including me, and an English couple. We all lived in the three-story apartment building. The couple were disconcerted by having three Peace Corps colleagues who couldn't speak proper English." [1999]

10

IMAGE VS. REALITY—GHANA I SPEAKS UP

How Many Ghanaian Friends Do You Have?

Almost two years to the day that he first came to Ghana, Shriver returned. Between April 1961 and April 1963, the Peace Corps had become a reality and now had programs in forty-four countries; the first Ghana teachers project was in its twentieth month and Ghana I was near the end of its tour of duty. Shriver was accompanied by Peace Corps/Washington staff members Franklin Williams and Richard Goodwin whom we came to look on as Peace Corps Image missionaries, revisiting issues that, in our own minds, had been settled by our performance over the previous year and a half. The Shriver party met with some of the group in Accra and went on a tour along the coast through Cape Coast, then up to a real "bush" location—Asankrangwa—and returned to Accra via Kumasi.

George Carter spoke of the visit:

"It was very interesting—I expected when I knew Shriver was coming that there were a lot of things about my project he wasn't going to like."

I asked George if Peace Corps/Washington felt that we weren't living up to the complete image of the Peace Corps:

"I don't believe that there was any 'this is what a volunteer ought to be like' kind of prescription. Different people had different ideas and they tended to fall into two camps [job first vs. meeting natives]. But Shriver was much too clever to let one of these points of view prevail over the other. During his visit, Shriver never expressed to me any dissatisfaction with what was going on in the Ghana project." [2000]

The high point of Shriver's visit was Asankrangwa (population less than 2000), where Frank Guido and Sam Selkow were teaching and thoroughly enjoying both the school and the modest pleasures of the town, especially the Mexico Bar. Frank described the occasion:

"We had a visit from Shriver and company—Frank Williams was there. They went through the village with us. They were surprised at how many people we knew and how many knew us. They went to the Mexico Bar [where] they enjoyed themselves with the High Life music and dancing. I think it was there that they decided they were going to offer us jobs with the Peace Corps when we returned. Shriver took back with him one of my monkeys.

"Richard Goodwin was there. They stayed with us at our houses. We weren't showing off anything and we weren't hiding anything. The chief met Shriver. There are pictures of Kennedy in the chief's compound. The chief made a presentation in our honor—it was a leopard skin to go to the President." [2000]

As we later said, "Shriver got the monkey and Frank and Sam got Peace Corps jobs." Without planning it, they had certainly given the Shriver entourage an almost ideal Peace Corps event—PCVs closely mingling with village people, in touch with the local chief and traditional customs, and, only incidentally in the eyes of some of the visitors, teaching at the secondary school. Shriver may have kept a balanced view of the project but Williams and Goodwin managed to strike raw nerves in talking to many of us.

Bob Scheuerman commented in his second interview with Brewster:

"Frank Williams was very upset because we associated with the Europeans as much as we did. How many, he wanted to know, how many African friends do you have? ... I think his attitude is a little bit more radical than Shriver's. Everybody that I talked to that had talked to Frank Williams said, that's the first question he asked him, 'How many Ghanaian friends do you have?'" [1963]

George Coyne: "There was a fellow—Goodwin I believe his name is—he came up to Kumasi with Shriver and his group. You'd ask him questions and doggone it he was very flippant—just give you a pat answer. [Later] a few of us cornered this guy Goodwin. Now they had just come back from Asankrangwa and he was talking about impact. He said that in his opinion there was more impact in a post like Asankrangwa where they had just witnessed dances and this sort of thing than at, say, Cape Coast where contact with the village chief and the customs was very limited. Well, doggone it, this made us mad. Here we are, all right, so we aren't going out and we aren't wearing kente cloth and that sort of thing, eating fufu and all the rest of it, we are here and we make the point—if you are really talking about impact—so you make a superficial impact with some of the people in the village—the real impact is on the kids that you are teaching. These are the people who will be running the country later on, who are going into the Civil Service, who are going to take over the schools—this is impact. It's something you are not going to see today or tomorrow but in the future.

"... later on, after we had talked to Goodwin for about two hours, then we sat around and talked with Shriver. He was the same Shriver that left us back in Washington; he said pretty much the same things, that is, you are going [to Ghana] to do a job. [In Washington] we had heard speeches about goodwill ambassadors, etc., but Shriver got up and sort of squelched all that and he said, 'Now you are going out there to do your job whatever it is; if you don't do your job, we'll pull you out of the ball game.'

"[But] Shriver's party—it seemed they had a vision of what a PCV was supposed to be and, damn it, here they were talking to PCVs—not what they are supposed to be but what they are and they weren't looking at us, they weren't listening to us." [1963]

Alice O'Grady: "People in Washington seem to feel, at least from the picture we got from Shriver and his gang, that our job was to be making, winning, friends and the teaching was secondary. I don't think any of us feel that way." [1963]

The question of the Peace Corps Image is a persistent one and has cropped up in many places since the Peace Corps was started in 1961—and it still does. As recently as April 15, 2001 in an article in The New York Times, titled, "'Dot-Coms' Loss Is Peace Corps' Gain," Abby Ellin wrote, "Clearly it takes a certain kind of person to commit to 24 months of living in a mud hut, earning a meager monthly stipend."

There was a contemporary voice in Ghana that also spoke on the question. In December 1962 the first issue of 'The Spark' came out. It was a newspaper published by the Bureau of African Affairs in Accra and expressed the radical point of view of the Convention Peoples Party. The first issue carried an article on the Peace Corps:

> Applied to Africa, the [U.S.] search is not for 'new frontiers' but for new forms of subjugating the young African states, and the Peace Corps is part of that neo-colonialist plan.
>
> Before going to Africa, Peace Corpsers are given special training which, besides knowledge in their respective skills, includes lessons in 'good behavior' in Africa. For Peace Corpsers are required to act as diplomats where regular U.S. diplomats are unwelcome. They are told to make friends with the natives....

On this 1963 visit, Shriver met again with President Kwame Nkrumah. He was accompanied by William Mahoney, the U.S. Ambassador, who described the meeting in official cables and cablese:

"Nkrumah greeted Shriver very courteously, although somewhat more reserved than customary in my discussions with him. Shriver began by recalling he [was] here two years ago and Nkrumah first chief of state to endorse Peace Corps. Inquired whether Peace Corps useful. Nkrumah replied by saying mathematics and science teachers badly needed, adding in course discussion that GOG [Government of Ghana] short of 'teachers to teach teachers,' agriculturalists and public health educators.

"Shriver raised question CIA, saying PC being criticized around world and he has been called number one spy. Said PC has nothing to do with CIA and that President Kennedy has given him direct personal assurances no one from CIA in any way connected PC.

"At close 40-minute conversation, Shriver asked whether PCVs who now concluding two years in Ghana could see Nkrumah before they leave—would be most disappointed otherwise. Nkrumah agreed, said he would have reception for volunteers on lawn; would work it out with me. Nkrumah gave every indication of wanting Peace Corps continue here."

I had a highly parochial view of Shriver's visit. By April George Carter had asked me to return to Ghana the next September to be a Field Officer in the project. He had a tentative OK from Peace Corps/Washington but, at that time, the practice was that no overseas staff position was finally approved until the candidate had been personally interviewed by Shriver. His visit gave George and me the opportunity to get this done. However, there were a few minor stumbling blocks along the way. Although I had a good reputation as a PCV, George felt that my beard [my God, not that again!] might be a problem. Taking a surprisingly conservative stance, he suggested I shave off the beard before meeting Shriver; it was his reading of the current organizational culture of Peace Corps/Washington that beards were verboten (beard = beatnik = pinko = who knows what?). I told George I'd take my chances, just as I was; just let me speak to Shriver. George delayed my face-to-face meeting with Shriver as long as he could.

When we would meet in Accra during vacation time, Jim Kelly and I had the custom of going to the best restaurant in town and luxuriating over dinner—soup to nuts, cocktails, cognac, cigars. That place was the Ambassador Hotel. This particular April evening, Jim and I had settled comfortably in at our table and were not thinking about nor discussing Image. Out of the corner of my eye, I noticed George Carter leading Shriver and his party into the dining room, heading for a large table beyond where we were sitting. George walked them right by our table without giving the slightest nod or gesture of recognition. The next day at the office, I kidded George about it and he just laughed weakly and hid behind his pipe.

Time was running out and avoidance was no longer possible. On the last day of the visit, George asked me to accompany him to the airport where Shriver and the others were sitting in the departure lounge waiting for their flight to be called. It was a jovial crew, augmented by several Hausa traders, peddling artifacts, fly whisks, and snake skins. I quietly took a seat next to Shriver. The table conversation had focused on one particular trader and a snake skin he was offering for sale at $50. The banter was about who could get the skin for the lowest price.

Before the contest could be settled, most of the party went to check in for their departing flight and Shriver looked around and said, "Where's this guy Klein I'm supposed to interview?" I made myself known, turned to him, and went into my pitch: "I really would like to work in the field for Peace Corps in Ghana and I think I'm uniquely qualified." I tried to continue with a reference to being a New York City teacher for five years and a PCV for two, and so on but was repeatedly interrupted by Shriver and the Hausa trader continuing to bargain over that damn snake skin.

It was finally time for Shriver to check in and we stood up to walk over to the counter. He whipped out a fifty-dollar bill, gave it to the trader, took the snake skin, and nudged me in the ribs, saying, "Tell 'em I got it for twenty bucks."

Thus was I introduced to the corridors of power, and my lifelong belief in not taking things too seriously was instantly confirmed. The next morning, George Carter told me that I had been approved by Shriver. Then, George said, "Now, maybe you'll stop fighting City Hall." And I immediately shot back, "Not a chance."

Through the years I've wondered about getting this job. Was it me or was it the snake skin?

The Termination Conference

When Ghana I gets together in a group we're like a critical mass of atoms in a nuclear reactor—we collide at random and generate a lot of heat. But we served as individuals, partied in small clusters (except for that one time at Swedru) and rarely gathered in a group while we were in Ghana. The first time was in April of the first year during the History teaching crisis (remember, Desist) but we were subdued by the seriousness of the meeting. The next time was September of the second year when we gathered to greet the arrival of Ghana II. On that occasion we acted like modest but battle-scarred veterans as we were busily checking out the new kids on the block. Finally there was the Completion of Service Conference in May 1963 in which we were invited to interact, express our opinions, and let Peace Corps/Washington know what our point of view was. The report of the Conference tells the story:

"The Ghana I volunteers believed they were in a situation where the job was clear and their long range contribution to Ghanaian development was unmistakable. As a result, they placed a very high premium on the importance of excelling as teachers. They pointed out that Ghana had invited them to teach and was paying their full salary to do a professional job in the classroom.

"There was unanimous resentment in the group over what they believed to be a basic tenet in Peace Corps Washington philosophy—that the classroom work of the teacher is important—but only as a means of bringing the volunteer into contact with the community outside of his [sic] school.

"Conclusion: The Volunteers are convinced they made a significant contribution to Ghanaian educational development. And if they had it to do all over again, almost to a man [sic] they would join the Peace Corps and return to serve two years in the secondary schools of Ghana."

As Nate Gross recalled, "At the termination conference, one of the discussion leaders asked, 'Do you feel your two years here was wasted? You could have been at home, getting ahead, getting married, getting a job, and starting a family and a mortgage.' Everybody burst out laughing—it sounded so preposterous." [2000]

A More Personal Assessment, Thanks to Brewster and Rafe

After the Completion of Service Conference at the end of May 1963 we returned to our schools to complete the third term of the second year and to prepare for our departures. Starting in the middle of June, Brewster and Rafe retraced their 1962 steps and stops throughout Ghana to do a second interview with each of us. Coming so close to the end of our tours of duty, these interviews produced introspective comments about the personal meaning of the experience as well as self-evaluations of personal performance in the schools. All these remarks are dated June 1963.

Ray Spriggs had just gone through a personal crisis trying to phone home and get information about his ailing mother. He finally got through to find out that it was not as serious a medical emergency as he thought but it was a harrowing week. Ray was still willing to talk:

"I tell you, Rafe, before this week, I didn't want to stay here and I didn't want to go home; you know, I wanted, I wanted to be home but I didn't want to leave here to get there.

"I've seen a country, something different, and it's very different and that, that really, you know, opened my eyes to a few things about my own personality which are bad and which are good and a few things about the world around me which I didn't and wouldn't have understood before. But I'm not sure that's good because it's more confusing now—not just confusing—a greater insecurity now than before because I don't know where I'm going. Before this, if I hadn't come here, I'd know the community and at the end of the school year know I'll be back, maybe work for the summer, take a vacation in Mexico. But now to go back into that rut would just kill me, kill my meaning in life." [1963]

Alice O'Grady in speaking to Brewster the year before, had unburdened herself of the woes of a strike and a stoning. In 1963 she was more reflective:

"Something I feel very strongly is that I'm a very different person than I was when I came out and it's not just because I'm two years older. I mean I feel like I've really grown up; I feel so much more self-assured for example and I think this is because of my experiences here. I plan to go back to my old crowd at home and whether being a different person will, I mean, will I look at them differently, will they look at me differently. I don't worry about it but this has occurred to me but I feel much happier.

"I'm pretty sure they'll be the same; they're still doing the same thing, you know; Lamplighters is what I mean, my old crowd. It excites me really to go home and see the new Alice in the old environment and then really seeing how much I've changed." [1963]

Jack Lord talked of the effect his teaching had on the students:

"They were not at all accustomed to being asked questions in class. One of the students explained that the first time it happened he was just absolutely terrified. He'd never dreamed such a thing could happen—that he'd be asked to get up in class and answer an open-ended question, not just recite a memorized piece of text. It feels even worse when there's no clear answer.

"But after two years they were on to that; they were used to that. And I think more than 'Why do rivers meander' was the main thing. It wasn't that we brought knowledge of Geography but I think a more effective kind of teaching that's better for the kids in the long run." [1963]

I discussed the same topic with Brewster:

"This year ... I have a feeling of more accomplishment as far as teaching but I see more evidence of real progress with English on the part of some students. Outside the classroom I've come to know the students much better, so more often now, we'll sit around and talk, and I can see where their—or I can hear—where their English is quite good. They'll ask me to correct them and they'll consciously seek out talking [situations]. I don't want to give the wrong impression. There are 120 students here. In the social life I talk about with the students, I think that less than twenty are involved. This is a family but it's also based more on personality than on achievement in the class. Those that are willing to seek me out, will sit down with me, or come join the activities we're engaged in and just are not too shy and are willing to make mistakes in English—those are the ones." [1963]

Furthermore, what my students lacked in polish, they made up in picturesque expression. I quote from letters written to me in August, just after my brief return to the U.S.

Barnabas: "Sir, if you were to see my face on this sheet, you would detect how sorry I am to draw your attention to this fact. Very unfortunately, we could not publish the paper. All the paper we had was used for the exam. Moreover, Mr. Hutchinson had no time to type for me."

Grace: "The chewing gum that you bought for me has remained only three. I have kept them. I will not chew them because when they get finished I will not have any."

Bennie: "If I had not eaten before you left, I would not have eaten for the whole day because I was sad at your departure."

Bob Krisko spoke of personal change but took it a step further and tried to think of what it meant in terms of his being back in the U.S.:

"I feel a little bit unsettled about going home, 'cause I'm going back to all this turmoil. Here there's no racial barriers and you feel very free. At home, just the idea that somebody who could be my friend here, if I went home, people would ostracize both of us or at least try to get me away from him. It just seems so juvenile. Well, no, because children don't do that; seems so 'adult.' "

SWSS and the Banana Man Say Goodbye

During the last few months of our second year, we were busy. We had to complete our third term of teaching, pack up our personal effects for shipment, and say our local farewells. The Peace Corps called us together in Accra at the end of May for five days during which we had medical examinations and the Completion of Service Conference. My departure was simplified by the fact that I was immediately returning to Ghana to start working as Field Officer. Since I led a fairly spartan life at SWSS and was not a collector of African art or artifacts, I had very little to pack and nothing to ship home. Having an adopted family at SWSS—Adu and the Juaboso gang—made it easy to leave many things behind for others to use—a radio, kitchenware, a typewriter—that was it. Before entering the Peace Corps I had lived in five different apartments in six years so I was accustomed to throwing away, giving away, packing up, and moving on.

The staff, students, and the Board of Governors had a farewell party for Dave Hutchinson and me. We were each given a full-size man's kente cloth, a lavish gift, as we sat, smilingly, while people said nice things about us. I was proud to hear Barnabas, as the school's Senior Prefect, give his speech. He had indeed become my nephew and I his uncle. He was among the best of the students I taught at SWSS. Some excerpts:

"Mr. Klein, the old man of the first batch of the Peace Corps, accepted his appointment and arrived on campus September 29th, 1961. Since his arrival, he has been working untiringly to help establish this school. His classroom teaching is beyond description and his outside projects are simply marvelous."

After listing and describing the projects, Barnabas spoke of Dave: "Though he spent the first term studying his new environment, his outside project within the school the last term is unspeakable. He is the horticulturist of the school. Under his supervision we have planted flowers all along the paths. Some are blooming now and others are sprouting."

He concluded, "Your hard work here becomes useful only when we study harder, go on to university, and become useful citizens to our own Motherland. We promise to follow your footsteps, so that in the future we may also become other Mr. Kleins or Mr. Hutchinsons of our country of Ghana.

"May the good God guide you safely home, give you long lease of life to work for the younger generation."

The Banana Man also gave me a gift to guide me home safely. It was the only goodbye that brought tears to my eyes. One of the last days at SWSS, there was the familiar tentative knock on the bungalow door. I opened it to welcome Mr. Asare—this time without a stalk of bananas on his head and dressed up in a neat white going-to-church suit. He presented me with a small, hand-painted carved figure on which he had painstakingly inscribed, "My Jesus." Bennie, convenient translator, told me that Mr. Asare had carved the figure to protect me in my travels and to assure my safe return. Bennie also said that Mr. Asare had been learning English and wanted to say something to me. Banana Man took my hand, looked at me with a smile, and said, "Mr. Klein, I love you."

The day I left SWSS, Dave and I were in the Jeep (you can be sure, I was driving) and just about to leave the school compound when we saw that our way was barred. The students had lined themselves up across the road. When we stopped, Adu came forward and said that it was a Sefwi custom to bar the way of a departing friend until he promised that he would return. All smiles and good feelings, I gave the required pledge and was on my way.

Finally Getting to Meet the Wizard

As promised to Shriver and Ambassador Mahoney in April, Nkrumah held a reception for the departing Ghana I group at Flagstaff House on July 9, 1963. I missed the event because I had left Ghana at the end of June to have enough time for home leave before reporting to Peace Corps/Washington mid-August to begin work as Field Officer. In the interviews I conducted in 1999–2000, people had surprisingly little memory of the occasion. After two years in Ghana of almost daily news comments and publicity about Osagyefo, Dr. Kwame Nkrumah, President of the Republic of Ghana—Redeemer—Founder of the Nation—Light of Africa—I expected descriptions comparable to those of our meeting with President John F. Kennedy in August 1961. But the meeting with Nkrumah is mostly recalled as a formal, low-key occasion.

George Carter had advised everyone to wear dress or jacket and tie, to drink and eat in moderation, and not to do or say anything stupid. I think of it like Dorothy, Tin Man, Scarecrow, and Cowardly Lion finally meeting the Wizard of Oz and learning, to their dismay, that he was, after all, just a human being. However, meeting Nkrumah was certainly an appropriate coda to our volunteer service. It was his request to Shriver in April 1961 that set the whole scenario in motion that led to our spending the two years in Ghana as Peace Corps teachers. We had much for which to say thanks, and little to regret.

Were We Successful?

The original Peace Corps Act of 1961 stated three goals for the new agency:

1. Helping the people of interested countries in meeting their need for trained men and women.
2. Helping promote a better understanding of Americans by the peoples served.
3. Helping promote a better understanding of other peoples on the part of Americans.

Although Peace Corps/Washington had developed a Division of Evaluation, under the journalistic leadership of Charlie Peters, when we completed our volunteer service its style was free-swinging and intuitive; it did not do corporate accounting. Our success could be measured by many highly personalized standards but, true to our anti-establishment bias, we felt that we were the best judges. Concerning Goal 1, we had certainly helped Ghana meet its need for trained teachers. Within two months of our departure, Ghana was employing over 120 Peace Corps teachers (of course, no History) and requesting more. Goal 2 evokes memories of the nagging Image arguments—counting how many Ghanaian friends we had just seemed wrong to us. We knew we had worked in Ghanaian environments, alongside Ghanaians, and moved freely about Ghana (not keeping head counts as we did so). The human quality of the friendships we'd made were not a thing to be quantified and certainly we wouldn't go out to meet people because we had been directed to do so. Years later, when I became Director of the Peace Corps in Ghana, a literal head-counting approach had begun to creep into Peace Corps/ Washington thinking as they adopted a project development system called PPBS (Planned Program and Budget System). I remember having to complete a report in which I was to count "the number of host country national contacts per volunteer." Without a moment's hesitation, I made up numbers: 43 contacts x 190 PCVs = 8,170. No one ever challenged me on it. Goal 3 was one that naturally emerged in our day-to-day lives after we were back living and working throughout the U.S.— talking about Ghana was easy to do and, if you have a few hours to spare, I can show you my collection of 500 slides of Ghana.

Now we went on with our lives, most of us changed, matured, emboldened by our experience and with an enduring sense of gratitude for the Ghanaians who were so friendly and delightful a part of that process. Years later, Newell Flather said, "I don't think any of us will ever be exactly what we were before we went— it's impossible."

11

THEN WHAT?

After 1963

What happened to us after the two pioneering years as Peace Corps Volunteers? It's clear that the Peace Corps experience brought new opportunity and direction to many in Ghana I. Ever-persistent Brewster Smith had continued to keep in touch with the group, doing a follow-up study via mailed questionnaires. He shared his results (and address lists) with us. In April 1964, less than a year after completing Peace Corps, more than half the group was in graduate school, with a party-provoking cluster of ten in Manhattan alone. In the fall of 1963, returned volunteers were a hot commodity with Admissions and Scholarship offices, especially at those schools with newly created or re-energized programs in African Studies. Six people received Ford Foundation Peace Corps Fellowships and at least another fifteen scholarships or teaching assistantships at top-notch schools throughout the U.S.

Back in 1961 the Ghana Ministry of Education had been concerned with the academic credentials of some of the group, those with degrees from little-known colleges such as Johnson Smith, Berea, Spring Hill, Monmouth. Well, now they would be impressed to hear Stanford, Columbia, UCLA, Penn, or Syracuse. At the same time, four of us were working for the Peace Corps—two in the field and two in Washington—and that number would eventually rise to sixteen. George Coyne was still on his way home from Ghana, having decided to spend six months on a kibbutz in Israel; Valerie Deuel, also. Only two people had returned directly to secondary level teaching—Bob Krisko, who was tooling around Kansas City in his XKE, and Darleen Malcolm. Through the years after 1964, sixteen of the group became college professors and eight taught and did administration at the secondary level.

But these are just the numbers and names—behind them are the individuals. Thanks to Brewster we got a sampling of comments about the transitional period from the returned questionnaires in April 1964. Brewster had shared them with us, without attribution. Here is a sampling of responses to the question, 'Have you talked to … groups about Ghana or the Peace Corps?'

"I showed slides to the youth groups at the local church just a week after I returned. They were orderly and cordial, but viewed everything with an air of incredulity, for just the month before they had slides from a missionary from the Sudan Interior Mission, and all his slides showed 'naked savages' living in 'huts and grass hovels' and although the people were portrayed as civil and kind, they were definitely 'unsaved.' They couldn't believe the pictures of the students in western dress and they were amazed at the curriculum their African counterparts had to endure."

"… I went out to Westchester County to talk about the Peace Corps in Ghana. The ladies (it was the village's Women's Club) were most interested…. I had expected a rather TIME-[magazine]oriented conservatism … but there was nothing of the sort. I thought it was a success … although the president of the club, in private conversation, betrayed her true feelings and stated categorically that most African natives weren't ready for independence, just 'as our Negroes aren't ready for full equality; they have to prove themselves, first.' I didn't ask her how she had 'proved herself.' "

" … I feel in the end that Volunteers from Africa must be spokesmen for Africa—most Americans are so damn ignorant about Africa. I also try to convey my deep personal commitment to my life in Ghana—this perhaps should be the end result of the Peace Corps, with the Peace Corps being the means of getting you there."

"… The experience of speaking to groups has been useful if only in the sense that it has awakened me to the attitudes and misconceptions midwesterners have of the rest of the world."

Under the heading, Problems of Readjustment, Brewster quoted these responses:

"The problem was to stop thinking in terms of a Ghana situation where things were done on a small scale and there was a lot of personal contact with noteworthy events—the Peace Corps itself was a 'noteworthy event' and I miss being a part of it."

"… I was looking forward to getting home and found it very pleasant. Some things annoy me such as the American feeling of superiority and narrow-mindedness about many things but this was no surprise to me. Hot running water and telephones that work still send me into ecstasies."

"Mainly, at first, I felt differently toward American Negroes—as if I had, by living among Black people for two years, become one of them. But since I had no way of communicating this to Negroes I felt uncomfortable at being regarded as just another white person. I was very aware of Negroes around me, and you might therefore say that my race-consciousness had increased over what it was before I went to Ghana."

"As for the U.S.—at first I tended to idealize Africa (my brother called me 'an African snob') and it was not until [Kennedy's] assassination that I began to feel 'This is my country—and somehow or other I have got to come to terms with it!' I guess the hardest thing to 'take' about Americans, in general, is their brash optimism, ethnocentricity, and lack of sensitivity—but there are many exceptions."

And there's at least one dramatic example of 'reverse culture shock':

On her return to the U.S., Sue Glowacki went into a Macy's department store to buy a raincoat. She asked a salesclerk where she could find a raincoat and the clerk replied, "Oh, the entire floor is raincoats." And Sue burst into tears.

Even after 39 years, people harbored strong feelings about what having been a Peace Corps Volunteer has meant in their lives. Dick Maze, Howard Ballwanz, Don Groff all reflected on this.

First, Dick Maze: "It was one of the most profound experiences of my life in terms of what I thought of the world prior to that, what I knew about the world prior to that and what I knew about the world after that—much more international-minded and much more open-minded after that experience. I grew up in Republican Iowa and I'd got to the end of a corn row and that was it. The schools were good in Iowa but it's middle America—you're out there in the middle of a very provincial society, with a 'blinder' view of the world where things seemed much simpler. There was a simpler model than what really existed. I know politically I changed. I was a conservative Republican before I went into the Peace Corps: you know, if you work hard in life, you'll succeed." [2000]

Dick went way beyond the end of the corn row in his career. He earned a graduate degree in Ecology at New Mexico State and for a year worked in the central Pacific Ocean on "islands where people don't normally go," on a Smithsonian biology survey. He returned to Ghana under the auspices of Teachers for West Africa (funded by Hershey Chocolate) and taught for two more years. Then for twenty years he was a consultant in International Environmental Planning, conducting surveys throughout the world—a long way from Iowa.

In response to an inquiry from me about the effect of Peace Corps, Howard Ballwanz wrote in 2001: "Profound—the Peace Corps experience confirmed my belief in the common humanity of all. We can toil with, teach and learn from others whose culture is different but valued by us. Peace Corps service propelled me through my M.S. in Ed. in '65 and my search for a Ph.D. because I was sold on African Studies. Geography of Sub-Saharan Africa ... has been my bread and butter over the last 32 years at Montclair [University]."

For Don Groff the effect of Peace Corps was a more complex matter, as he explained: "I guess the direction my life has taken in very overall terms was not greatly affected. I probably wouldn't have taught high school Physics for a few years if it hadn't been for the Peace Corps experience. But I guess in terms of attitude about the world, what sort of place the world is and what sort of place I have in it, or what sort of place the U.S. has in it, it's made a big difference. I guess I see the world as kind of a big place that has the U.S. and a bunch of other countries; the U.S. doesn't have first dibs on everything the world has to offer."

After returning to college to complete a degree in Electrical Engineering, Don has continued to work in the field of electronics. "For a few years I worked for a company that had an assembly plant in the Philippines. I was over there a couple of times—I mean the details of that activity were not at all Peace Corps-like but the way I approached it was kind of Peace Corps-like. I worked with the technicians who worked in this factory—guys who spent their days testing electronic equipment—but I felt I was much more able to communicate with them; I was much more 'simpatico' than my [American] colleagues. I went out with the techs in the evening and partied a little bit.

"In dealing with Japanese engineers I think the Peace Corps experience was very valuable in helping me understand why we didn't understand each other—not just the basic linguistic problem—the guys we dealt with all spoke a sort of English but my colleagues didn't understand that you can't throw slang and sarcasm around and expect it to be understood or accepted. Based largely on a couple of years in Ghana teaching kids whose English was not all that good, you learn techniques for communicating and determining when you're not communicating. That's probably as important as communication itself." [2000]

Don ended our interview humming the melody to *Yen Ara Asase Ni* and reminded me that he was one of those who was in the front ranks of the group actually singing, upon our arrival in Ghana in August 1961. He couldn't translate the song title for me but compared it, as song and anthem, to 'America the Beautiful' in the U.S.

Frank Guido went from a planned career in microbiology and medical research to inner city education; his Peace Corps experience was part of the change. "You don't learn things except over a period of time but you have to be open to the learning and I think that's what the Peace Corps did for me. It opened me to understanding more about what was going on in America, in society.... I realized that perhaps the biggest problem we were facing in the U.S. was the racial problem and the racial problem could only be solved through education. I chose to work in a Black school [Benjamin Franklin High in Philadelphia] ... my emphasis was on challenging the students intellectually because a lot of times they don't get that. In fact, they responded to it. I was non-threatening to them in terms of their work and we'd constantly talk of how they had it in them to achieve.

"Then I was offered the chance to start this new school from scratch. I had the opportunity to travel around and look at other programs across the U.S. But some of the things that were included were the result of my Peace Corps experience— included in the design of the school from the very beginning was volunteerism; that students had to earn credits not only academically but in service to the school and the community. And that was directly from the idea of the Peace Corps—offering your service to improve things. I was committed to creating an environment where interracial and intercultural students could be in a positive place." [2000]

In 1992, The Franklin Learning Center was selected as a National Blue Ribbon School by the U.S. Department of Education.

Back to Ghana and SWSS

I returned to Ghana in early September 1963 and was greeted at the airport by Barnabas and Bennie—a happy reminder of the Juaboso connection. I had escorted a new group of Peace Corps teachers, just beginning their tours. During their first weeks in Ghana there was the now-routine Ministry of Education orientations with a few lectures and a lot of bus touring along the coast and up to the site of the Volta Dam. Then, out to the schools. In one of my first letters home after my return, I was already revealing my priorities in my new job as Field Officer:

"I probably won't get up to Sefwi for a week or so, since there are other matters to be worked on [like the job I was hired to do]."

I did figure out how to combine work and Sefwi family, as I reported October 2:

"Another field trip completed (my third so far)—I went Mpraeso to Kumasi to Dunkwa to Sefwi and managed to visit 21 volunteers in 5 days.

"Returning to Sefwi was an absolute delight. Although the road is still as miserable as ever, the warm greeting that awaited me was worth any journey. I arrived just before the students' lunch and a bunch crowded around my car to greet me. Like little kids, they became terribly shy and, one after another, came up and shook my hand, saying *Akwaaba* (Welcome).

"After lunch, I went to the dining hall and was introduced to the 'raws' (the new students) and then spoke briefly to the entire student body. I reminded them how they had 'barred my exit' in June and how I had promised to come back within 3 months. I also commented that my vacation with my family in my village of New York had been a good one and that was why I looked so fat.

"I happened to arrive in time for the second anniversary bonfire on Saturday night. SWSS opened officially just two years ago! I visited with the new PCV and my friends in town; Adu had me over for a fufu and groundnut stew dinner. It was really like old times."

Then a weekend trip to Wiawso at the end of October and so it went through the ten months I was back in Ghana until my transfer to Kenya in July 1964. George Carter left Ghana in March 1964 and returned to Peace Corps/Washington to become a Regional Director. (In late 1966, after five years with the Peace Corps, George was recruited by Tom Watson to become an executive with IBM.) The new Director in Ghana was Frank Broderick (the job title was no longer Peace Corps Representative). In December 1963 I wrote home a bit wistfully:

"My new life here in Ghana is still strange to me. I'm still not sure if I like it better than life in Sefwi where things were quieter and I had a better idea of what I was accomplishing from day to day. That my new work is successful is unquestioned (Carter has several times complimented my work)—whether it is as satisfying and, in the long run, as important, I'm not sure."

Franklin Williams, then Peace Corps Africa Regional Director, had asked me if I would accept a transfer to Kenya. Peace Corps was starting its first program there (including a large group of teachers) and I was well qualified to be on staff during the developmental stages: seven years' teaching experience, including two years as a Peace Corps Volunteer, one year as a Field Officer. In accepting, I had the thought that I might be on a track that could well lead me back to Ghana, perhaps even as Director of the program. I have always taken a critical look at any administration under which I worked (the U.S. Army, the New York City Board of Education as well as Peace Corps/Ghana), to see how sensitive and responsive they were to the needs of 'the troops in the trenches.' I was ready to try my hand at being an administrator, my way. Part of it was also the common fantasy, "Well, if I ran the zoo, then ..."

My boss in Kenya was the Peace Corps Director, Tom Quimby, who soon became the Africa Regional Director in Peace Corps/Washington by mid-1965, replacing

Franklin Williams who in turn had been appointed U.S. Ambassador to Ghana. As my tour ended, I returned to the U.S. (via Ghana, of course), still working for the Peace Corps but with my new position unspecified. During my two years as Field Officer I had worked under two people who then became Regional Directors in Peace Corps/Washington (Carter and Quimby) as well as for the current (1965) Director in Ghana, Frank Broderick. They all endorsed my candidacy when I was nominated in November 1965 to be the next Peace Corps Director in Ghana. This was better than even my wildest French Foreign Legion daydreams. From the day I first thought of joining the Peace Corps in May 1961 to this moment, I had the feeling that many good things in my life had fallen into place. What I had done, what I was doing, what I was about to do were all the result of actions I had taken, ideas and opinions I had expressed—it was what I wanted to do. However, before I could attain the heights, there was Franklin Williams to deal with. Ambassador Williams, who had to approve my appointment, had some personnel choices of his own he was pursuing but they did not work out. However, in the process, my final approval and departure for Ghana were delayed until February 1966.

On February 21 I returned to Ghana, again greeted by Barnabas and Bennie. President Kwame Nkrumah was overthrown by a military coup on February 22, my first full day on the job. I remember the Peace Corps driver picking me up at my residence that morning to take me to the Peace Corps office. He greeted me and said, "Please, sir, the government is being overthrown." It was for me, sentimentally, a sad day because Ghana and Kwame Nkrumah were so intimately entwined in my experience since 1961. The Peace Corps in Ghana had always been non-political and had, with reasonable modesty, helped meet skilled manpower needs; our status was not threatened by the coup. If anything, we were soon asked to increase the number of volunteers.

That it was not a blood-bath coup was illustrated by my experience on that morning. I was being driven to the Peace Corps Office, which was located next door to National Police Headquarters on Ring Road—this was the nerve center of the coup with the best countrywide communication system. It was ringed by armed soldiers, favoring the coup. As we neared the office, a soldier, waving a rifle, gestured for us to stop. We did and I rolled down the window, so he could see clearly inside the vehicle. The soldier said, "Have you been searched?"

I responded, "Yes, we have!"

He said (with a friendly wave of his rifle), "Drive on."

I ran the "zoo" for two years, visited SWSS a little less often, resisted some changes and instituted a few others. Blocking ill-conceived suggestions for change was really a matter of avoiding the Ambassador, who seemed desirous of continuing his Peace Corps Image campaign from his new position. Franklin Williams would travel on official visits to small towns and villages throughout the country and, on his return would call me into his office and say, "Bob, I think we should have volunteers in every one of these villages, doing community projects, working with agricultural co-ops." And I would say, "Yes, sir, we are exploring that with the appropriate ministries." I don't think he believed me. One day, he called me to his office to meet David Acquah, Principal Secretary of the Ministry of Social Welfare.

When I arrived, the Ambassador introduced me to Acquah, saying, "Bob, I think you and David should be developing good village programs with Social Welfare." David, bless his soul, said to Ambassador Williams, "Oh, Mr. Klein and I have had lengthy discussions already and if there are programs that can utilize Peace Corps personnel, we will certainly let you know."

Brewster Smith had visited Ghana in 1967 and in his diary is a story I had forgotten:

"Bob was recently back in the States ... [and] saw Jack Vaughn, Shriver's successor, who said that he assumed things were going well in Ghana because when he asked the Ambassador about the program, the Ambassador had nothing good to say. This reflects an interesting situation: the Peace Corps is eager to maintain its independence of the Embassy. Everybody apparently regards it as a fine thing that Bob is such a diametrically opposite sort of person to the Ambassador. There is minimum likelihood that the Ambassador and Bob could ever form a coalition or that the Ambassador will dominate the program."

The changes I introduced were designed to minimize the organizational distance between volunteers and staff. I changed my residence to a modest housing area in town, accessible to visitors from out of town and within walking distance of the PCV hostel. I did the same with the office, moving it to a downtown building above a Lebanese trading company and near the commonly visited shops and stores. With whatever staff I had, Deputy, Field Officer, Doctor, I strongly encouraged them to spend one-third to one-half of their time in the field, visiting volunteers. But the real joy of running the zoo, living in a rambling old house, was that Barnabas, Bennie, and Grace could come and live with me, a part-time arrangement based on their continued schooling.

In the long run, I came to believe that Ghana I's original insistence that "we are only teachers" was OK but too limiting. I was fortunate in that Jane Meleney had joined the Peace Corps/Ghana staff. She had served in northern Nigeria as a PCV and considered her staff work as an extension of what she had striven for as a volunteer—service and involvement. Discussions between the two of us helped to define a creative new teacher training program, in which PCVs could at least be introduced to the possibility of involvement beyond the confines of the prescribed teaching role. With Jane's unflagging help and guidance and with the cooperation of the Ministry of Education, we developed a comprehensive in-country training program for the penultimate group of teachers I worked with as Peace Corps Director in the summer of 1967. Peace Corps/Ghana retained its good reputation in Washington, in spite of or maybe because of the expressed differences between Ambassador Williams and myself. It was still a Peace Corps tradition, after six years of growth, to allow for experimentation in both programming and training.

The model we developed was as follows: After five days of staging, paperwork and immunizations in Washington, the trainees flew directly to Ghana for their training and selection. They spent two weeks together for orientation and basic lectures on Ghana history and education. Then the trainees were assigned, in groups of seven to ten, to village centers away from Accra to live with Ghanaian families, practice teach in the local middle school, and have intensive language training (in a setting where they could immediately put it to use). At each center we assigned an end-of-tour PCV as mentor and counselor to the trainees. They were chosen because as PCVs they had successfully taught, had become involved with the larger community, had learned some vernacular, and were articulate enough to express the possibilities of being a PCV in Ghana. We weren't pushing Image but rather trying to encourage a broader individual outlook.

This innovative training program was a success. My own sense of it was that it was a better way to make use of the first three months of a Peace Corps Volunteer's limited twenty-four month tour of duty.

This approach to training was still in effect in Ghana in 2007 and is the common pattern in worldwide Peace Corps training today. I awaited some indication that the Peace Corps/Washington staff shared my feeling about the program. My answer came four months later in a letter commending me for the in-country training. The commendation was based on the fact that the overall program costs were one-fourth of what they were for equivalent stateside training! That was when I knew, with absolute certainty, that I could never work in Peace Corps/Washington (and I never did).

When my tour of duty as Peace Corps Director in Ghana was over, I returned to the U.S. and became a foot soldier in the War on Poverty, participating in one innovative program after another, moving on as funding dried up in one sector and resurfaced in another. I trained VISTA volunteers, was Education Director of a New Jersey storefront school project for urban high school dropouts, developed and ran an alternative Master of Arts in Teaching program for the Urban Education Corps. I kept in touch with the Sefwi family.

In 1970 I organized and led a two-week summer study group to Ghana, abandoning them at one point to run off to Wiawso for two days.

In 1973, being "at liberty," I went back to Ghana, this time with my wife, Carol (whom I met when she was a PCV in Ghana, naturally) and our two young children. Sarah was 3½ and Ben 2½ years old. We found someone to rent our house in Montclair for two years, bought tickets on Pan Am, and flew to Ghana. Once there we found teaching positions at the Presbyterian Training College in Akropong and, after lengthy and confused negotiations with a bewildered local Peace Corps staff, we re-enrolled as volunteers from the field. Barnabas (now Kwaku) visited us from the U.S. where he was doing his doctoral research in educational psychology at Rutgers University in New Jersey. Bennie was soon to leave for Dakar to pursue further studies in French. Grace was married and was about to join her husband to teach in Nigeria to get better pay and greater availability of goods. Adu had gone to the Ivory Coast to teach for the same reasons (he died there in the early 1980s).

In 1986 Kwaku and I went to Ghana to take part in the 25th Anniversary Silver Jubilee of SWSS. Being back was at first depressing because economic conditions were not good and the continued droughts in the Sahel had drastically reduced food supplies. But when we finally got up to Wiawso and SWSS, the gloom disappeared as I met one after another of the young (now not so young) people I had taught from 1961–63. I remembered many of them (with help from Kwaku) and they remembered me. The fabulous mural maps on the walls of the school buildings had almost disappeared, one covered with a tropical fungus that attacked the paint, the other painted over during a zealous school clean-up campaign.

In 1991 I went back to Ghana as part of a small delegation of former volunteers who were invited by the Government of Ghana to celebrate thirty years of continuous Peace Corps assistance. This visit was saddened by the recent death of Bennie in his mid-forties; he had been an Assistant Headmaster of a secondary school.

And, in 2006, successfully recovered from heart surgery the year before, I was hosted by Kwaku for an extended visit, much of which was spent in Sefwi, the school and Juaboso. When I've gone back on these later visits, I consciously prepare myself, saying. "I'm not returning to do a comparative study of third world development since the '60s." That frees me to enjoy the company of the many former students and friends I encounter. It is joyful to be sitting at Kwaku's house, drinking a beer, and looking up to see yet another visitor. I look at a 60-plus-year-old Ghanaian man and suddenly a 'gestalt' kicks in. Within the aura of graying hair, wrinkles, portliness, I suddenly see the face of the 15-year-old Nelson Ntaadu or Anthony Owusu. Veneration wears thin quickly and conversations soon turn to family, career, personal history. Of that generation I taught, many have done university and then left Ghana to pursue greater opportunities in Germany, U.K., U.S. But many have stayed (none as farmers in the Sefwi district) and become merchants, teachers, government employees. We talk more of the present than of the past.

Of my three Ghanaian 'children' (Kwaku a.k.a. Barnabas, Bennie, Grace), Kwaku came to the U.S., completed a doctorate at Rutgers, and pursued a work career in higher education administration in the U.S. (mostly in New Jersey and New York). He returned to Ghana almost annually and, in retirement, divides his time between the two countries. Bennie studied language in Senegal and in France, encountered personal demons, and died young. Grace became a middle school teacher, married, went to Nigeria with her husband to teach. They had six children and, when Nigeria began to expel the Ghanaian teachers, she was abandoned by her ne'er-do-well spouse. With the children, Grace returned to Ghana where, against incredible odds, she managed to stay employed and nurture her family. We lost track of her but when I went in 1986, Kwaku and I were able to find Grace in Accra and visited with her at the modest home where she lived. Out paraded six beautiful, well-dressed children ages four to 14, all eager to meet 'Uncle,' all speaking beautiful English. I thought to myself, "What strength Grace has; she is truly Mother Courage."

I look forward to my next visit to Ghana, maybe for the Fiftieth Anniversary of the Peace Corps and of Ghana I (and SWSS).

Through the Years

Through the years, trying to stay in touch with the fifty individualists who were Ghana I has been like trying to track satellites in space with an amateur telescope—brief images flash across the sky and suddenly look familiar. Some of the group have disappeared from our shared pool of contacts and information. As of this writing, five have died—Ken Baer, Frank Guido, John McGinn, Ray Spriggs, and DeeDee Vellenga. Starting in 1986 we held reunions every five years or so, and more and more of our stories emerge each time we get together. As we've gotten older, we have spent very little time at reunions singing Michael, Row the Boat Ashore because our lives have not been dull or static, and so every five years we have a lot of catching up to do. On the other hand, someone has claimed that the only crowd they can find to show their Ghana slides to is at the reunion. Taking a look at Ghana I, twenty-five to thirty years later, there are three overlapping clusters; (1) educators; (2) internationalists; (3) everybody else.

Almost twenty settled in to careers in education, mostly at the college level, with some echoes of the Ghana experience. Howard Ballwanz has taught African Geography; Tom Peterson exotic languages; DeeDee Vellenga and Penny Roach both Sociology with an emphasis on Women's Studies and Africa (both returned to Ghana several times to conduct research); Richard and Antonette Port taught and did curriculum development in English as a Second Language in Nigeria, then Hawaii (they utilized traditional Ghanaian folk stories—Ananse Tales—in an ESL text).

Laura Damon, who taught at several colleges, commented: "My most enjoyable years of teaching were at Niagara County Community College. The reason, I think was … there was a similar commitment. Those boys in Ghana wanted to learn; they really wanted an education with a capital 'E'. Their whole communities were paying their tuition and not just Mom and Dad. There was a similar commitment on the part of the students at the community college. They couldn't afford to go to Yale or Princeton or Harvard but they knew that they wanted a good education. So a community college answered their needs. As the African students had done, they pushed me to the limit, asking why, why, why." [2000]

The internationalists had careers either overseas or with agencies whose focus was the developing world; many were in Africa. Jim Kelly, after a stint as Peace Corps staff in Cameroons and with the U.S. Mission to the United Nations, worked for AID; was AID Director in Ethiopia and in his career, of necessity, became an expert in famine relief. After retirement, he continued as a consultant in that field and was instrumental in creating a program called FEWS (Famine Early Warning System) which collects worldwide data on food supply-related information such as long-term weather patterns, local food production and storage capability, availability of food transport vehicle in an area in case of famine—the information is available to any agency working in famine relief to facilitate more timely responses to crises.

More modestly, a large group of us had Peace Corps careers, some in Peace Corps/Washington, most in Africa. Peace Corps was not and is not a government career service and we moved on to other things. The additional time in Africa was a mixed bag for some. As Frank Guido and others said, in relation to working in Nigeria, Malawi, Kenya, Tunisia, Cameroons, "I was homesick for Ghana."

Nate Gross recalled his experience working for Peace Corps in northern Nigeria and the effect it had on his career choice, which initially was to enter the Foreign Service: "In Nigeria I saw enough of foreign service life to know what their officers did every day; also, having to explain our Vietnam policy. I wasn't comfortable with that. Peace Corps reinforced my attitude about public service, wanting to do something helpful, not just make money.... In Nigeria I met a young Foreign Service officer who I got to know. Then I saw the down side of Foreign Service. The coup had taken place and there was a military government. His job was to go out to the Officers' Club every night and drink beer with all the young officers, so if there was another coup or whatever happened he would know all the people. Man, he got tired of that. One time it was 45 nights in a row—this is a job?

"I concluded it's a fascinating life style, wonderful social life, always going to nice dinners with interesting people from other countries but, over the long term, between homesickness and being a bit too uprooted, I decided to go urban U.S. instead of overseas." [2000]

Later, after completing a degree in Urban Planning at Harvard School of Design, Nate worked for the District of Columbia government in the urban planning and development office.

Alice O'Grady, ever the restless one, had a different experience working for the Peace Corps and an unplanned return to Ghana. Brewster Smith visited Nigeria in December 1966 and there met Alice. In his diary, he wrote: "[Alice] has been Deputy Director of the Regional Peace Corps office in Ibadan for a year and a half and seems to love it … she looks blooming, in a loose semi-Nigerian dress made of Yoruba cloth. Evidently, Alice had arranged her life so that she has other activities besides being a Peace Corps official. She has been active in a light opera society doing Gilbert and Sullivan and now a Donizetti opera. She also founded and edits a weekly sixpence magazine, 'What's On in Ibadan.'"

After three years in Nigeria, Alice returned home but then wanted to return to Ibadan during the Biafran War to work in a hospital. Alice flew to Accra and from there tried to arrange a visa to re-enter Nigeria, but without success. She thus found herself back in Accra, without funds. So she found a job teaching at Accra Academy (a secondary school) and stayed for four years. After other adventures, by 1995 Alice was deep into writing an historical novel set in Ghana and returned to Ghana to do research. While there she visited Accra Academy. Alice continues the story:

"When I went back to Accra Academy, there was a big pile of broken furniture in one of the two school quadrangles. I asked the Headmaster why it was there and he said that the carpenter wasn't keeping up with repairing broken furniture and he had to keep it there because they now locked that section so people wouldn't carry it off for firewood. So, I said I'd like to repair it—chairs with legs off, simple kind of stuff. I said I'd like to invite students to help me and I'll bring some tools and nails. It ended up, I think, that classes were assigned to join me afternoons for the two weeks I was there.

"The students kind of vied with each other. I kept a record of how many pieces we repaired, so we had a little competition. That was kind of fun. We repaired 'em all. I was asked to come to a morning assembly after we'd finished and I was presented with their songbook and something with my name embroidered on it and a scrapbook of photographs, perhaps—I think so. The Headmaster announced that the Alice O'Grady Project had not ended because he noticed that the boys liked to write on the walls and they are going to buy paint and the boys will paint their school.

"And the boys applauded. I asked the Headmaster afterwards why they'd applauded. He said, 'I guess they liked the idea and it's going to be called the Alice O'Grady Project.'" [2000]

As we gather for our next reunion, I'm not sure what new stories I will hear. We still talk less of what it all meant and more of what we have done and how we've enjoyed it, in 1961, in 1967, in 1995, and today. Most of the group are at or near traditional retirement age but few have settled in to somnolent golden years. Few have lost the inner spark that first got them to accept the challenge of joining the Peace Corps in 1961—a sense of adventure and a desire to 'do the right thing' by helping others. The achievement of being first, being Ghana I, is a modest one but we lived "on the side of angels." A year before her death, DeeDee, in her annual Christmas letter to friends in 1983, quoted William James:

> I am done with great things and big things, great institutions and big success, and I am for those tiny, invisible molecular moral forces that work from individual to individual, creeping through the crannies of the world like so many rootlets, or like the capillary oozing of water, yet which, if you give them time, will rend the hardest monuments of man's pride.

Kwaku and me in Madison, WI, 2009.

Reunion in Gloucester, MA, 2002.

On Bass Rocks, Anani pouring libation at Reunion 1996.

Brewster at Reunion 1996.

Tom L. and Bob S. at Reunion in Tucson, AZ, 2007.

George and Ruth at 2002 Reunion.

Reunion in Gloucester, MA, 2009

APPENDIX

GHANA I (data as of 1961, with Initial Teaching Assignment)			
Volunteer	Hometown	Education	School in Ghana
1. Carol Armstrong	Bala Cynwyd PA	BA Mt. Holyoke MA Harvard	Tamale Teacher Training College
2. Kenneth Baer	West Los Angeles CA	BA Yale MA U Cal/Berkeley	Ebenezer Secondary Schl (Accra)
3. Howard Ballwanz	Libertyville IL	BS Northern Illinois U	Swedru Secondary School [G.E.T.]
4. Susan Bartholomew	Minneaplois MN	BA Boston U	Swedru Secondary School [G.E.T.]
5. Meryl Blau	New York NY	BA Brandeis U	Ghana National College (Cape Coast)
6. John Buchanan	Lewisburg PA	BS Penn State	Akim Abuakwa State College (Kibi)
7. Lucille Carmichael	Grosse Pointe MI	BA/MA U Michigan	Korforidua Secondary School [G.E.T.]
8. Barnett Chessin	Paterson NJ	BA Paterson State Coll	Kukurantumi Secondary School [G.E.T.] (Tafo)
9. George Coyne	Plainfield NJ	BS Rutgers	Sunyani Secondary School [G.E.T.]
10. Laura Damon	Buffalo NY	BA Smith College	Opoku Ware Secondary School (Kumasi)
11. Ophelia DeLaine	Hollis NY	BS Johnson C Smith U	Opoku Ware Secondary School (Kumasi)
12. John Demos	Cambridge MA	BA Harvard	Okuapemann Secondary School [G.E.T.] (Akropong)
13. Valerie Deuel	Berkeley CA	BA U Cal/Berkeley	Accra Girls Secondary School [G.E.T.]
14. Peter Dybwad	Leonia NJ	BA Wesleyan	Akim-Oda Secondary School [G.E.T.]
15. Newell Flather	Lowell MA	BA Harvard	Winneba Secondary School [G.E.T.]
16. Marian Frank	Pittsburgh PA	BA Oberlin	Yaa Asantewaa Secondary School [G.E.T.] (Kumasi)
17. Susan Glowacki	Schenectady NY	BA Cornell	Swedru Secondary School [G.E.T.]
18. Donald Groff	Strasburg PA	BS Penn State	West Africa Secondary School [G.E.T.] (Accra)
19. Nathan Gross	Fremont NE	BA Beloit College	Swedru Secondary School [G.E.T.]

20. Frank Guido	Philadelphia PA	BS Temple U	Asankrangwa Secondary School [G.E.T.]
21. Roger Hamilton	Arlington VA	BA Harvard	HalfAssini Secondary School [G.E.T.]
22. Susan Hastings	Malibu CA	BA Stanford	Yaa Asantewaa Secondary School [G.E.T.] (Kumasi)
23. David Hutchinson	Russell KY	BA Berea College	Tarkwa Secondary School [G.E.T.]
24. James Kelly	Milton MA	BA Boston College	Tweneboa Kodua Sec School [G.E.T.] (Kumawu)
25. Robert Klein	New York NY	MA U Chicago	Sefwi-Wiawso Secondary School [G.E.T.]
26. Robert Krisko	Kansas City MO	BS U Kansas	Korforidua Secondary School [G.E.T.]
27. Loretto Lescher	River Forest IL	BA Rosary College	Swedru Secondary School [G.E.T.]
28. Thomas Livingston	Wood Dale IL	BA U Illinois	Ghanata College (Dodowa)
29. John Lord	Springfield IL	BA Harvard	Navrongo Secondary School [G.E.T.]
30. Darleen Malcolm	Belle Rive IL	BA S Illinois U	Yaa Asantewaa Secondary School [G.E.T.] (Kumasi)
31. Richard Maze	Carroll IA	BA Iowa State Teachers College	Bogoso Teacher Training College
32. John McGinn	Alameda CA	BA/MA U Cal/ Berkeley	Kadjebi Secondary School [G.E.T.]
33. Steve McWilliams	Aurora CO	BS U Colorado	LaBone Secondary School [G.E.T.] (Accra)
34. Marion Morrison	San Francisco CA	BA Rice U	Okuapemann SS [G.E.T.] (Akropong)
35. * Edward Mycue	Boston MA	BA North Texas State College	Acherensua Secondary School [G.E.T.]
36. Alice O'Grady	Chicago IL	BA U Chicago	Dormaa Ahenkro Secondary School [G.E.T.]
37. Thomas Peterson	Wilmette IL	BA U Wisconsin	Navrongo Secondary School [G.E.T.]
38. Antonette Port	Stoneham MA	BA Boston College**	Sogakope Secondary School [G.E.T.]
39. Richard Port	Stoneham MA	BA Boston College	Sogakope Secondary School [G.E.T.]
40. Maureen Pyne	Chicago IL	BS Spring Hill College	Holy Child School (Cape Coast)

41. Penelope Roach	Hyde Park NY	BA Vassar MA American U	Okuapemann Secondary School [G.E.T.] (Akropong)
42. Robert Scheuerman	Bison KS	BA Fort Hays State U	Bishop Herman Secondary School (Kpandu)
43. Sam Selkow	New York NY	BA Columbia U	Asankrangwa Secondary School [G.E.T.]
44. Michael Shea	Eau Claire WI	BS Marquette	Akim Abuakwa State Coll (Kibi)
45. Georgianna Shine	Kensington CT	BS Central Connecticut State College	Tema Secondary School [G.E.T.]
46. Ray Spriggs	West Chester PA	BA Lincoln U	Fijai Secondary School (Takoradi)
47. Dorothy Vellenga	New Concord OH	BA Monmouth College	West Africa Secondary School (Accra)
48. Martin Wallenstein	Brooklyn NY	BS Brooklyn College	Navrongo Secondary School [G.E.T.]
49. Carol Waymire	Santa Rosa CA	BA Santa Rosa State Coll	Yaa Asantewaa Secondary School [G.E.T.] (Kumasi)
50. Ruth Whitney	Quincy IL	BS Marquette	Yaa Asantewaa Secondary School [G.E.T.] (Kumasi)

Notes to Appendix

* Ed trained at Berkeley and was selected. He went to Ghana but had to return to the U. S. within the first month because of his father's serious illness; he did not return to Ghana.

** Awarded B.A. with credits accepted from Berkeley training.

1. Arnold Zeitlin was deselected during training because his degree was in Journalism; by the end of the first month of the project, he came to Ghana as a Peace Corps Volunteer and was assigned to teach at O'Reilly S S.

2. [G.E.T.] indicates a Ghana Educational Trust school.

3. Trainees at Berkeley not selected for Ghana project:

William Austin   Robert H. Eisenman
Bruce A. Bloomfield   Donald Erickson
Patricia Brooks   Francis Michalski
Charles Dirks

ACKNOWLEDGMENTS

Cover photo © AP Images, used with permission. Other photos courtesy of The National Archives and personal friends. The author wishes to thank the John F. Kennedy Library Foundation for research support. He also owes a deep debt of gratitude to both Betsy Sandlin and Phyllis Noble without whose professional guidance and gentle nagging this book would not have been completed. Special thanks for inspiration and encouragement to David Apter, George Carter, and Brewster Smith.

This image is a traditional Ghanaian *adinkra* symbol meaning "Remember the Past."

CPSIA information can be obtained at www.ICGtesting.com
233531LV00003B/16/P